Len McCluskey, General Secretary Unite the union

The dispute at Grangemouth petrochemical plant in 2013 was a unique episode in British industrial relations. As is often the case in such disputes, thousands of workers, their families and communities faced an uncertain future, with only their trade union there to fight for them. What was exceptional was how this dispute ended up stretching far beyond the industrial arena to embroil both Scottish and UK governments in what ultimately became one of the most compelling power struggles of our time, as private and commercial interest pitted itself against the national and public good.

Relations between the Unite union and Ineos had been deteriorating for some time prior to the company's decision to drive Ineos Vice Convenor Stephen Deans from his job in October 2013, with requests for meetings to discuss pensions and other matters regularly rejected by the employer. Mr Deans had served Grangemouth and his Ineos employers loyally for twenty-five years, and two future investigations would later show there was no case to answer against him. A loyal employee and a dedicated Labour party activist, and a very decent man, he suffered tremendously at the hands of a media that was determined to find wrongdoing where there was none.

Regrettably, what developed in the following months went on to entangle the Labour Party leadership, Police Scotland and my union in a pseudo-crisis of the political classes' own making, which only acted to conceal the true nature of the scandal exposed there: the inappropriateness of private ownership over essential energy supplies, and the true anti-democratic nature of the decades-old policy of transferring national assets into private hands. There are many brutal lessons to be learned from these events, but foremost among these must be how one individual billionaire can accrue the power that allows him to shut down a country's petrochemical and refinery operations.

And yet this book covers far more than those tumultuous months in 2013. Mark Lyon grew up in a BP family home during the days when the Grangemouth plant was publicly owned and provided for all of its surrounding communities. He charts the enormous changes from those days politically and economically for the communities directly affected by the onset of privatisation, and considers how we might reimagine the key issue of ownership in the twenty-first century. Mark serves with distinction as Unite's vice-chair and as one of our most respected lay activists. With this book he has done the movement another service.

Pat Rafferty, Unite Scottish Secretary

Much has been written concerning the Ineos dispute in 2013, some of which comes close to the truth, but most of which does not get anywhere near it. The right-wing media had its own agenda of course – not just from a corporate perspective, but as a political objective as far as the trade union movement is concerned.

This book will take you on a journey through time back to when the site was in public hands and when corporate responsibilities to the community really mattered. Back to when we had social clubs where people interacted, and to a time when workers appreciated the loyalty of their company and what their company stood for.

Have those times changed?

Well you will make your own judgement on that having read the book. This book gives you the true picture of what really took place in 2013 and in the lead-up to that period. It is written by a man who had spent most of his working life on the Grangemouth site and who ultimately paid a heavy price for doing nothing other than trying to do the best for the people he represented.

So – read the book, draw your own conclusions. And having done so I am sure you will soon identify where the truth really lies and that it is not in the propaganda that has been spouted over the years.

Andrew Murray, Chief of Staff, Unite the union

My bookshelves are full of the memoirs of working-class militants from the first half of the twentieth century. More recent autobiographies by leaders of the labour movement seem to be much rarer.

That is one reason why Mark Lyon's decision to tell his own story is so welcome. The voices of those at the sharp end of industrial life are too seldom heard nowadays – it is one measure of the labour movement's retreat over the last generation or so, alas.

This is an important story too. It underlines the old wisdom that in the class struggle there are few irreversible victories, no permanent defeats. The Lyon story is of fighting for the rights of working people against a greedy and rapacious employer focused solely on the profit margin.

Continued on page 235

The Battle of Grangemouth

A Worker's Story

For Wendy, Ross and Louise and my gorgeous granddaughters, Molly and Abi.

I also dedicate this book to everyone who has ever held the position of trade union representative. This volunteer army sacrifice much and give their all to improve the lot of workers, yet ask nothing for themselves. They meet on shop floors, in draughty village halls and in the back rooms of pubs to organise and combine as they work tirelessly to make things better for their brothers and sisters. Your contribution is magnificent.

The Battle of Grangemouth

A Worker's Story

Hugh Mark Lyon

Lawrence and Wishart
London 2017

The most evident characteristic of our time and country is the phenomenon of industrial centralization, which is putting the control of each of our great national industries into the hands of one or a few men and giving these men an enormous and despotic power over the lives and the fortunes of their employees and subordinates – the great mass of the people; a power which eviscerates our national constitution and our common law ... a power which, though expressed in terms of current speech as the right of employers to manage their business to suit themselves, is coming to mean in effect nothing less than the right to manage the country to suit themselves.

From *An address to the public*, issued by the advisory committee, the knights of labor and the amalgamated association of Iron and Steelworkers, Homestead PA, July 1892

Contents

Acknowledgements   1

Introduction   3

1   The rise and fall of a workers' paradise   6

2   Things fall apart   18

3   Enter Ineos   38

4   Billionaire on benefits   61

5   The Falkirk Labour Party affair   90

6   The build-up of the plot   120

7   The execution of the plot begins   141

8   The company move in for the kill   159

9   After the strike   171

Epilogue   202

Cast of characters   220

Timeline   223

Index   229

Photographs are between pp128 and 129

Lawrence and Wishart Limited
Central Books Building
Freshwater Road
Chadwell Heath
RM8 1RX

Published in association with Unite the Union
© Hugh Mark Lyon/Unite The Union 2017

ISBN 978-1-912064-00-7

British Library Cataloguing in Publication Data.
A catalogue record for this book is available from the British Library

Acknowledgements

I want to thank my family for their love and support and for putting up with so much over the last couple of years while I was writing this book. Not once did you waver or question the path we were on.

To my friend, Ian Proudlove, I say thanks.

I also want to thank all at Team Unite for their unconditional support over the years and for the solidarity of comrades from other unions and associated organisations. My great fear is that I miss someone out by including names, but there are people I need to say thanks to and mention. My thanks go to you Pat Rafferty, Howard Beckett, Tony Woodhouse, Len McCluskey, Stevie Deans, Brian Jones and Karie Murphy.

Thanks to all my stewards past and present who worked, and still work, with me in Grangemouth. To Jim Mowatt, Linda McCulloch, Scott Foley, Jackson Cullinane, Tony Burke, Michael Connarty, Neil Findlay MSP, Leo Gerard and all at USW, Cliff Bowen and Colin Mckay, Alan and Gary Lamont, Tam Conroy, Roger Stelfox and all the troops on my national committee.

And thanks too to our Unite executive, and the fantastic Linda Addy and Irene Dykes, Graeme Smith and the STUC general council, Scot Walker and the Scottish regional committee, Stephen Wright at Fair Pley for 'the ballad of Grangemouth', Canon Leo and to every single person, union member or not, who conveyed their support to me over the last couple of years and provided light in some of the darkest of times. Thanks also to Amanda Campbell for help with the photographs.

I want to thank all at the legal team who helped me and mine and who bring credit to their profession by giving balance to the equation: Patrick McGuire, Lindsay Bruce, Kenny Gibson, Alan Argue and the mighty Engelman. With you all there, it should really have been declared 'no contest'.

I thank all the good people I have worked with over the years from the management team at Grangemouth, John Williams, Robin

McGill, Dougie Rae and Amy Smith. To all the fine individuals who worked with our union in a cooperative and compassionate way, I say thank you.

I want especially to thank Barrie Clement for his writing expertise, guidance and patience, and Andrew Murray for his advice and help in so many ways. Thanks also to Sally Davison for editing the text, and to everyone who has deliberately or otherwise slipped a thought or idea into my mind for the book.

I hope I have not missed anyone from my list. There are so many friends to thank. I give my gratitude, sincerely and humbly, to you all.

HML

Introduction

THIS BOOK SETS out my reflections in the wake of the 2103 Ineos dispute at Grangemouth.

It is a part of the broader story of our national assets being handed over to private individuals for their own profit, and the mismanagement of resources that nearly always follows – although the Ineos management are perhaps in a class of their own when it comes to disastrous decisions.

This particular story began long before the much reported dispute itself, and it certainly has not ended yet. The trouble at Grangemouth really began to escalate in 2005, when the Ineos group bought the Grangemouth petro-chemical complex from BP, once a nationally owned company but by then already wholly in private hands.

Jim Ratcliffe, a man who displayed what many would describe as eccentric, arrogant and authoritarian behaviours, is the founder, chairman and chief executive of Ineos and he holds 60 per cent of the shares. Ratcliffe is the spectre who haunts this book. He never forgave Unite for successfully protecting the pensions of the workforce at Grangemouth in 2008. From that point on, he embarked on a crusade to punish his employees and to dismiss their main representatives (of whom I was one).

The core event of this story concerns Ratcliffe's manoeuvring to provoke a strike in 2013, swiftly followed by the announcement that he would close the Chemical site if the workforce did not immediately accept greatly reduced terms and conditions. His claim was that the company could not survive economically without such sacrifices. And he also amplified tales of the company's financial woes to win grants and loans from both the Scottish and UK governments, and even to blackmail BP into reducing their rates for feedstock gas supplied to his chemicals plants. All this could be best described as corporate brinksmanship.

Throughout the book, I describe the unfolding events as a 'plot' by those at Ineos. I use that word in its widest meaning. It would give too much credit to Ineos to say that they foresaw all that would unfold, and orchestrated this entire matter. They certainly responded to events, however, with the clear intention of removing myself and Stevie Deans from the site, gaining every possible financial advantage from the situation – and with the clear intention of exacting payback for the previous dispute of 2008. For me this is their 'plot'.

The events that unfolded were also exacerbated by the presence of gutless managers who, driven by fear, co-operated with the plot and told Ratcliffe exactly what he wanted to hear.

As part of the plot they exploited a row in the Falkirk Constituency Labour Party to smear the name of plant deputy convenor Stevie Deans, and eventually they drove him to resign from his post under the enormous pressure and personal distress he felt. So the book also includes a chapter giving our side of this often misrepresented story.

This is not a technical document full of facts and figures, but, rather, my take on events. I hope I have avoided the finished article looking like a pie-charted academic report. The account is not set out in strict chronological order, but I will try to provide some sense of flow over the years.

The story is really quite remarkable, and readers may think parts of it are exaggerated or motivated by vitriol. My promise to you is that I will set out my reflections with integrity. I will try to avoid colouring the events with the outrage I still feel at the treatment of our Unite members at the Grangemouth site.

Much has been said about what happened at Grangemouth, and the question of blame has never been far from the surface. Monday-morning quarterbacks have often let us know where we went wrong. Let me make my position on this clear from the outset. There are things I would have done differently, and I am sure our branch members and committee would say the same thing – but I am saying this only with the benefit of hindsight, and, what's more, anything I would have done differently would have been solely with the intent of making our campaign of resistance even more effective – not less.

I consider that all the blame for the long-term damage that has been done to our factory, the community and the Scottish and UK economy lies fairly and squarely with Jim Ratcliffe's Ineos.

The events described here have driven me to the conclusion that it is lunacy to allow a single company – let alone an organisation effectively run by one man, with sole custody of decision-making – to control nationally important assets such as the Grangemouth complex.

But all this is only a small part of the progression to disaster that is currently taking place in the UK. This story really concerns retrograde industrial and political change in the oil and chemical industry in our country. Readers can derive their own conclusions from this particular example as they please – but don't be surprised if you see parallels with workplace situations you or your friends have faced.

One key question that arises for me is who it is that should be called to account for the damage these changes are doing to the country. Is it the selfish, self-absorbed and terminally greedy who should be pilloried, or is it the disastrous political, legal and social framework which allows such behaviour to prevail?

Why don't we start out on the story – and I will see you on the other side for your thoughts.

Hugh Mark Lyon January 2016

CHAPTER 1

The rise and fall of a workers' paradise

The ters o' the workin class!

BY WAY OF a personal introduction I thought I would tell you a bit about my family and where we all come from. When else would I get a chance to document such affairs? But I will try to guard against self-indulgent forays into python-esque style commentary on how hard life was, and how we got up before we went to bed and walked twenty miles to work – all uphill – and then walked uphill back home again ...

My mother's side of the family were McMonagles and they came to Falkirk from Ireland around the turn of the century. Their story was probably pretty typical of the time. They settled in a tenement flat in Garrison Place. The area was just known as 'the Garrison' but it no longer exists, having given way some years ago to the general Post Office. My grandmother Mary would tell us that the block backed on to a modest lodging house and she was a bit afraid of the men who would come and go at all hours. These were not homeless men, you understand, these were mainly working men, away from home and making a few bob in the industrial areas of Scotland to send back to their families. The McMonagle family took in such a man as a lodger even though they were very overcrowded already.

My great grandfather Manus worked on the roads and the kids delivered milk to help make ends meet. They said that it was definitely a case of first up best dressed, and they often went barefoot. (I know, John Cleese would be proud already.)

The experiences of their family were probably like many at that time in that life, played out in episodes of uncertain fortune. Over the years tuberculosis took some, and America also took a few.

Some went on to become teaching professionals and others, like Mary, worked hard all their lives, not just to support the family but also to provide further education for siblings. There was no discrimination in these opportunities. The way things played out was mostly based on age, and it was just how things were. My grandmother was one of the cleverest and most academically gifted people I knew, but her place in the order of Garrison life meant that she was inevitably on course to be engaged in honourable manual labour all of her life.

Mary McMonagle worked in service as a cook and housemaid for a family in Falkirk called the Allens, who were lawyers in the town, and she stayed in the big house in the servants' quarters. She never said much about her treatment and I don't know that she was unhappy, but she did recall being reprimanded once for talking in the basement where she slept. She was apparently talking to the dog. I always thought that let you know the relationship and painted a picture.

When she was in her late teens she sailed to America to take up a similar post with a family in New York. She went on her own, and it must have felt like travelling to the moon. She settled for a time and later recalled how they would spend the hot summer months in the Pocono Mountains. The family must have been wealthy I guess.

On a trip to the US in 2013 I visited the Tenement Museum in the Lower East side of Manhattan, to see if I could find any information on my Irish relatives, and to take in some of the history of the many immigrants from different cultures and countries for whom the building was their first accommodation. In its time the building was filled with German, Eastern European, Italian and Irish people as well as many others. I recommend this excellent museum to anyone who has the chance to visit it.

Anyway, Mary came home a few years later, and bumped into a previous acquaintance, George Vincent Harvey, in Camelon Main Street. They were married not long after.

My grandfather George was an iron moulder and a union man. I don't mean he was an activist, but everyone was a union man or woman in those days and the better for it. He worked in R&A Main's Gothic Works, one of about twenty iron works in Falkirk, including the famous Carron Iron works where the cannons of the Napoleonic wars were struck. All the foundries are gone now, and a

Tesco supermarket stands on the site of the Mains Gothic works. Most of them closed in the early 1960s. George got a barometer when he left, and a pension just big enough to deny him free National Health glasses under the means-testing regime of the time. After that he went on to work in the Bison cement works until he retired.

My grandmother Mary worked on in service, but no longer lived in the big house as she and my grandfather were raising my mother and aunt, and she also worked for Mathiesons the bakers in a café in Falkirk called the Tudor House. She worked there until well into her 70s, serving food in the canteen. She was allowed to bring home cakes if they were broken, and it is amazing the number of confections and vanilla slices that get damaged in such a venture! But nothing was ever proven. Pies were also on the menu, and George would always ask the same question when it was pies for tea … 'What is better than a pie?' …. The answer of course was … 'two pies'. He was right enough.

My paternal grandfather, Hugh, was also an iron moulder and union man, but he died quite young and I don't remember much beyond that. The Lyon family had come to Falkirk from Glasgow for the same reason working-class people always move area – for work. My grandmother Bridget came to live with us when I was very young after she suffered a stroke, but, sadly, I don't remember much about her either.

Industrial occupations were hard on the body, and most young men in the Falkirk area leaving formal education early found their way into the foundries. The only blessing from foundry work was that it was a reserved occupation in the Second World War, and both my grandfathers were spared the horrors of frontline conflict as they made munitions and acted as fire-watchers in the factories.

My Great Uncle Tom was not so fortunate. He saw active service in the Normandy landings. He was married to my Great Aunt May who was a Lyon, and they lived in North Berwick. Tom was a soldier, gas lamp lighter, gardener, handyman and a boxer, – though my father reckoned, judging by his face, not a very good one. May was a nurse during the war and continued to retirement age, and after that she took lodgers in the summer, utilising their home as a guest house. She also moonlighted for the local undertakers and would be called out at all hours to tend to the recently – and sometimes not so recently – departed. She told me once that an unfortunate had passed away with the electric blanket left on, and had gone to their eternal rest looking like a grill-striped sirloin.

Hardy folks with gallows humour were clearly the order of the day.

Hugh Lyon, Hugh Lyon, Hugh Lyon and … Hugh Lyon

My Da Hugh, one of a continuing line of Hugh Lyons, gave me a number of books during his life. One of them was *The Ragged Trousered Philanthropists*, and I read it twice through right off the bat. I have reservations these days about the book's criticism of workers, and the assertion that they deserve all they get because they accept their lot and don't seek to change it, and sometimes even defend it. I think this a harsh assessment now and a bit simplistic, but it is fair to say that Tressell blew me away at the time.

Another book my Da gave me was the *History of the Scottish Horse and Motormen's Association* (known as 'the carters'), written by Hugh Lyon. This was my Great, Great Uncle, who was the general secretary of this union, which was a predecessor of the Transport & General Workers' Union (T&G). I was heavily involved in unions long before he gave me this book, so I have a romantic notion that the commitment to workers' rights can run in the blood, and that any small contribution I can make could somehow add to his legacy. Sure, there were some raised eyebrows at the Scottish carters' ambivalent attitude to the 1926 general strike, but I choose to view any such criticism in the context of a growing union with sound enough direction and principle.

In 1918 Hugh Lyon was president of the Scottish Trades Union Congress (STUC), and he was heavily involved in the spread of trades councils, as well as support of the Labour Party. He substantially grew the carters' union and undoubtedly improved the lot of his members.

My parents Hugh and Cecily lived in Camelon near Falkirk, and they had both been employed in the tar works before moving the few miles to Grangemouth when my Da got work at the chemical complex. My sister Mhairi and I were brought up in the town of Grangemouth.

A SPELL BEHIND BARS

We had a happy and stable childhood, but I have to confess that my cousin Mairi, sister Mhairi and I did all spend time behind bars – at what was effectively a borstal, near Edinburgh. The Her Majesty's Facility in which we were banged up and did our time was St Joseph's Approved School near the town of Tranent.

You see, our Auntie Betty was one of wardens, though she was known as a house mother, and she ran one of the blocks where offenders who had served most of their time lived prior to their release. New offenders had to live in one of the older blocks, a very cold and hard place without much in the way of home comforts.

I spent most of my time with the inmates, and was asked the same question dozens of times: 'what are you in for?'. My street credibility with my cellies was a bit dented when I revealed that what I was in for was ... visiting my dear Auntie Betty.

If you did not know Betty you might be forgiven for thinking she was also a bit hard, but nothing could be further from the truth. She looked after the boys like her own, and even took some of them home at weekends to give them a taste of the home life that many of them had never experienced.

My memory of the block she ran was of a clean and warm atmosphere and surroundings, and the constant smell of freshly baked bread and scones. Most of the young inmates were in for a bit of truancy or petty crime, and I have no memory of any threat of violence.

We – the St Joseph's three – went there during the school summer holidays to stay for a few weeks, and it was quite an education. This would never be allowed now of course – the child protection agencies would most likely be immediately called in – but I look back at that time with fondness, and we all still laugh about it now when we meet up.

Many of the lads clearly came from difficult backgrounds and were not as lucky as we were – living as we did in the safety and security of the 1960s Socialist Republic of Grangemouth.

I sometimes wonder where those lads are now.

The Socialist Republic of Grangemouth

The Grangemouth refinery and chemical site is actually a collection of production factories or 'plants', and anyone visiting the east coast of central Scotland will probably have seen the cooling towers and the continuous clouds of steam rising from the complex. The first plant was built in 1924, and since then the site has been operated under a number of names and guises, but until 1987 it was always at least partially state-owned. The different organisations that ran it can be considered as evolutionary steps towards the eventual temporary but stable ownership of BP.

Grangemouth was the financial pearl of the Scottish central region in the 1960s. Although the socioeconomic conditions were beginning to move in the wrong direction, the situation was still a long way from the major calamities to come.

Later on in life I once went on holiday to Poland. You can enjoy cherry vodka, fine beer and jazz in Krakow. And I also had a very sobering and memorable visit to Auschwitz-Birkenau – which I think everyone should see at least once during their lifetime. Another afternoon was spent on a visit to the suburb of Nowa Huta, and it is this political and social experiment that is most relevant to my story.

Nowa Huta was built in the late 1940s as a model communist village, with a state-owned steel plant that was central to the community. There was work and housing for all. Social events and interaction were provided for all the workers.

But in the stated objective of being a town devoted to workers' interests, Grangemouth succeeded in the 1960s where Nowa Huta failed. Grangemouth was as close to a workers' paradise as you could get at that time. OK, the petro-chemical works was not designed for that purpose at all, and you can pick holes all over that assertion – but bear with me.

British Petroleum was a wholly nationalised entity at one time. I will spare you all the history of the company going back to the Persian Oil Company in 1914, but the bottom line is that in the late 1960s BP belonged to you and me and all the other citizens of the UK.

My father worked for the Chemical division of the company, in the laboratories, and we were very much a BP family. We lived in one of the modest yet comfortable four-in-a-block flats that the company had built to accommodate the workforce. You see, part of the workforce had relocated there from places like Broxburn, a town to the West of Edinburgh where the company had in the past operated shale excavation and refining. So, in response to the need for homes … they built them.

All the homes had huge gardens front and back, and good-size rooms, and it was obvious that the design was made very much with families in mind.

For those who wanted to work for BP Grangemouth but not to relocate, the company provided a free bus service from all around the old shale works to bring workers in every day.

My folks paid the very reasonable rent direct from my dad's wages, and the homes were serviced and maintained by the plant's maintenance crew.

The company directly employed glaziers, plumbers, carpenters, gardeners and general handymen. If you needed a repair or had any difficulty in your home, you could call the plant and they would send out Bob Hope (real name) to appraise the situation and organise the necessary work. This was not under-the-table work. This was the official tenancy arrangement to ensure safe, comfortable and well-maintained homes for the valued workers.

Somehow, the thinking has changed, so that it is now inconceivable for workers engaged in such honourable professions to be retained in-house. I am willing to bet that you are saying right now, 'oh yes, they contracted all that out at our place years ago'. The thought that house maintenance would be done by someone from a factory workforce, or gardening be done by retained workers, has become inconceivable in most companies. Why is this?

The 'experts' with the flipcharts would tell us that this kind of work is not 'core', and we need to concentrate on the vital or 'core' functions of modern business. This is, of course, nonsense.

I don't know exactly how much cash has been harvested from the oil game in Scotland, but I do know it's a massive amount, and I think it is right that the money should be used to benefit everyone involved. Twee and old-fashioned as it may sound, why shouldn't workers who are, for instance, gardeners and janitors enjoy security of employment and industry-appropriate wages, pensions and benefits?

Let me tell you about the gardeners at Grangemouth. Since they were dispensed with in favour of contractors the services have declined, and become of much less focus and importance. This is not because the contract gardeners are incompetent and lazy – quite the reverse –

it's because the stated aim is to pay less attention to this important work and to dismiss it as non-core. This is an example of poor management.

The upshot of this policy is that years later the site has suffered from a series of events which have been dangerous and damaging to its profitability and environmental performance. These events have led to incalculable losses for the bottom line of the business and I will tell you why ...

There is a problem at sites like ours for the pipes that lie in trenches. If soil and vegetation is not controlled and is allowed to build up and engulf these pipes, you get what is called 'under lagging corrosion'. In other words the pipes rust and eventually fail and release whatever is in them (and you don't want that in a petrochemical site, trust me). Because of the 'non-core' label on gardening services this has happened big-time at Grangemouth. Incidents have included massive environmental leakages, which have resulted in closing down and restricting production, and presented a danger to both the workforce and the public. Is gardening core? I think it very much is.

If the cost of these incidents had been avoided, the company could have easily afforded the employment of all the services in-house, with brilliant wages, benefits and pensions – and with change to spare. This is false economy on an industrial scale.

At that time there were far more workers and families dependent on the plant than there are today, and it undoubtedly generated considerably more community and economic benefits than anything seen now.

My favourite story from the time was told and retold by my father on countless occasions, but I never tired of hearing it. It has no doubt evolved and been modified and exaggerated over the years, but this is how it goes ...

My dad called this guy he knew 'old man D' – I don't think he appreciated that old man D was younger than him. Old man D and his wife Bridget lived in the BP houses near us. Some maintenance issue had come up in the house, and Bob Hope was summoned to have a look. When Bob was ushered into the front living room he observed that a service hatch from the kitchen had been cut right through the front-room brick wall – as was, fleetingly, the fashion in those days. I think the idea was that you could pass your fish fingers straight through without having to take the five or six steps that would transport you from the east to the west wing of the dwelling house!

The dialogue …

Bob Hope	There is a hole right through this wall here [pointing with horror, surprise and confusion]
Old man D	Yes [with indignant inflection]
Bob Hope	But this is a load bearing wall
Old man D	Yes
Bob Hope	But you need permission to alter the houses
Old man D	Yes
Bob Hope	But did you get permission?
Old man D	Yes [still indignant and now impatient]
Bob Hope	But, but, but … who gave you permission?
Old man D	Bridget …

As the site was so close the maintenance guys would come out to make repairs on old-fashioned Pashley bicycles like the one in *Open All Hours*, and I can remember seeing them going up and down Oswald Avenue where we lived while going about their business. Looking back, it was as if the company tentacles were reaching out into the community and everyone felt very much part of it.

If you were to look back over copies of the local newspaper, the *Falkirk Herald*, you would see a big contribution from BP in funding local projects and the like. To this day the part of BP still in Grangemouth sponsors the local children's day.

Further up Oswald Avenue was the BP club, conveniently located and purpose-built by the company for the enjoyment of the workforce. Leisure sections included a bowling club, fishing section and snooker club. They also built two very well-used tennis courts (not for tennis of course but football, this is central Scotland after all).

The licensing hours were different in those days but I understand that a few pints would always be poured and ready on the bar for the end of the back shift at ten o'clock in the evening, so that if they wanted the troops could have a glass of beer on the way home.

The BP club was where the retired members and other pensioners in the area met for lunch and some social interaction, and it was also where the company held Christmas parties for all the kids in the area.

One year my big mate Louis and I went to the Christmas party, and after the obligatory film show, games and lashings of jelly and ice cream big Santa finally arrived. Louis and I were full of expectation as the gifts were handed out. I was thrilled with my cowboy outfit, hat, felt waistcoat and two shiny pistols (remember it was common in the 1960s and 1970s to give toy small arms to children). But the best was yet to come ...

Someone had mistaken Louis for Louise, and when my big mucker peeled back the festive wrap what did he find ... A plastic tea set! Fantastic, and everyone agreed it was the best Christmas ever.

We were aged 23 at the time.

The site canteen was also open for retired members to have lunch for free, and it was mainly widowers who congregated there every day to socialise and play a few hands of cards. I don't know why this example is so much in my mind, but it just seems to illustrate the low-cost but thoughtful actions of a company whose soul and philosophy is a million miles from that of Grangemouth Ineos today.

Mind you, there was class segregation in operation in the canteen at this time. The restaurant was split into an area for the boiler suits and an area for the white-collar staff, and behind closed doors there was an oak-panelled chamber which was commonly known as the 'Golden Trough'. This was where senior managers were silver-served their lunch by waitresses in traditional black and white.

My late father swore by BP. He only bought petrol from BP stations, and would drive by any other stations to find one. He felt part of the company, and I think he and my mother were thankful for a decent living and the chance to bring up their family in a secure and pretty comfortable environment. I think everyone who worked there felt more or less the same.

The fall of the empire

In 1975, with the help of a government loan of some £375 million, the fully-nationalised BP built a pipeline from the North Sea to bring oil and gas via several waypoints to Grangemouth. Significant deposits of oil and gas had been discovered, and an economic boom was predicted. Her majesty the Queen visited Grangemouth to ceremonially commission the pipeline and receive the first barrel of oil.

BP was made up of a number of entities, and three of them were present in Grangemouth: Oil Exploration, Chemicals and Refinery. All were state owned. They are all entirely privatised now. I always return in my mind to the work of Tressell when thinking about this. Tressell asserts that if it was feasible for the ruling classes to gather up all the air in the world and put it in a giant gasometer, they would. They would find a way to declare ownership and charge the great unwashed like me and you by the lungful.

I know it is a fanciful notion that some greedy selfish megalomaniac would build a massive tank for nothing but personal gain, but you get the idea of what Tressell meant.

The parallels with North Sea oil are also obvious. How can it be that a section of the population can seize and declare that the oil belongs to them – a geological accident, a global resource? I apologise for my perhaps unsophisticated grasp of this – but can anyone explain how that happened?

When the company was publicly owned there was a logic to how this all operated. The idea that the revenue could be harvested for many decades, and used for the progress, betterment and prosperity of all UK citizens, was very attractive one.

In his *Official History of North Sea Oil*, oil industry expert Professor Alexander Kemp of Aberdeen University argues that in the early 1970s there was a general consensus within the Labour government that a national oil company was needed, and that thought should be given to permanent public ownership of the oil fields.

Clearly this position was rejected.

In fact, the Labour government at the end of the 1970s, with a nudge from the International Monetary Fund, sold off 17 per cent of BP (in 1977). It was Labour, not the Conservatives – as you might be forgiven for assuming – that kicked off the process of privatisation of this company.

As we know, Margaret Thatcher became prime minister of the newly elected Conservative government in 1979 and enthusiastically picked up the privatisation agenda. In her memoirs she states that there were a number of reasons for pursuing privatisation, but a central aim was to 'reverse the corrosive and corrupting effects of socialism'.

As is also well known, her programme of privatisation was extensive, and the national assets were systematically flogged off, one after another.

With the radical, extremist and frightening philosophy that was at the heart of Thatcher government decision-making, it is not surprising that many of the economic difficulties we all now face can be traced back to this period.

It is certainly true that the events at Grangemouth 2013-14, and the problems that continue to unfold at the site, can, at least partially, be traced back to these origins.

In 1977, at the time of the first sale of shares, the criteria specified that a 'golden share' would always be held by government, given the strategic, economic and structural importance of the oil industry. The thinking set out was that government would need to make sure that the assets were run with the national interest at the heart of the agenda. The idea was to ensure that the company did not fall into the wrong hands and be run for selfish interest, or be subject to poor decision-making; and that the vital importance of security of supply and national revenue would always be considered in any directional or strategic change.

Clearly, this is also not what happened.

The golden share principle was abandoned in the course of the Thatcher government and the entire company was gradually sold off. The last of the BP shares were sold in 1987.

However, as we shall see, the desire to halt public interference in the course and direction of the markets has never been regarded as applying to tax breaks, business grants and the underwriting of loans for the immensely wealthy.

CHAPTER 2

Things fall apart

My apprenticeship

I STARTED AS AN apprentice at BP in 1980, just the era of stability was drawing to a close. When I finished my apprenticeship in 1984 there was no job for me, and when I eventually returned to the site in 1988 the period of change and decline was in full swing.

This is probably a good place to say a little more about the Grangemouth complex, which is one of the largest manufacturing sites in the UK. It is broadly split into two areas – the oil refinery, which makes products like petrol, diesel and fuels for aircraft, and the chemical site, which utilises petrochemical by-products from the refinery to make products such as Ethylene (used to make plastic) and industrial alcohol (used in pharmaceuticals). The site has two power stations, as well as laboratories, stores, workshops, water treatment areas and a transport infrastructure. The products made at the site are distributed by road tanker, or by ship from company terminals in Grangemouth Docks, or by train from the company rail terminal, and in plastic pellet form in bulk containers by road.

The main raw materials used on the site – crude oil and hydro-carbon gas – arrive by pipe from the North Sea or by ship from Finnart Ocean Terminal in the West of Scotland. The gas from the North Sea pipeline arrives at the same time and in the same pipeline as the oil, and the main purpose of the refinery is to split oil into its component liquids. This is not a particularly complicated process and mainly involves heating and cooling oil streams to separate the various compo-nents of the crude oil. There is also a 'cracking' process, whereby heavy or thick oil products are made into lighter or thinner and more valu-able liquids. This process is very important since it upgrades the value of each barrel of the oil and also produces feed material that is used in the other chemicals plants.

But though the process itself is not too complicated, the equipment and controls that operate in the blue-collar processing and mainte-nance areas are – and the workers who maintain and operate the plants are highly skilled. The people who work at the site include hands-on maintenance technicians, manufacturing technicians, chemical and maintenance engineers and a range of skilled manual employees.

When I started BP had a system for attracting apprentices. There was a major fault in it – they only sought male candidates at the time – but apart from that the idea was not bad. The company visited local secondary schools and offered an aptitude test to all the leavers who wanted a technical job. I took that test in 1980, and after a further interview and medical was offered a start in the refinery as an appren-tice welder.

I had also been offered an apprenticeship as a motor mechanic under an initiative facilitated by local authorities in the area, and I was a little bit torn between the two offers because cars were a big interest of mine at the time. But the main reason for choosing BP was the experience of my father. He worked for BP's chemical division, and although it was a completely different and separate operation, the warm feeling around the company was the main reason for my decision.

I started in summer 1980 at Workshop 'B'.

At that time there were about 35 apprentices in the refinery and approximately the same number in the chemicals plant. They were directly employed from day one, of course. We had safety inductions, new boots and boiler suits and a tour of Grangemouth, as well as Finnart Ocean Terminal. We also had a boat trip to Hound Point in the middle of the Forth near the bridges, to see the place from where processed crude oil was exported by ship around the world.

We also had a presentation from Trevor George, who was the branch secretary of the Transport & General Workers Union. We left with union cards and copies of the site agreements. My union was actually the GMB because of my trade as a welder, but the T&G were also strongly organised on the site and were party to agreements across the refinery, covering different trades and disciplines.

At this juncture let me draw your attention to an article published in the *Telegraph* on 3 November 2013, quoting Jim Ratcliffe on 'my battle with the union':

The union issues on the Grangemouth site date back to the Seventies. Only three weeks ago, half a dozen friends and I were guided on rocky trails through the high Alps in Italy on mountain bikes. One participant, Tony Loftus, who had been the operations director for Ineos's predecessor, Inspec, revealed in a discussion about the troubles at Grangemouth that his first job after a chemistry degree at Manchester University had been as a graduate trainee on the Grangemouth site in the early Seventies. He said, quite spontaneously: 'When I was in Grangemouth, there were no problems, we didn't have any strikes, and management did as they were told.' Little has changed since, and today the site struggles compared with its German counterparts.

This tired, predictable and clichéd reference to the idea that the unions ran the site in the 1970s – management did what they were told and all change and progress was halted by us – is quite revealing. This is nonsense, and it is also a very dangerous attitude that has been enormously damaging. The reason for pointing it out at this stage is to identify from the beginning one of the revealing and major fault lines in the disastrous events of 2013.

In fact, many of the calamitous events of 2013, as well as the lead-up to them, would have been avoided if Ratcliffe's assertion about our union had been correct. In fact, because of our misplaced trust in the competence of management, we sometimes acquiesced in their decisions when we should have contested them.

In any case, as will become clear, big decisions were later made on the basis of this false assertion.

The truth is that the organisational changes to the site over the years came about not so much by evolution as by revolution, and when this happened most of them were not supported by the unions because the proposed changes were not for the better and were unhelpful to the business. But this did not stop the changes happening.

To suggest that all these changes occurred in a climate where unions ran the show is, quite simply, wrong and ludicrous.

The next time I am cycling through the rocky trails of the high Alps in Italy I will be thinking about all this.

I will return later to the dramatic changes at the site over the years, and the reality of industrial relations at Grangemouth, but for now let's go back to Workshop B.

Cowboys and elephants

Workshop 'B' was the boiler shop, and there were about 30 boiler-makers, 30 welders, half a dozen gas welders, three blacksmiths and maybe 20 craft mates working there. All directly employed by BP of course. If there is a more vital and core part of oil production than high quality fabrication I can't think what it would be.

Today not one of these roles is in-house at the site … Not one!

The work was hard in the fabrication workshop in the 1980s, and the men were fairly hard too. They were all men by the way. In the years I spent there I do not remember a single woman being employed in the workshop. Shocking as that is, it was not unusual for heavy industry at the time in the crafts known as the 'black trades' – the shipbuilding trades. Fortunately this has changed somewhat – and this is one real change for the better.

Another heartening change is today's culture of tolerance. In my experience, there was undoubtedly an undercurrent of sexist, racist and religious bigotry in the workplace at that time. This was not by any stretch everyone's position, but the reason I mention it is that it is encouraging to think that at least some progress has been made over the years in that regard – many of the comments made then would not be tolerated now.

The workshop was full of characters, and there is no doubt that this helped morale and led to increased productivity and welfare within the workforce. Everyone's favourite was Arthur Robertson. Arthur had been a fine welder but was of advanced years by the time I started, and had a dual role as both welder and entertainer. He was known as the cowboy due to his love of John Wayne and Jimmy Stewart, and he could often be heard singing such songs as 'The man from Laramie'. I had the great pleasure and educational opportunity of spending a whole summer refurbishing a tank in the refinery in a team with the cowboy himself. We operated from a tent-like structure known as an elephant. The tank, I remember, was more rust than metal – a portent of things to come and an illustration of BP's poor maintenance strategy even then.

The site at this time also had chauffeurs and a fleet of black Austin Princesses, and one of the drivers we will call Tam McN. On one occasion Tam, who had a bit of a weakness for the drink, had been dispatched to collect someone from the airport but the flight had been delayed. By the time the poor guy arrived, he had to drive himself and Tam back to the site, for safety reasons. Thankfully Tam was not to be dispatched from employment, but he had been busted to the role of labourer in the workshop.

During my apprenticeship I was honoured to be invited to attend at the Golden Trough in the canteen. Unfortunately this invitation was not to have lunch, but, rather, to climb below the floor to repair a steam leak. The honour had no doubt been bestowed because I was the most junior welder at the time. The underside of the canteen was not a pleasant place to be, and there was only about two feet of headroom between the ground and the floor. And the smell was really bad. The task was accomplished while lying on my stomach in an inch or two of condensed water from the leak. When I lifted my welding helmet at one stage, I was eye to eye with the biggest rat I have ever seen and I was out of there in a big hurry – much to the amusement of my industrial companions who had been anticipating such an encounter.

The appearance of troublesome rats at the site continues to this day.

In telling a few stories I don't want in any way to trivialise the men and their work in the excellent workshop. The site was a happy but also very productive place to be.

'Modern' HR processes have sought to remove such characters and diversity and to develop standard employees. This is folly and without doubt a big mistake.

It was big news on the site at that time if anyone left to go to another job, and the company benefited greatly from the loyalty and devotion of the workforce. In contrast to this, in the months following the 2013 dispute the attrition rate was phenomenal. It was not quite a case of asking the last person to leave to turn the light out, but it was not far off. At one stage the attrition rate was approaching 50 per cent in some sections of the workforce.

The mismanagement and ineptitude that led to this situation will be explored and discussed further on in this book.

In the 1980s the 'D word' had a major influence over the way the work was undertaken – 'Demarcation'. This word is seldom used now, but when it is, it is uttered in hushed tones. But I think the practice of demarcation is safe and sensible.

Why don't we ask NHS doctors to change the oil filters on ambulances? The answer is … for obvious reasons.

Some of the specialist work done by boilermakers and welders in the workshop was unbelievable in its complexity, and actually, in some cases, its beauty. The workshop could turn out almost anything, and most of the maintenance pipework and structural fabrication was carried out in-house.

In their own time, and with materials and engineering expertise provided by the company, the troops once built a hyperbaric chamber. These are used to help people suffering from medical conditions such as multiple sclerosis. Rather than being made by machine, the vessel was hand-rolled by eye by the boilermakers, men of immense skill and experience. It was a joy to witness such creativity.

The move to cut costs by asking for 'flexibility' across all sections of the world of work has some merits, but it has had the detrimental effect of diluting fantastic skills and making everyone to some extent a jack of all trades. At one stage recently a suggestion was made at the site that the workers who operate the plant and equipment should carry out weeding and vegetation control, in order to save £30,000. This workforce had already been dangerously depleted by a mass exodus, and were already working excessive hours. They were also below the safe core numbers required to operate the site's highly hazardous equipment. This kind of proposal is reckless nonsense.

As part of the agreements on site in the early 1980s, any contract workers on site were paid the same as in-house workers. This was called the 'domestic agreement', and it unashamedly protected against casualisation. But it also had the effect of paying contractors on a fair basis.

Another protective agreement was called 'the trigger': before contractors were asked to work overtime, all the in-house craft workers of that discipline had to be offered the work first. These agreements appear quaint and old-fashioned now, but maybe that is what is wrong. These agreements incentivised the retention of a permanent workforce.

Needless to say, not one shred of any of these agreements is still in place now. More evidence of half-baked ideas from the high cycling trails of the Italian Alps.

At that time wage negotiations were conducted separately by the craft unions and the T&G, which represented most of the process operators and craft mates. The process of wage bargaining was pretty conventional when I started work, but dramatic change was on the way in terms of flexibility, reduction in employee numbers, outsourcing and the use of contractors.

In the early 1980s apprentices were not allowed into union meetings until the final year of their training under local union arrangements, but this changed over time. Once I was allowed into meetings it was fascinating to finally get involved. I had wanted to be engaged in union activities since that presentation from Trevor George when I first joined the company, and especially after living through the disgraceful treatment of the miners in the state-sponsored assault on them in 1984. That made the union feel even more essential and relevant to me.

Sadly, the beginning of the process that eventually led to the complete closure of the fabrication workshop had begun by 1984. It was the reason I was not kept on as a tradesman when my apprenticeship ended. Because of this I did a welding test with one of the local contract firms, and then took up a position with them a couple of weeks prior to my scheduled leaving date.

Four years on the road

Between August 1984 and August 1988 I worked as a contract welder with a number of companies. I was pretty lucky never to have a day without employment during this time – I survived countless lay-offs. These four years were a big education for me and I met some brilliant people. In my opinion life continues to be hard for the men and women who provide this expert resource for the industry to call on. The casual nature of work for these fine people is very difficult in terms of life planning, and the treatment of contract workers at some sites is far below anything that is acceptable.

I acted as a representative on some of the sites I worked on, and now that the despicable blacklisting that went on has come to light I often reflect about the attitudes. A common phrase used against employees who had displeased management was 'you will never work in this town again'.

Two incidents that took place during this period – in March 1987 – had an effect on everyone involved, including me. On 13 March, when I was working in the refinery, sub-contracting for an electrical company, a fire took the lives of two contractors. The cabins of the small fabrication company I was employed by were sited quite close to the incident. It was horrific and harrowing.

Then on Sunday 22 March I was scheduled to be back at work, and I got up in the morning ready to go to the site. A massive fire could be seen from the roadside outside our house in Oswald Avenue, which was located within sight of the factory. The Hydrocracker plant had exploded at 7am in the morning, and a crane driver – who was actually at the wrong plant by mistake – had been killed outright.

Later in life I ended up studying health and safety and acting as a safety rep, and these incidents had a lot to do with my ongoing interest in safety.

At the time of the dispute in 2013 the company destroyed all our best-in-class safety systems and committees on the site, driving these changes through on the back of threats to close the plant. At that time there were many false accusations made against me and other union representatives, but the most sickening of all of them was the assertion that my almost anorak-type interest in safety was driven by the political aim of using safety as an industrial relations weapon. I will say much more on this later.

Anyway, during these four years I worked around Grangemouth, including at the BP site, and did a bit of travelling as well, until I applied for a job back at Grangemouth again because of the insecurity of contract work and my plans to get married to my partner Wendy. I took the aptitude test, had an interview, and started back in August 1988 as a process operator.

Wendy and I were married on 9 June 1989 and now is as good a time as any to tell you that my son Ross Hugh was born on 10 June 1990 and my daughter Hannah Louise was born on 15 September 1992. Ross and Louise are very different people, but Wendy and I are proud of them both, and love them very much.

By the time I returned to the site in 1988 it was almost unrecognisable. Dramatic changes had taken place. If the unions were trying to tell the company what to do and totally resisting change then they were definitely going the wrong way about it. (The Italian Alps indeed!)

A changed environment

The site changes over those four years included the total closure of the fabrication workshop, the relocation or redundancy of everyone in it, and the outsourcing of carpenters, glaziers, gardeners, canteen workers, a big chunk of the maintenance workforce, riggers, scaffolders, chauffeurs, and more.

Our Unite director for education, Jim Mowatt, has a saying that in good companies there is sometimes a reduction in the workforce, but workers should be piped ashore not made to walk the plank.

In the end all the affected workers at the site had been accommodated, but the fact remains that a significant number of good quality in-house jobs had been lost.

Agreements like the 'trigger and demarcation protocol' were also gone, and so was the domestic agreement protecting contractors at the site.

It was also around this time that BP began to contract out tanker drivers to external firms.

The story of the site is one of constant change and resultant job reductions. I don't want to go into detail about all the company reviews over the years, but it felt as if a programme of redundancies would be initiated every few years – that this was the 'BP way'. The difficult issue for our unions was that employees came to expect – and even plan around – these early retirement programmes. People could retire at age 50 with a reasonable pension and up to 27 months' pay as a lump sum, depending on service.

With these incentives in place it was sometimes more a question of a race for the door than an industrial campaign to preserve the jobs.

When I started back in 1988 I was assigned to the hydrocracker plant (which was still being rebuilt following the fatal explosion), and life went on for a while. The plant makes and upgrades oil-derived products like petrol, diesel and kerosene for fuelling aircraft engines. Over the years I trained on all the posts, including all aspects of the operator's job.

In the early 1990s BP – following the UK political and sector trend – moved to de-recognise the unions for the purposes of collective bargaining. Unions at a number of other refineries in the UK had already been de-recognised, and the company embarked on a relentless campaign to dismantle the standing arrangements.

The company talked about lack of investment, and offered a six per cent pay rise and a lump sum to union members in return for giving up their rights. A number of meetings took place, and communications were sent directly to members' homes setting out the company position.

It always struck me that the odious practice of sending out communications to employees' homes was designed to hack away at the security of families and to infiltrate the most sacred of relationships, in the hope that pressure would be applied from home so that the company would have its way.

Members were not given a yes or no vote on de-recognition. Instead they were bombarded with consent forms and asked to sign up. After months of this campaign the company managed to get 61 per cent of members to sign up, and then they de-recognised us. Campbell Christie, general secretary of the STUC at the time, described the BP action as a mixture of threats and bribery.

It was a very difficult time at the site, but BP was astute, it has to be conceded: after this period of conflict, they immediately moved to build bridges with union members and union representatives. This is what any sane, sensible and stable organisation would do in such circumstances.

There was no move to industrial action at the time of de-recognition – and a number of opinions have been expressed over the years on that. The bottom line is that the company had navigated through this process and got what they wanted.

In fact, during the many decades BP owned the refinery and chemical plants there was, I think, one token strike, in the 1970s. Apart from that, there were no strikes. This trend continues to this day at the BP-owned exploration site in the town. Sure there are contrasting positions and robust debate, but no real unrest. Industrial conflict arrived at Grangemouth on the same horse that was ridden in by Ineos.

Following de-recognition BP then set up consultation forums. These were dreadful and ineffective, of course, but they were at least asking for opinions from the workforce, and these bodies were filled with union members.

European Works Councils were also set up, including UK consultation meetings, so our union representatives were also involved in these.

And our senior stewards were still engaged in councils dealing with pensions, and continued to act as trustees of the schemes.

One element of union recognition maintained by BP was in safety representation – including the position of safety reps and the committee structures involving both management and unions. Given the hazardous nature of the business, it is absolutely vital that strong and robust representation from the workforce is in place. I will come to the irresponsible and dangerous actions of Ineos in this regard later, but for now it should be noted that the destruction of safety structures and committees is potentially life-threatening, and this was one of the most disturbing and foolhardy elements of the events of 2013 and beyond.

During my studies of health and safety over this period I gained a NEBOSH (National Examination Board in Occupational Safety and Health) certificate, and was awarded both parts of its diploma – a degree equivalent. I have since gained chartered status of IOSH (Institute of Occupational Safety and Health) through continuous professional development. (One of the Ineos managers, Declan Sealy, was later to suggest that I had studied in my own time for about five years just so I could use safety as a political weapon!) Around 2005 I was offered a job as a safety manager by BP, an offer that was fronted by Grangemouth site manager Gordon Grant. I have to say I was briefly tempted by this offer, but the draw of my trade union work was too much.

One of the positives of BP, in contrast to Ineos, was that it was open to sponsoring this type of development. Ineos withdrew all this kind of assistance for people like me. One of the company's first acts was to scrap the system whereby management paid for professional subscriptions – at a stroke weakening links with other specialists in the sector and undermining access to the industry's collective intelligence. From now on people would have to pay their own fees. I did pay them myself incidentally, and the company got the value of this big time.

I was also asked to take up a directorship with 'Cogent', which was the Skills Sector Council set up by the government to facilitate training in the oil and gas industry. As part of this I contributed to training plans and direction across the whole of the oil sector. This was really interesting work. My drive was to bring about training at an appropriate level to admit a diverse population to the industry. I think there was a real bias towards academia in terms of recruitment selection, and this continues to this day. A good selection of craftsmen and women were, in my opinion, the backbone of the industry, and I strove to move the training agenda in this direction.

The HR function in our industry is often out of touch completely, and there is an insistence on psychometric cleansing, as I would describe it. This involved a barrage of nonsensical psychological recruitment tests, with no identifiable relevance to the industry.

Despite all this upheaval at the site, it more or less hung together, and the vast majority of employees remained in BP Grangemouth employment. The safety performance of the site was by no means brilliant, but it was reasonable, and was improving as a result of the hard work of our representatives and the attitude and culture of the company.

This is in stark contrast to the disastrous position at the site today.

During the anti-union phase of BP's reign, people came to be paid different wages for doing the same job. It was one of a number of retrograde changes which created ill-feeling and poor teamwork. All this had a negative effect generally on every aspect of performance, and this process of decline ultimately contributed to the downfall of the forced de-recognition and new arrangements.

In the end this industrial relations experiment to de-recognise our unions failed, and collective bargaining was restored when conditions were aligned across the site (see p32). And the inequality and injustice that had resulted in the site's terms and conditions was corrected. The key point here for me is that oppression and removal of basic rights can prevail for a time but not forever. Many commentators predicted that the unions would be forever in the wilderness after de-recognition. But that did not happen – and ultimately the situation at Ineos will also be reversed.

When I think about all the changes at the site that were imposed on us, I keep coming back to that assertion by Ratcliffe and Loftus that the union was in charge!

1997 and all that

By 1997 my big mate Ian Proudlove and I had become stewards. He was minute secretary and I was vice chair of the branch within a few years (a meteoric rise eh?). We were also heavily involved in the Labour Party and had been campaigning hard for a change of government. Our minds were very much on the manifesto commitment to restore the right to collective bargaining, with minimum standards enforceable by the Central Arbitration Committee (CAC).

Thankfully the Tories were heavily defeated and, yes, we did stay up for the heart-warming scenes when Michael Portillo lost his seat.

Ian and I had been located in the same area of the refinery when I returned to the site in 1998 and had hit it off right away. Ian became a steward before me and encouraged me to get back involved with the union. Between us we have seen it all, holding every branch position, attending some meetings with hundreds to talk about wage deals and others with three men and a whippet on a wet Wednesday night when the football was on the telly. We've been to disciplinaries and grievances, and dealt with the irrational and the eloquent, poets and maniacs, and the terminally stupid. There have been glorious gestures that buoyed us for weeks and selfish acts that crushed us. There was blood and tears, laughter that made you sore inside, gallons of beer in the Mahratta public house and enough management bungling to last a hundred lifetimes. We have sat side by side for decades through all this and I am the richer for it.

Ian is a superb tactician and the most professional of union representatives. We differ on the 'old firm' football divide between Celtic and Rangers, but as aficionados of Laurel and Hardy we are united as sons of the desert: 'Why don't you do something to help me!'

A number of things were going on at the site around this time.

BP 'reviews' seemed to take place time and again. The latest thinking was to depart from the separate-business model and to merge the refinery, chemical and exploration units into one Grangemouth managed site.

One example that will give you a sense of these reviews was the refinery maintenance strategy. The constant reviews were not always about job losses or the future of the plant. On this occasion a certain maintenance 'expert' came to the site from America, and brought with him the gift of 'run to destruction' maintenance.

The thinking here was that it could be more cost-effective to run equipment like pumps or compressors until they broke down, blew up or exploded and then fix them. In so doing the cost of regular preventative maintenance schedules would be somehow saved.

It seems even crazier than it sounds when I reflect back on this – but that was the thinking. Obviously our union protested in the strongest terms at all kinds of meetings and forums, but the practice was adopted.

To cut a long story short, the refinery ended up on its knees. Thankfully no one was badly hurt, but the plant was like a disaster zone. A guy called Tony then arrived from Australia to be the refinery manager. We liked him. He was small on talk but big on expletives and he went ballistic when he saw the state of the place. In the

Hydrocracker area there were no spare pumps as they were all in bits. Tony shut the plant down and refused to start it (big cost to BP) until all the maintenance had been carried out and the plants made safe.

The awful and depressing thing about this story is that so many managers went along with all this without protest. They must have known it was wrong. Think about your own car – it's always best to change the oil before the engine seizes.

But managers often feed off each other when someone comes up with the latest crackpot idea. It's like a cloak of confidence. There is a saying in safety circles that 'there is nothing more dangerous than a confident idiot'.

Such intellectual jewels of progressive thinking were usually rolled out at meetings with the message that this was it! We have cracked it now. This time next year we will all be millionaires. (To quote British blues band Rev Doc and the Congregation, 'If trouble was money, I guess I'd be a millionaire'.)

These guys would show up and use words they clearly had only the weakest grasp of – along the lines of 'centralisation, leading to improved synergies and cost saving by economies of scale and collective learning and the sharing of best practice'. It was all utter guff. And the next time you saw them they would be arguing that the only way to go was 'deep and integral, demand driven services'. It's the future!

Almost my favourite was the myth peddled by consultants who liked to produce 'ice breakers' at the start of meetings by asking someone the question 'What did the cleaner, who was sweeping the floor, reply at the NASA space centre when JFK asked what he was doing?' The contrived and fictitious answer is of course: 'I am putting a man on the moon'.

Now clearly this never happened. Someone sweeping the floor when the President was visiting? I don't think so. But I always thought the correct response would have been: 'I'm sweeping this floor for minimum wage, and, as a result, I can't afford healthcare or to send my kids to college Mr President.'

This was nearly my favourite, but the hands-down winner came from another refinery which will remain nameless. The company had come up with the slogan … 'Feedback is the breakfast of champions'.

This one will never be beaten.

But to return to the issue of unquestioning compliance – a rep of ours once told me about a manager that he'd had an argument with about yet another new initiative. As usual the manager stoutly defended the latest fad. The rep had known the manager for decades, and they had seen dozens, or maybe even hundreds, of small and large initiatives implemented over the years, and yet this manager had never found any of them disagreeable. Not any of them! As the rep asked, is that even possible?

Those words stuck with me because such passive obedience is not only distasteful, undignified and worthy of contempt, it is also very dangerous in an industry like ours.

This is why independent and well-trained union reps acting freely on behalf of the workforce are so valuable. Good employers welcome and embrace this, and engage robustly and openly with them. But the Dickensian mill-owner model, with no respect for the workers or their expertise, produces the type of dangerous decline in safety performance that is now evident at Ineos Grangemouth.

Aligning conditions across the site

BP now began to look again at union/management relationships, prompted by two factors: the drive to manage the three businesses as one, and the impending legislation giving us the chance to restore collective bargaining.

The task of aligning the businesses was not easy, and our differing union arrangements in each division did not help. All the differences had arisen historically, partly in reaction to different sector trends and partly in reaction to the way the company had lurched from one initiative to another, sometimes in response to the usual range of industry 'benchmarks'.

The pay in the refinery was miles ahead of the chemical plant. Some of our operators doing very similar jobs were as much as £10,000 adrift. The agreements on terms and conditions were also completely different – from holiday entitlement, to specific payments for certain tasks and conditions, to the cost of the canteen and all points in between.

The shift system was also different in each division. Employees in the chemical plant worked a twelve-hour pattern, the refinery an eight-hour pattern. The shift allowance payment was miles apart as well.

Refinery operators had additional payments of 6.3 per cent of salary a year. This was because they had been forced to work in self-managed teams following de-recognition. The payment was in lieu of overtime payments for sickness, holidays, training and the like.

The maintenance teams' set-up, practices and procedures had also been subject to similar changes around this time.

When overtime was paid, it was at 1.67 times the basic rate for refinery workers and 1.75 times the basic rate for those who worked in the chemical plants.

All the HR processes except group ones were also different – for sickness absence, maternity and so on, and dozens and dozens of other policies.

There were entirely different domestic and Europe consultation bodies and works councils, and the pension structures were also different.

The companies were managed by three separate management teams, with three general managers.

Our branches were totally independent of each other. One T&G branch represented members in the refinery and exploration sites, the other branch represented people who worked in the chemicals sites. There were also different branch practices. For example there was a convenor in the chemicals plant but not in the refinery.

Anyway, you get the picture – bringing all this into one structure was not going to be easy.

The first step was for the company to bring together our union reps and to ask us to operate in one consultation structure. I was heavily involved in all this because Trevor George, our long-time branch secretary, was not in good health and was handing over some of the duties to Ian Proudlove and me.

The company brought in an American consultant to facilitate talks to assist in bringing together all the contrasting issues and to provide training on the process of change. Pretty expensive I understand, but it did help to provide a place to start.

I had argued from the minute this process started that we would have to have aligned wages and conditions, and a return to full collective bargaining. You would have thought I had taken leave of my senses from the way this assertion was received. It was considered unachievable. The company were the principal sceptics, but they were not the only ones.

In time everything was aligned as I had predicted. It just made sense that this would happen. I could see no other possible outcome if the site was to be run as one business. I am not telling you this to let you know how clever I was, but because it is important to our story – the move towards equality started to take root and grow from then on.

It's important to talk about some of the main kinds of re-alignment so that you can get some sense of the dramatic and difficult changes we were involved in.

Wading through treacle

During the alignment process, all the employment and pay policies had to be scrutinised, adjusted and agreed one by one, line by line, clause by clause. If you had put an animal through this torture they would have sent for the RSPCA. Eventually the process was completed after months of laborious work, as well as the – not insignificant – task of securing agreement from our members.

As if we had not suffered enough, we had completed a job evaluation process just prior to the talks on aligning the plants, placing members and jobs in a proposed structure to go to the branches for their approval. This was little more than a horse-trading exercise, but we had worked hard as a union to place jobs fairly. To be honest the result looked suspiciously like the position prior to de-recognition.

Some of the most contentious issues in the alignment process were the removal of fixed payments and the change to straight overtime rates. This was much fairer, and more lucrative for our members, but there was, as always, a healthy debate and differing views.

Negotiations started with two T&G branches in the room and one set of company representatives. However, despite management's efforts to present one position, it was clear that the company was all over the place and subject to pressure from the three separate entities.

After many meetings, much messing around and lots of unpleasantness, we got to the end of the matter. Trevor George was still our branch secretary and he was leading for us. The process on the final day of negotiations went like this … First of all the company produced a spreadsheet with all the existing pay rates for individuals and where they worked (without names). What a mess it was! The pay range was all over the place. In the short time the company had enjoyed control over individuals' pay, the inequality among people doing the same job in the same areas was unbelievable. If ever a negative example for performance-related pay was needed, this was it.

The spreadsheet also set out the proposed new grading, and where members would sit in it, and then how members would be positioned after adding some cash. After this proposed adjustment all the chemical members would have big rises, but in the refinery branch something like 270 members would lose out. It would have been very difficult to ask our refinery members to agree to this, and Trevor then dropped the immortal words 'what happens to the number of people who would lose out if we put five hundred pounds on each grade?'.

I remember it as if it were yesterday.

A man from HR, who we used to call the Professor, fed the data into the financial sausage machine with the extra £500 added to each grade, and it came back with the result that the refinery members would then have about 50 people who would lose out. Not easy for us, but deliverable, and in all cases right and equitable and just.

The company reps looked at the numbers and each other. Trevor whispered to me 'not far away', the laptop performed one last check and … Hey presto … Computer says yes! (Or so we thought.)

At a meeting the next day for some other talks, HR manager Brian Wishart was obviously uncomfortable. What's wrong? we asked. He said they had checked the numbers overnight and they were slightly out. How much? we asked. £45 million, he said. I jest you not friends – they were £45 million of the Queen's English pounds out on the calculation!

We did not call the HR man the professor quite so much after that.

In the end my mate Ian Proudlove, who has a good grasp of mathematics, came up with the solution. He proposed that the grades would survive, but the rises would be capped over a couple of years for those gaining most, and there the settlement would lie. There was the small matter of asking the members to agree to all this of course.

We went to two mass meetings, one for the chemicals members and run by the chemical stewards, and our one in the refinery. I don't think the chemical stewards were actually carried shoulder high up the Bo'ness Road, but it was not far off.

We, on the other hand, had a more difficult afternoon. I was the branch secretary by this time as Trevor had stepped down. Ian and I had to explain the importance of wage equality and how this would strengthen us in the long run. Not everyone was delighted, but I was really proud of the stance taken by the majority, and we achieved an overwhelming mandate to go ahead as proposed.

If you think the wages issue was difficult, the shift pattern nearly scuppered the whole deal. There is nothing more contentious than working patterns. People organise domestic and social events round shift systems – their golf, fishing, bowling and so on. Their holidays are planned years ahead, and members looked ahead to what shift they were working at Christmas and New Year, football ties and lord knows what else. We heard it all.

There were two main systems to align, the eight-hour and twelve-hour shift pattern, which were totally different in every conceivable way. Meetings took place, and email forums were set up asking what folks thought (big mistake). Our branch had a standing order that the shift pattern could not be changed except by a two-thirds majority. This was very difficult, but we eventually persuaded the members, in the interest of unity, to accept a straight vote on a possible four patterns – and we got there.

A hundred and one issues like this consumed us, but you get the picture.

The other alignment issue was, of course, our union structures. To cut a very long story short, there were two branches, with two sets of personalities and ideas and history – but we did eventually get there. We ended up with two conveners, but over time we moved to one. By 2013 I was convener, Stevie Deans was branch secretary and vice-convener, and Ian was branch chair. We also had – and still have – the most fantastic and hard-working stewards and safety reps committees.

I would like to point out here that the full-time status Stevie and I 'enjoyed' did not originate at our request. Initially the company asked us to go full-time for set-piece issues, and over time this gradually became the norm. The positions were eventually consolidated as part of the evolving facilities arrangements and agreements. I think something was lost by not being on shift and on the factory floor every day, but the practicalities and volume of work made this pretty much impossible.

It is also worth pointing out that I had been scheduled to begin training to become a panel operator at this time, but I did not have the chance to take up the role because the company asked me to come off shift. The role I had been scheduled to take up involved controlling the process from a computer console, and attracted a much higher salary than that of outside operator, which involved more manual work. My reason for mentioning this is not to request a place on the list of national martyrs based on my significant loss of earnings over the years, but merely to give you a sense of my involvement and motivation. The company lackeys, led by the chief executive Ratcliffe, have since labelled this as my personal agenda.

Anyway, no matter how you cut it – whether you address these issues from the floor of a mass meeting or from the saddle of a bicycle in the thin and crisp mountain air – none of this was easy. The industry and our site was changing rapidly.

CHAPTER 3

Enter Ineos

The last days of BP

IN 2001 BP announced that up to 1000 of the existing 2500 employees would be made redundant at the Grangemouth site. A number of processes would close in the chemicals plant, as well as the 'Number One Crude Distillation Unit' in the refinery (keep that one in mind, it comes into the story later – see p180).

The day this was all announced was memorable for two reasons. The first reason was the shocking enormity of the proposed job losses, and the second reason was that this was 11 September 2001, the day that the twin towers were destroyed in New York.

We were at the old BP club that day to hear the company announcement when the unbelievable news filtered through.

There were also plans announced that day to outsource some departments, including our water treatment sites. One of the principal management arguments for this centred on environmental considerations. The company proposed using 'grey water' rather than purified town water, on the grounds that this was friendly to the environment and much less expensive.

We listened with incredulity to the nonsense the company was offering. They said they would drill wells under the Forth estuary to find such water and install pipelines to the local canal, and that they would take water from a local river called the Avon. We instinctively knew this was not going to happen. Needless to say, none of this has ever been implemented.

Gordon Grant much later told us that the threat to move to grey water had assisted in reducing the cost of purified clean water when negotiating the price from the council, even though the company had never had any real intention of doing so. Pretty shocking behaviour.

After meeting with the members we resolved to resist compulsory redundancies by any means necessary. This would potentially include industrial action. We also prepared reports on the safety implications of the proposed cuts, and made representations to the Health and Safety Executive (HSE).

To cut a long story short, BP eventually came to an agreement with us on phasing in the reductions and reducing the number of job losses. We also worked hard on the safety aspects as a union, and found a way through this further difficult and unpalatable business.

The deal to save so many people's jobs was signed, rather bizarrely, in a bedroom in a local hotel called the Leapark, between myself and Colin McLean, who was general manager at the time. Dougie Rae, an industrial relations coordinator who had been instrumental in brokering this deal, was also in attendance. The room had been cleared of all furniture that day except for a table and chairs placed in the centre for our use. It was a very strange setting but the agreement was signed within the hour.

The deal had, pleasingly, been done behind the backs of management representatives in McLean's team, and it was obvious how sick and betrayed these zealots felt the next day when McLean and I met them to tell them the good news. Imagine being disappointed because working people were not going to be made redundant?

Many non-union employees benefited from our deal as well, and I was glad we had insisted that the company did not differentiate. I just sometimes wish that people who choose not to join our union would at least acknowledge the force for good that our organisation is.

I personally represented members in dozens and dozens of appeals against redundancies, and this was one of the most difficult periods of my life. People were terrified for their families and it was very upsetting. We found out that one of the company managers had been at a local hotel walking around with a baseball bat pointing to names on a list on the wall and gleefully identifying employees who were targeted to lose their jobs. It was disgusting and brutal behaviour.

Happily, between volunteers and jobs saved, extended leaving dates and some work between the lines, I don't think any of our union members were driven out. I don't think the same could be said for all of the staff employees.

I should also say that I was proud that our members accepted a one per cent pay rise at this time, which was way below inflation, in exchange for saving more jobs.

One of the most touching episodes of my time at the site came from all this. I had declined working on a big plant overhaul programme on the part of the site where I worked. Typically, these happened for a few months every few years, and everyone made a good few bob working extra hours. But this time the maintenance programme coincided with the raft of redundancy appeals, and I had declined the overtime so that I could concentrate on helping the members with their cases.

At the end of all this I was about on my knees, and then the troops from my plant said they wanted to see me. I fully expected yet another set of problems to be landed on my desk.

When they gave me a substantial sum of vouchers so my wife and I could have a nice holiday I was overwhelmed by their thoughtfulness and kindness. It's not often I am lost for words but I was then.

The job losses were eventually reduced to – a still disastrous – 700 or so, but it is near impossible to calculate the loss of contractor, agency and suppliers jobs resulting from the site shrinkage. It was a considerable blow to the community.

Our union members and all our representatives were faced with challenges never before faced but we proceeded with great flexibility, pragmatism and integrity. This working attitude continues to this day, as you will see later in the book.

It is worth saying that, on reflection, I can see that the cost-cutting moves were most likely well thought out preparatory steps in a plan by BP to exit manufacturing in Grangemouth. But we did not know that at the time.

Innovene ... the IPO that never was

In spring 2004 BP announced that its Olefins and Polymers division was to be spun off as a separate company. And in November 2004 it added two refineries to its new business – Grangemouth and Lavéra, in France. In April 2005 it created from these the 100% BP-owned subsidiary Innovene. In September 2005 it announced that Innovene shares would be traded on the stock exchange in an IPO (Initial Public Offering).

The new company from the beginning encompassed sites across the world and included the chemicals part of our site. That constituted probably between a third and a half of the workforce and about half of the footprint of the Grangemouth complex.

This was massive news at the site, and once more caused real uncertainty and insecurity. After all the work that had been done to align the site, now we had the latest lurch to split and sell.

Preparations began to be made for the establishment of the new company and the extensive consequent changes to operations at the Grangemouth site. The position of our members in the chemicals branch was initially to oppose the spin-off, and a campaign of resistance began. I attended weekly meetings of the stewards and our excellent Labour MP Michael Connarty. I have to say I had a slightly different opinion on the spin-off. Even though there were a million and one concerns to be addressed, I felt that remaining in a company that did not want the factory would not be sustainable in the long run.

However I was employed in the refinery, which at first was not included in the new company, so I kept my opinions to myself and supported the chemicals branch campaign 100 per cent.

It was not that long before things changed dramatically. The IPO idea was scrapped and Ineos was taking over the lot, including the refinery as well as the chemical business. Our branch members found themselves in a different situation altogether.

A mass meeting later and we were not exactly pleased at the Ineos takeover, but we were working towards it and securing terms, conditions, agreements and pensions for our members.

Matters like positions on European Works Councils were sorted in short order, and we got down to a 'traffic light' system to track and secure conditions. This meant that all the employment conditions, from canteen to pensions, were turned 'red' by us. They were then turned amber when under discussion, and green when confirmed transferred. Pretty much everything was green by the time of the sale in 2005.

However we made our concerns clear to the House of Commons Scottish Affairs Select Committee on the sustainability of the new set-up. Our evidence centred on concern over the future financial security of the site, but no obvious government intervention took place. No assurances were sought from Ineos, and no conditions for the sale even indicated.

Our concern arose because we knew that the economic survival of individual elements of the oil and petrochemical sector were inextricably linked. There are three broad sectors, which were all represented at Grangemouth at the time of the sale.

There is the exploration part of the business, which encompasses everything from drilling the seabed for oil and transporting it by pipe to the shore, the initial processing of the oil and its distribution as stabilised crude oil to refineries.

Then there are the refineries, which take the crude oil and convert it into fuels such as petrol and diesel, and feedstock flows for chemical production.

Finally there is the chemical business, taking feed from the refinery and from the exploration business and making chemicals. These are used to make plastics, for instance, or industrial alcohol.

All these sectors are cyclical in terms of demand and profitability, and it is common for one or more of the three to be making a loss at any one point. It is highly unusual for all three to be making a loss at the same time, and this is why multinational companies like Shell, Esso and BP were historically active in all three. If the chemicals sector was depressed then the refinery business would typically be making good money. Exploration has pretty much always done well – but not always. I am old enough to remember oil at $10 a barrel, which seemed inconceivable in 2014 when oil was routinely traded on the international markets at well over $100 a barrel. But the dramatic drop in oil price in 2016, to under $30 at one stage, demonstrates this point well.

The point is that a company with a footprint in all aspects of the oil industry is well placed to ride out the highs and lows of any one sector by being able to draw on financially strong parts of the business to temporarily subsidise the less profitable ones. When a company is only involved in one part of the chain, it makes it financially vulnerable.

Many of the multinationals decided to get out of the manufacturing end of the business around this same time, to concentrate on exploration and oil trading. In my opinion there were two main reasons for this 'strategic' move. The first was a short-term outlook that the oil price would always be relatively high and that any investment would be better placed in exploration and crude oil handling rather than in manufacturing, where recent profit margins had been lower.

The other important reason was the safety liability at manufacturing sites, and the damage to company reputation and shareholder confidence when accidents happen. An example of this is the explosion at BP's Texas City complex in 2005, which killed 15 people and injured more than 170.

It is ironic, therefore, that the biggest reputational and financial damage to BP occurred in its crude oil business, in April 2010. A huge explosion at the drilling rig Deepwater Horizon in the Gulf of Mexico caused what is regarded as the biggest marine oil spill in history. It is sometimes forgotten amid all the environmental discussions about the disaster that 11 workers lost their lives. It has been said that the incident came close to 'killing the company'.

I am sure the same corporate assurances were given to governments, regulators and members of the public alike over the safety of drilling in the Gulf as are currently being offered over fracking and unconventional gas extraction.

All this is precisely why the golden share principle was enacted – to avoid such a carve-up; to avoid companies which own nationally important businesses abandoning key sectors in favour of the fast buck.

Obviously the real solution to the damage caused by such short-term profit-seeking would have been to retain public ownership of all the assets, but in the absence of this, and with the golden share gone, the profitable sections have been retained by BP and the manufacturing end thrown to the wind.

There is a danger when 'two-bit' outfits, especially when they confuse ambition and capability, are able to get hold of these strategic assets. When there is the inevitable downturn, the business, jobs and economy are put at risk.

At the now defunct Coryton refinery, for instance, BP might well have ridden out a few years of loss-making and the cost of an overhaul, in the expectation of better days ahead, and being in possession of the financial clout and knowhow necessary for survival. It also held a diverse set of interests, enabling it to balance temporary losses against other sections of the portfolio. The now defunct Petroplus, however, having bought the refinery in 2007, closed it five years later as a result of mismanagement and lack of running capital.

After the Coryton refinery was discarded, BP continued to harvest billions from the exploration assets it had retained.

It was national economic suicide to allow the mixed portfolio of the once publicly-owned, and once golden-share-protected, oil, gas and chemical industry to be so mismanaged, and to be left open to the vagaries of the market.

ICI is a further classic example of a laissez-faire attitude towards key industrial sectors. There is no doubt that the management of the enormous entity that was ICI had its critics. But the organisation was able to support internal business divisions in short term difficulties by using the sum of all its parts and resources. The history of ICI after its sale to Dutch multinational AkzoNobel is one of sell-offs, division and subdivision, resulting in closure after closure.

In Grangemouth there was a site run by ICI where many thousands of people worked. It covered miles of land with many diverse, inter-related and productive plants. Today the site has withered away to a few scraps of activity operated by different companies. The work is valuable and important to the town, but the site is now a dim shadow of its former self.

At this stage, however, I will make a statement you may search high and low within Ineos to find any other employee making …

I am glad that the refinery and chemicals plants at Grangemouth were sold to Ineos.

Yes, you read correctly. It is clear beyond doubt that a group of responsible adults (government ministers maybe?) should have stepped in when BP started to back out of manufacturing, to ensure that the overall profits of the industry were used to support the entire industry, and not just to provide short-term gain for shareholders. However, in the absence of such good sense, it would have been even worse if the chemicals division had gone to IPO. I am sure that the new company would have struggled badly during the recession as a stand-alone entity, and would have been subject to shrinkage or worse. I am also convinced that the refinery would have been sold to Petroplus instead of Ineos as part of the same disposal strategy, and would have been liable to the same fate as the Coryton refinery.

BP was, in any case, resolved to exit these companies. It was inevi-table that they would have done so at some stage.

It's just my opinion – and it's a bit like saying would you rather have thumb screws than hot needles in your eyes – but I think we have been landed with the slightly lesser of two evils.

The point is, though, that there is no regulation in place to prevent random acts and spurious decision-making having a massive and irre-versible effect on factories and the people who work in them, or rely on them for their livelihoods.

Where is our coherent manufacturing strategy? In 2013, on behalf of our union, I asked this question of Ed Balls, then Labour's shadow chancellor, from the floor of the TUC congress. I inquired whether a Labour government intended to install a minister for manufacturing if they were elected. I didn't get an answer.

It's quite big isn't it?

Ineos bought the whole of the Olefins and Polymers chemical business and two refineries for a reported $9 billion, according to the Ineos website. Yet when its representatives first arrived on the site they told us that not one hour of due diligence to appraise the condition of the plant and equipment had been undertaken.

It appears that the deal was signed and sealed in short order. BP CEO, Lord John Browne of Madingley, proclaimed that it was a good deal all round – as I remember, he said it was the best of a number of good deals.

No doubt it was, for you, Johnny boy!

All the money used to buy the business was borrowed from banks, every bit of it. The whole shooting match was bought by a company with no refinery experience, in what is a cyclical and volatile business. BP's profit centres were now weighted towards oil exploration, in common with all the 'wise' money, and there were projections of a further move in that direction. There was a serious recession just round the corner. What could possibly go wrong?

Another problem when BP sold off the site was the loss of managerial experience and competence. This did not happen all at once – it is still continuing to this day – but the employment status of managers and technical specialists at Grangemouth was immediately downgraded. As you would expect, some of the most senior managers were on the lifeboats back to BP right away, but over the years many talented and ambitious people have continued to leave, from a desire to pursue their careers with credible and well-known multinational companies.

Today, the trickle of leavers from the site has become a flood.

It is probably best not to say too much about the remaining management team. At least they are obviously content to stay on, and most of them try their best to be fair.

Tom Crotty, an Ineos director, came to meet us at the site shortly after the sale. We were genuinely welcoming as we felt let down and abandoned by BP, and thought it was at least of some comfort that this company, Ineos, wanted to own the site.

We still have a laugh when we think back to the day Tom arrived. Having seen the Grangemouth site for the very first time Tom looked up in childlike wonderment and commented, wide-eyed and breathless: 'It's quite big isn't it?'

Priceless. Bear in mind they had paid $9 billion for the businesses ... Critics would maybe say that an extensive programme of inspection and due diligence prior to the sale would have been appropriate.

I also have a movie running in my mind where wee Lord Browne, in a camel coat and with his trademark cigar, has made a drawing with crayons for Jim Ratcliffe, to show him how grand it all was – alas, only in my mind. But you get the feeling the plants were sold on like a fifth-hand Austin Allegro, but for Aston Martin money.

The serious side of this is that the plants, many of which were already built when Paraffin Young was still a paperboy, were now fully laden with debt to be paid off before grossing a single dollar. These plants must have paid for themselves over and over again during many decades of production with BP. Many of them were built with pre-decimal money, and yet here we were, placed in a position where crippling debt was strangling the business.

Someone said at the time that the sale of these divisions to Ineos reminded him of an ant trying to swallow an elephant.

At the time of the Ineos take-over it was clear that BP had underinvested in maintenance in some areas. One example was the tank farm, where products are stored and blended. At the time of the sale this area was not in good condition at all – believe it or not, nearly a decade later the maintenance and repair programme was still ongoing. Ineos told us that BP had given them a substantial amount of money to undertake the project. I don't know how much, but that is what they told us after the sale.

None of this represents sensible management by any measure. If you wanted to jeopardise the future of the factory this was the way to go.

I remember meeting a guy from Petroplus at an environmental and energy conference in Edinburgh, just at the time when they were contemplating buying Coryton from BP. The man from Petroplus was obviously pretty excited about the whole thing and looking forward to getting the keys. He was surprised when I asked him if he had seen the tank farm yet. I don't know where he works now but it sure is not Coryton, and he certainly knows why I asked him that question. The BP Coryton tank farm, it turned out, was in the same poor condition as the one at BP Grangemouth: it is clear that BP had followed a path of minimal maintenance of such equipment. You have to conclude that this neglect took place in anticipation of selling on the refineries and other manufacturing sites.

'Let the markets decide'? Well they had as far as Grangemouth was concerned. In the absence of any government control or overview, any joined-up manufacturing and economic strategy or intervention, or even the seeking of any guarantees, the site that reportedly accounts for more than 10 per cent of Scotland's GDP had now been precariously placed on a cliff edge.

We met a few times with the aforementioned Tom Crotty at this time. One of the things he told us was that Ineos did not believe in the use of consultants. But Price Waterhouse Cooper and T.A. Cook were engaged within months in order to identify cost-cutting to the tune of 20 per cent.

Tom also told us that Ineos wanted to invest in the site and maybe build new plants. We were very keen to engage and assist with any of that. In the event, of course, plants were closed rather than built and the chemicals site in particular is now much reduced. A proposed bio-diesel plant failed to materialise, and the overall story is one of dramatic decline.

The other thing Tom identified almost immediately was that the company wanted to close the final salary pension scheme. This was extraordinary: the scheme was in surplus and we had received assurances that it was secure at the time of the transfer, a matter of weeks previously. Tom explained that Jim Ratcliffe did not believe in such pension schemes. He thought they were old-fashioned. The economics of our scheme was therefore not the relevant issue. Jim just wanted to close all such schemes in Ineos.

We were also granted an audience with James Arthur Ratcliffe just after the sale, in early 2006. He came to the site and we were allowed to actually meet him! He was very untidy and dishevelled, and his remarkably floppy hair was also of some note. What might have been a thrilling experience was somewhat tinged with disappointment, however, as his manner was somewhat unpleasant: he treated us as if we were something the store cat had dragged in. I remember well the exchange and the approximate words I used. I told him that we welcomed the sale, and asked only that we would have a seat at the table so we could work well together. We also asked for assurances on investment at the site and corresponding job security for our members.

He just kind of grunted as I remember, and the historic liaison was soon over.

I will return later to the pension dispute of 2008 (see pp53–60), but you can see that from the very first moment the die was pretty much cast.

LETTER FROM STEVIE DEANS TO THE CHAIRMAN OF THE COMMONS SCOTTISH AFFAIRS COMMITTEE 21 JUNE 2007

Thank you for your letter dated 21 May regarding your inclination to follow up on the evidence that was given in July 2004, November 2004 and January 2005 on the implications for Grangemouth of BP's plans for its petrochemical business.

You will recall that the main focus of the trade union evidence given to the committee was on BP's original intention to sell only the Olefins & Derivatives business at Grangemouth and retain ownership of the Refinery and the Kinneil/Dalmeny Facilities, and the effect that this would have on the Grangemouth site, as well as the local and national economy. The trade union was particularly concerned, at the time, with the possible detrimental impact on the continuing safe, efficient and profitable operation of the site and the negative effect that de-integrating the businesses at Grangemouth could have on the long-term viability of the site and thus the Scottish economy.

As you are no doubt aware, since the report on this matter was compiled, BP went on to sell the whole of its Grangemouth Complex to the chemical company INEOS – excluding only the Forties Pipeline System Terminal at Kinneil and storage and shipping facilities at Dalmeny/Houndpoint.

In many respects the Ineos approach to business has been a welcome change from that of BP. There has been some investment in remediation of the site infrastructure and announcements have been made on further unconfirmed investment – a proposed Bio-Diesel plant and expansion of KG ethylene plant. Unfortunately though, almost immediately after purchasing the site, Ineos embarked on cost cutting exercises. The first was when Price Waterhouse Coopers were engaged to identify cuts of 20% in non-manpower fixed costs and then another consultant, T A Cook, were engaged to assist with a project to ensure that the site is profitable at the bottom of the business cycle through identifying operational/maintenance cost cuts, including manpower resources. These and other issues give the trade union great concern as to the future of sustainable, safe and efficient manufacturing at the Grangemouth site.

Not least of these other issues is the concern on which we gave evidence to the committee previously, the de-integration of businesses at Grangemouth. The Ineos philosophy is very focused on business divisions and they have imposed a model of management and organisation on the site which could arguably have worse consequences than the initial de-integration proposed by BP.

The organisation at Grangemouth site is now divided into four separate and autonomous businesses which report directly to CEOs offsite – Refining, Olefins, Polyolefins and Enterprises – with a central services organisation that is supposed to co-ordinate and run the site as one single operation.

We believe that the issues that were raised in our previous evidence to the committee regarding de-integration of businesses at Grangemouth are just as valid today, if not more so, given the Ineos business model that has been imposed on our site.

The issues pointed out in your letter are particularly acute with regard to the Polyethylene business and the proposed closure for 'economic reasons' in December of the Innovene 2 Plant, which produces High Density Polyethylene, with production being moved to a plant in Belgium. The company have also made it clear that they believe that the remaining Polyethylene plant, Innovene 4, is underperforming according to their measures, which gives us great concern over the future of this plant.

There are also a number of health and safety issues which give great concern to the trade union and some of these are linked to the site de-integration. There are a number of issues particularly related to the legacy that BP left us with through the years of cost cutting, de-manning, underinvestment and lack of preventative maintenance. The latter is now manifesting itself in failures of particular equipment, extremely high levels of overtime being worked, skills shortages and also the previously unknown phenomenon at Grangemouth, of large numbers of people leaving and going to work elsewhere.

In conclusion, I would like to thank you for revisiting this matter and would ask you to contact us at any time if you require any further information.

In 2007 our plant vice convenor Stevie Deans wrote to the chairman of the Commons Scottish affairs committee on our behalf as a follow-up to the evidence we gave at the time of the sale (see pp48–9).

The letter set out our general observations and predictions. No one could have then foreseen the utter disaster unfolding, but readers will see that we were very uneasy at that stage, and that we were indicating continuously to the political world that all was not well. No political intervention, that I can identify, occurred at this stage.

Portents of trouble

It turns out that Ineos has a formulaic approach to cost-cutting after they buy a business. They talk about this on their website, boasting about how they take businesses and reduce costs and turn around the factories and generally save the day. This is not borne out by the facts. The Grangemouth site was profitable when they bought it. The pension scheme was substantially in surplus, and the factory was far bigger than it is today in terms of plant and equipment, and had a stable and highly skilled workforce. Ineos ownership has been very negative and damaging for our site.

Union colleagues from other sites owned by the company contacted us at the point of the takeover and made a couple of key observations. After relaying jocular commiserations (at least we thought they were joking at the time), they told us about the company's proud boast that 'Ineos is not a paternal company'. We had to work that out, but we now realise that what they were saying was that there was no warmth in the working relationship. Warmth is my own word here, but what I mean is that the relationship was always about paying only whatever they had to, for as much work as they could get. And if you took ill or could no longer continue, whether because of age or some other reason, you should just quietly go.

Our colleagues' words have often come back to mind over the time Ineos has owned the site. The declared position from Ineos is that good pensions are not acceptable, and they have also savagely destroyed the long-standing protection employees once enjoyed at our site for those in ill health. Their dismantling of agreements in these areas has been devastating for our vulnerable members and their spouses and children. These attacks on sick people constitute one of the most odious of all the selfish cuts they have imposed.

The other thing we were told by our Ineos union colleagues was the parable of the apple and the dinner money. The parable goes like this. If you give the school bully your apple, they want your dinner money. If you give them that they want your bus fare home. If you give them that it's your designer trainers. They will not stop until they have taken possession of your grandmother's stair lift. The only way to break this chain is to stand up and say No. We thought our colleagues must be trying to wind us up.

Between 2006 and 2008 the story of the take-over was one of review, poorly-founded assertions and ill-advised cost-cutting, with the consultants never too far away. Our technicians and non-collective but unionised staff workforce are highly skilled, diligent and competent, and the bulk of them stuck around during this time. The reason for this was that they had a voice and a say through their union, and still felt part of the Grangemouth site. Ineos were viewed as guests on our site, and even though some poor decisions and incompetence were evident, this was nothing new to us – our members were not overly bothered about who was the caller at the bull crap bingo.

The picture for middle and senior management was very different. The exodus of those able to hold their own in the global industry began almost straightaway. A number of senior managers went back to BP and gradually took their teams with them. Others who were mobile and capable took up positions with credible multinational players in the industry. The damage from this was not immediately apparent. But today I don't think it is too unkind to note that the Grangemouth site has not exactly been a magnet for the top management talent in the industry – and we have suffered badly as a result.

One of the outstanding issues after the sale was the loss of the BP share schemes: there was an implied agreement to make good on this. Yes I know, my lefty comrades, we should never have let a drop touch our lips – but the schemes were very much viewed as part of the wage package, and were mentioned during wage negotiations. Rightly or wrongly, but in any case importantly, our members were up in arms when Ineos told us there was to be no compensation for the loss of the schemes.

The short version of this is that we had mass meetings and lots of negotiations with the company, but eventually reached a total impasse.

A consultative ballot was carried out and members signalled by just short of 100 per cent their willingness to move to a full postal ballot for industrial action. Ineos backed down fairly swiftly. Everyone on-site – including staff members, many of whom were prone to bad-mouthing us – received two one-off payments of £3000, while a further £3000 was added to base pensionable salary.

It was pretty shocking to us, despite the successful campaign, that industrial action had come so close. BP had been on site for decades and I cannot remember ever before having such poor industrial relations, or having seen such deliberate brinksmanship.

Annus Horribilis

'touch ane touch a' tis better to meddle wi the De'il than tae tangle wi the bairns o Fakirk'

Motto of Falkirk

(*Translation: touch one and you touch all, it is better to take issue with the Devil himself than to engage in conflict with the children of Falkirk*)

During 2007 and 2008 we saw the crash and burn of the economic system around us, and the disastrous effect this had on mechanisms like the stock markets. The crisis has inexplicably led to the bedroom tax, cuts to welfare, disproportionate pain for people with disabilities and distressing effects on ordinary working people – all this accompanied by a narrative that 'we are all in this together' and must cut our cloth to suit. This was a situation brought about by, among other things, the rise of irresponsible and poorly-regulated lending to people who could not afford to hold such heavily-levered assets and were hopelessly out of their depth. Sub-prime lending of this type had collapsed the house of cards.

Reflect on that for a moment if you will – cash poured like water in loans to any joker who showed up in a bri-nylon suit and with an outstretched hand. Then, on finding out that the borrowers were totally incapable of managing the assets, everyone else having to pick up the tab.

Something worth dwelling on for a few moments?

At this stage, though, none of this had affected the Grangemouth site. There may have been indirect effects, but there was no obvious problem in relation to the crash.

However, as we have seen, in one of the first positions set out just after the sale, the company had signalled that it did not like the final salary pension scheme. This was a defined benefit scheme, i.e. the pension paid out was defined by an employee's final salary or other known factors when retiring. In such schemes the pension expected is far more certain than, for example, in defined contribution schemes. In defined benefit schemes the risk is, rightly, carried by the employer. In defined contribution pension schemes the pension paid out depends on the performance of the investments in a pension pot, i.e. the risk is all carried by the employee.

They began to make their move on the scheme in 2007, with a series of nonsensical presentations trying to justify its destruction. Their plan was to close the defined benefit scheme to new employees: the aim was to switch them to a defined contribution scheme with considerably worse terms.

Remember, the scheme was fully funded, the company was profitable and there was no reason at all to close it except on the grounds of political and philosophical dogma.

There was also a small matter of a missing £40 million. Let me tell you about it …

In the complexity and confusion of the transfer, and all the work relating to our traffic-light system for ensuring we secured our conditions, there had been a failure to examine the amount transferred from the BP pension scheme into the new Ineos scheme (which at the time was called the Innovene scheme). I and colleagues had just assumed that whatever level of funding was in place would be transferred over, on a per capita basis.

This had not happened.

It was only when we got down to really scrutinising the numbers, and when Ineos started making bold assertions, that the question arose: where was our share of the surplus we had in BP? When I picked this up I wrote to Ian Fyfe in HR to ask what had happened. My crude assertion was that if you took the funding level and the number of people involved, then something in the region of £40 million had not been transferred over.

Ian Fyfe was famous for telling us, every time any opportunity came up, in any meeting, that he was a Grade 1 football referee. No matter what the meeting was. Every time he told us I died a little bit inside. My best memory about that was following a game in 2003 when Ian had been the man in black at a 2-2 draw between Motherwell and Partick Thistle. Apparently there were no less than 11 bookings and a sending-off. The excellent headline in the *Herald* read 'yellow is the colour as referee goes bananas' ('Fyfe' remember) – tremendous.

Anyway, 'Referee' Fyfe wrote back with words to the effect that, yes, the cost of buying the business would have been higher but for a decision not to transfer the pension surplus as well as the core funding. This was outrageous. Here was a company saying they wanted to close our pension scheme because of lack of funding, and yet they had reduced the cost of buying the company by leaving our share of the surplus with BP!

I think it is pretty obvious that Ineos had not envisaged that there would be a problem with this because they intended to close the scheme in short order anyway.

I described this action as theft. Our members had lost a big chunk of cash, some of it related to voluntary enhanced contributions. Ineos had saved cash on the sale – and our surplus, as far as we know, is still in the BP scheme. In 2008 I moved an emergency motion about this at the STUC at Inverness, and part of my contribution was to make plain my view that this was theft. Our union later quoted me and – rather predictably – a tiresome move was then made to file for defamation against our union. In the end we clarified that this was not theft: it was just that we no longer had the cash and Ineos had benefited and so had the BP scheme!

Ineos would later, during my tribunal application, put the blame for this failure to transfer the cash on BP: they said that BP had refused to do a deal unless only the core funding (100%), rather than the whole funding including the surplus (115%), was transferred across. They then went on to say that Ineos 'could not afford to independently inject £40m into the fund'. I think an important point to make on behalf of all my Unite brothers and sisters is that we could not afford to lose £40 million from the value of our pension fund.

Over the years we were to realise that Ineos was very quick to resort to litigation. The same move to take defamation action against our union was made by Ineos in 2013, when the company unsuccessfully launched proceedings against Unite over an assertion that there was a climate of fear at the site (see p141).

In any case, let me just remind you that Ian Fyfe was a Grade One referee.

We ran a number of campaigns about the pension scheme during what was to become a costly and unnecessary dispute. We did all we could to avoid any kind of action, but, according to Gordon Grant, Jim Ratcliffe felt he had given in too easily on the shares dispute, and so he was absolutely determined to go all the way with this one. We were quite worried about this because we felt it was not a responsible, rational or business-like approach to the situation.

One of the campaign rallying cries we used during the pensions dispute was: 'Mind the GAP: Greedy employer, Affordable pension, Profitable company.'

During the dispute Jim Ratcliffe sent out an insulting email claiming that our personal agendas were in play, and that they could not invest with our attitude as it was. He also wrote that we were earning £60,000 a year. This, our members reported, caused all kinds of domestic bother, as husbands/wives/partners wanted to know where the other £30,000 was going.

Things rumbled on into 2008 and we tried to negotiate, and come up with ideas to avoid unpleasantness, financial arguments, etc. Our pension expert from the union came to the site to spend a couple of days briefing us on the broader issues. One of the important issues in all this was that we did not want to sell new recruits down the river. We did not want to have to look people in the eye and say we preserved our scheme but sold yours. This would have been disastrous for the individuals, but equally so for our branch.

The other more selfish reason was the knowledge that once a scheme closed to new entrants, it was pretty much a matter of time before it was closed to everyone. The balance of those in the old scheme and those outside it changes over a relatively short period of time, as people leave the company.

We took a motion to our branch saying that we wanted to proceed on the basis of three red lines. That there would be no two-tier arrangements. There would be no detriment to existing and future members. And any changes to the scheme would increase benefits.

Against our advice and better judgement a meeting was once again arranged between us and Jim Ratcliffe. This was acknowledged by everyone, including myself and General Manager Gordon Grant, to be a disaster in waiting.

Gordon Grant was not a Grade One Referee ... That was Ian Fyfe.

On the day of the meeting we were scheduled to see Jim after he had met with a group of allegedly independent workforce representatives. This group represented no one and were not even elected by any process you would recognise. As it happens we had a few good troops in there from our staff membership as spies, just to cover all the angles. But it was a pointless, toothless and utterly worthless forum.

(In fact Stevie Deans and I, together with others on our negotiation committee, were regularly asked by Gordon Grant to derail forthcoming 'independent' representatives' consultation meetings so that they did not need to go to them. We would then ask our moles to find reasons why the meetings should be delayed or cancelled, just to save Gordon going to them. We colluded in this way with the site management because it suited both us and them, but the point to note here is the regard with which these representatives were and are still held. The meetings Gordon was so desperate to avoid were apparently tortuous affairs that took place under the broad heading of consultation on workplace issues. Most of the attendees were hand-picked people, and they would ask the most tedious and insipid questions. Gordon could not be bothered with the process at all.)

Anyway, on the day of the 'disaster-in-waiting' meeting, big Jim had previously met the 'independents' in the fancy boardroom at the refinery. These 'representatives' were provided with lunch and were pressed to say how much they supported abandoning their right to a dignified and secure retirement in order to advance the company line. There were rumours that they also sang the company song.

After that management met us in a side room, and Tom Crotty told us in a kind of embarrassed way that there were still some sandwiches left. We declined the second-hand soggy offering and proceeded to business. Tom more or less fawned on Jim. The only things missing were sackcloth, ashes and a pig's bladder on the end of a stick, as Tom tried to cajole and humour his master like a seventeenth-century court jester. It was all very distasteful and undignified. Tom said to Jim … I think Mark and Stevie want to talk about the pension issue.

We said that we did not.

Jim sat side-on to us, eating grapes and desperately trying to look aloof and uninterested in what we had to say. Eventually he said words to the effect that he paid us wages and he gave us a bonus, what else did we want? I will spare you the rest of this excruciating exchange, but suffice to say it did not go well.

On another occasion Ratcliffe came to Grangemouth but did not meet with us to try to resolve the issue, as we had requested. Instead, he met with managers in the main office, and when he emerged the assembled picket line of about one hundred members spontaneously chanted 'Ratcliffe, Ratcliffe, shame on you'. Ratcliffe was later to complain bitterly to site management about this, saying that he had never been treated like this before. Gordon Grant later told us that Ratcliffe held a real personal grudge against some of us, which may go some way to explaining his discrimination against us later on. Personally, I was quite relieved at the time that the chant was not more expressive. The other thing I remember from that day was Gordon Grant holding an umbrella over the great man's head as he went to get his limousine – like some kind of servant.

Some time after the meeting in the side room, Calum Maclean met Stevie Deans and me. He told us that he was highly influential with Jim Ratcliffe and that he would most likely be in line to succeed him. He told us that Ineos had decided to allow the strike to go ahead – a strike we had desperately tried to avoid. He went on to say that once the forecourts were empty of fuel, the airports shut down and the whole country brought to a halt, the union would be forced to negotiate and give concessions.

I later quoted these words in a radio interview, and once more the legal card was pulled out, asserting that my comments were lies. Ineos threatened litigation unless the comments were withdrawn.

The difficulty for our Calum, though, was that he had repeated his words almost word for word to dozens of our members around the factory. We had something like fifty witnesses lined up to back us up. Needless to say management had to back down, but this gives you all sorts of clues as to the strategy being employed.

Next, the company laid down implementation dates for pension changes, and we were forced to ballot for industrial action. The ballot result came back in early 2008 from our fantastic members with something like a 98 per cent return and 97 per cent in favour of strike action or action short of strike. Stoppages were announced for 27 and 28 April.

We ended up going to the Advisory, Conciliation and Arbitration Service (Acas) in London, where we sat for days without any contact with the company. The only interest they showed was when they asked us to agree safety cover during the forthcoming strike. We were naturally disappointed that no attempt at all was made to engage in a discussion on avoiding the strike, but the prophetic words of Calum Maclean about the company's desire for strike action were never far from our minds.

We had already presented a stewards' recommendation to one of our mass meetings that safety cover would be provided in the event of a strike, and we also recommended that the plants should be kept on 'hot standby'. Just to explain – there are real hazards when plants like ours are closed down to cold and started up again, because of issues like thermal shock – a situation where different parts of the plant expand at different rates, causing severe strains and leading to serious damage, including cracks and leaks. We were convinced that hot standby, where plants would not be producing any fuel or products, but would be circulating and kept hot, would protect the plants and make it easier and safer to start up once the dispute was over. This has always been our position and remains so.

When we took our proposal for hot standby to the mass meeting we had been happy but not surprised by the very mature and responsible attitude of our members. We are always governed by the will of the members in our branch. The proposal from the floor had been not only to provide safety cover, but to provide full cover including manufacturing and maintenance technicians, all of which would be provided free of charge. We were very proud of the stance taken by our troops.

(As we will see, in the 2013 dispute the company crashed the units down to cold once we had been forced to announce strike dates, against our advice and against the advice of the Health and Safety Executive. This was one of the most irresponsible and dangerous elements of the company's actions at that time.)

We also insisted, with the full support of members, that not one pensioner, and not one hospital or any other area of the emergency services, would go without fuel. We also received a number of requests from Ineos during the strike to accommodate fuel supply in particular circumstances, and not one of these requests was denied by us. A recurring example was the company asking us to request our jetty dock workers to load fuel ships. We did so on every occasion.

A notable example I always remember was when Scottish First Minister Alex Salmond acknowledged this on the radio, when he noted that 'as we speak, the Border Thistle [a tanker ship] is steaming its way to my constituency'. (As a matter of fact it was still on the berth being helpfully loaded by our members free of charge, but you get the idea.) It did sail later that evening.

During the strike – which, regrettably, did eventually go ahead – the factory was reduced to the safe condition of hot standby over an appropriate period of time, and was then maintained and monitored by the experts – our members – throughout.

Unaccustomed to any form of action as our members were, they were magnificent. The walkout on the morning of the 27th, and the discipline displayed by everyone throughout the two days, was a joy to behold.

I also want to commend our Unite regional officer at the time, Pat Rafferty, and all the excellent sections of our union, who were just brilliant and who gave us unconditional support in our just struggle.

After the strike, the company put a note out called 'strike consequences'. One of them was that the bicycle-to-work scheme, where employees could buy a bike and have the payments taken off their wages above the line, was halted. Apparently this scheme had saved people paying some tax and National Insurance contributions. However, they may take our bicycles but they will never take our freedom! All the cyclists on site were quite simply devastated ... NOT!

I can only hope none of them were planning to go cycling on the high Italian Alps with Tony Loftus.

By the way, talking of bikes, another motivational wheeze from management at one point was the 'Livestrong' Armstrong stuff, inspired by the 'champion cyclist' Lance Armstrong, who was hero worshipped by one and all before it turned out that his success was down to illegal self-administered medication. Inevitably, our compliant, hero-worshipping management clique would come away with meaningless phrases like 'maintenance-strong', which clearly meant something to them, but nothing to the rest of the people on planet earth. They wore Armstrong-style yellow wristbands as well, good lord! On reflection, the only surprise really, with people like some of these at the helm, is that the site is still running at all.

Shortly after the strike, it was agreed to hold discussions with a view to agreeing the way forward, and the plants were started up right away, as you would expect. The company had taken all reference to closing the scheme off the table, and the dispute was broadly viewed as a very heavy defeat for the company. This is unfortunate, as it was not our stated intention to 'beat' the company: we just wanted to get on with life and industrial relations without conflict.

During the dispute an enlightening episode occurred at a European Works Council meeting in Brussels. Things were very strained and awkward with the company, but Brother Deans and I were elected reps to the EWC so we went there to present the views of members at the meeting, as you would expect. However, the idea of sharing dinner, breaking bread and taking wine with senior managers in the evening, while our members were still in struggle at the site, was just wrong and so we did not attend the official dinner.

To be honest, we always referred to the EWC meal as 'the excruciating dinner' anyway. We would rather have been almost anywhere else, but the reason we did not attend during the dispute was because we thought it was inappropriate.

You would have thought we had murdered someone by not attending this dinner. Ineos HR directors complained bitterly to the site management, who got it in the neck because they were for some reason blamed for our cheek at not conforming to the after meeting activities. It was implied that they should be managing us better. Gordon Grant raised it with us just to let us know, but he acknowledged that it was a big fuss about nothing. However all this gives you an idea of how they thought about us and our obligations as workers. It was as if we were some kind of indentured serfs to be governed in every respect including who we choose to eat with.

The company had chosen the pension fight in 2008 and had paid a heavy price for their foolishness. In the event a compromise was reached that was acceptable to our brilliant members. It involved significant changes to the scheme, but none that betrayed the general principles we had set down. Current and future members were protected. This should have been the end of that crazy period, but, sadly it looks as if the desire to 'get even' with us was just beginning. JFK once said that 'you should always forgive your enemies, but remember their names'. Well, we were hoping things could move on, but, alas, it was not to be.

As a longstanding student of Sun Tzu, a wise military strategist and philosopher in ancient China, I know it makes sense to try to depart the battlefield with the enemy rather than be triumphant and create negative energy for the future. This is why we wanted to compromise and let the company withdraw with dignity. Any other approach sets a course for future conflict – and this is why the company's subsequent actions in 2013 were unwise and illogical.

It was known at the time and reported to us by people like Gordon Grant and Ian Fyfe (who, it should be remembered, was a 'Grade One Referee') that James Arthur Ratcliffe was furious about the success of the industrial action. It is clear to me, and to the dogs on the street, that this ill feeling has been carried forward and been materially important right up to the current day

CHAPTER 4

Billionaire on benefits

Before you set out for revenge, dig two graves

Confucius

IN THE YEARS following the pension dispute, the site was subject to a constant negative campaign directed from the board of Ineos Capital (which of course took all its orders from Jim Ratcliffe). I was warned by the then Unite joint general secretaries, Tony Woodley and Derek Simpson, to watch my back, because during their meetings with Ratcliffe it had been made clear to them that he hated me personally. Tony and Derek expressed concern over my future employment at the site. How right they turned out to be!

Another aspect of this vindictive campaign was the steady replacement of Ineos employees with agency staff, bogus self-employed workers and contract workers. This was to ensure that the pension plan benefits were slashed as far as possible. The workers replaced in this way did not work in our union's collective bargaining units, but this was nevertheless a war of attrition which ultimately damaged the site over time.

The main problems this foolish strategy created were that staff members began to complain that the workforce was in rotation mode, with people coming and going as better offers came up. And this has, without doubt, damaged the site and seriously diluted the competence of the workforce. Once the genie was out of the bottle, individuals found that they preferred to come to the site for massive short-term pay rates, and then to move on, having pulled all the strokes within the law on tax avoidance. This may have been good for such individuals, but the functioning of departments on the site was in serious and dangerous decline.

Another regular occurrence was people leaving Ineos employment on a Friday with lump sum and pension in hand, and being back on Monday with agency status. This was wrong on so many levels.

This is not my assertion alone. A number of senior managers made the same observation, and complained constantly about the reluctance of Ineos to offer secure in-house contracts to replace leavers, their failure to replace leavers quickly, and the general decline in departmental capability that this led to.

When we consulted our colleagues on other Ineos sites in the UK and Europe, we could find no other site that was subject to the same level of scrutiny of employee recruitment. The Ineos chemicals plant at Runcorn and Seal Sands in the UK, for example, had far more discretion to recruit employees when vacancies arose, as did the Ineos sites in Germany. (This comparison was made possible through talking to union reps from those sites by telephone, email and at EWC meetings.) Managers at Grangemouth appeared to be just as frustrated by the situation as we were. The difficulty in recruiting people was confirmed, for example, by Gordon Grant and Ian Fyfe (who happened to be a Grade One Referee). Our strong sense was that Grangemouth was being singled out for extra scrutiny.

One of the key areas in the seemingly relentless drive to replace in-house workers with agency staff and contractors was the inspection of pipelines. The crusade to keep people off the books, and the general malaise at the site, drove some excellent engineers away, along with most of their department members. The site went into panic mode, as failed attempts to recruit began to bite. Our HR manager Helen Stewart, site director Gordon Grant and most of the section heads kept us up to date with all this.

And the problems were by no means confined to the department involving pipeline inspection. Between all our stewards and myself we could provide volumes of evidence of concerns of this nature, brought to our attention by site management.

As part of the plan to exercise unchallenged control over the site, every single employee brought on to the books had to be personally approved by Ineos Capital, on a case by case basis. The company told us this on site, and managers complained bitterly about their lack of ability to fill vacancies quickly, or with Ineos contracts. Projects like the KG flex project, which would have involved upgrading one of the chemical plants on site (now shelved indefinitely), were severely impacted by this mismanagement.

But this almost pales into insignificance when compared to the utter shambles the company has created at the site more recently, with pretty much everyone seeking employment elsewhere. Especially as this is combined with a reluctance of people from outside to join Ineos, given the toxic nature of the site in terms of its treatment of the workforce and uncertainties over the future of the business. If you threaten to shut a site down, as Ineos has done, the effects will last forever – or until you declare a complete and permanent reversal, admit your failings and apologise, and make efforts to repair the damage you have done in order to rebuild confidence and goodwill among your employees.

In this context, the contrived 2013 'survival plan' that Ineos management once boasted about – and which they made celebratory and triumphant films about – now looks pretty embarrassing. We told them what would happen, that the workforce would take their leave of the site after their plot was executed, and this is exactly what happened – and by the way I can think of no better way of describing the actions of the company in the run-up to the dispute in 2013 than as a plot.

Let me give you an idea of how Ratcliffe viewed the site. This snippet was shared with us by a number of senior managers. One time when Ratcliffe was up in Grangemouth with some other hangers-on, the site management took them to a restaurant in the fine town of Linlithgow. You can imagine the excruciating atmosphere at this event and the riveting repartee that would have abounded. The long winter evening must have just flown. I bet Jim had everyone in absolute stitches with his rapier sharp anecdotes. Anyway ... here's what happened. There was a guy at the dinner called Andy Hughes, who was the manager of two plants on the Grangemouth site. Andy was one of the good guys by the way. We liked him, as we did most of the plant managers. We had good personal and working relationships with most of them. Andy had previously worked for Ineos at Runcorn – another site where threats had been used to secure funding (see p64).

Anyway, Jim turns to Andy, in full view and earshot of all the other companionable dinner guests, and asks how he is finding Grangemouth compared with Runcorn. Andy says that he likes it, it is a very good site, and is staffed by good people. Jim shouts out right away, interrupting all the fascinating conversations that were going on up and

INEOS AND GRANTS (AND LITIGATION)

In 2001 the BBC ran this story:

> The new owner of the giant ex-ICI chemical plant at Runcorn is thought to be asking the British government for up to £300m in aid to modernise the plant and protect jobs.
>
> Ineos Chlor, which bought the plant at Runcorn in Cheshire from ICI in January, says it needs the money because of under-investment by ICI, the Sunday Times reported.
>
> The paper also said Ineos is planning a £65m legal claim against ICI, alleging that the plant is in a worse state than it was led to believe.
>
> The paper claims to have seen documents the company will present to industry minister Patricia Hewitt at a meeting on 30 October, stating that up to 133,000 British jobs are at risk unless the plant receives a cash injection.

In the end the Ineos Chlor factory at the Runcorn site was awarded a £50 million grant from the Department of Trade & Industry.

On 6 January 2004 the Telegraph *ran the story: 'Chemical firm wants £300m in aid':*

> The European Commission has approved a £50m grant from the Department of Trade & Industry to Ineos, the company that bought ICI's chlorine operations.
>
> The deal comes after Ineos, which owns the Ineos Chlor business, threatened to close the plant at Runcorn, Cheshire, which it claims would have meant the loss of 10,000 jobs. But the chlorine business employs only 1,800 people, with 1,450 of them in Runcorn.

'It is the soothing thing about history that it does repeat itself'

Gertrude Stein

down the table, and roars in a scoffing and incredulous way to one of his sidekicks at the other end of the table 'wait till you hear this – Andy says there are good people at Grangemouth. Ha, can you believe it?'.

Please bear in mind that the great and the good from across the whole Grangemouth site are sitting right there at the table. Apparently the only thing missing was the tumbleweed and a bloke with a black hooded cape and a scythe. No wonder the site was in decline, and the senior managers were demotivated – and intensely disliked Jim Ratcliffe.

To give you the texture and taste of off-site and on-site relationships among senior managers, I will pass on a story told to us by Gordon Grant and Helen Stewart about Jim Ratcliffe's injured leg. I don't know if the leg was broken or not, but it was apparently put in a plaster cast, so it must have been quite severely injured. Gordon and Helen were laughing about the injury, but the real focus of their mirth was that Jim had, against the specific advice of the doctors, taken off the plaster cast and replaced it with a ski boot. As Gordon said sarcastically, 'it's not like Jim to ignore advice and know better than everyone else'. All pretty distasteful of course – but our main conclusion from that was that the Grangemouth management must have really disliked this guy.

I had a monthly meeting with the refinery manager, Russell Mann, and his euphemistic observation was that he thought Ineos were not bad manufacturers, but they were terrible at people issues. This is perhaps the understatement of the decade, but it illustrates once again the organisational cracks that ran right through the management structures. I also met the refinery management team on a monthly basis, and a similar line was evident then. They mostly complained to me about the lack of recruitment, but also about the general lack of investment at the site. (Sharon Hooper, one of the refinery managers who attended these monthly meetings, once personally thanked me for saving her pension during the strike in 2008, and frequently urged me to keep up the good work. It is therefore disappointing to report that Sharon later gave false testimony against me which contributed to my unfair dismissal. I think it is worse somehow that Sharon would later place herself with the company in this way when she had been so critical of Ineos in the past, and of Ratcliffe in particular.)

Mark Durie, a maintenance manager who attended these monthly meetings in 2013, was central to an HR debacle that came to be known as 'donutgate'. Durie oversaw the work of a supervisor called Martin Proctor (who is not named in my tribunal papers), and under Durie's guidance Proctor treated one of our members badly. In the end Proctor's disciplinary action against our member was overturned by the union as set out below. The point here is that Durie was no friend of mine – he had advised on the disciplinary action, and in Steven Boyle's later statement at the tribunal he cited Durie as one of the witnesses he had consulted from the refinery meeting that led to my dismissal.

The bones of the incident itself are as follows. Proctor, under Durie's guidance, had stopped our member from working any overtime – to teach him a lesson for being late a couple of times when he was taking his kids to school. Naturally we took this up, and the sanction was then immediately withdrawn, but our Mark had now fallen out with us. The next day he decreed in a fit of rage that the whole team was now barred from using the company van to go and get cakes for someone's birthday during lunchtime (as was the normal practice). Once again his ridiculous stance was overturned – but not before we had had a meeting with all twenty or so of the departmental team, and not before Stevie Deans and I personally visited Greggs the bakers to procure a selection of cakes to distribute to all the attendees at the meeting. Members reported that they had never tasted a sweeter confection.

This is as good a place as any to tell you about another package of nonsense that has since become very sinister indeed – the trend for 'Behavioural Safety', which was beginning to sweep through workplaces between 2011 and 2012. Unite was very critical of Behavioural Safety, and published an excellent booklet on how to resist such dangerous schemes – how to argue against them and how to protect members where they had been implemented. Not long after I had been at a Unite executive meeting that had discussed these issues, I attended a European Works Council of Ineos, and – lo and behold – I had to sit through a managerial presentation setting out that Ineos too intended to put in place just such a programme.

In case you have not come across this managerial device, here is my interpretation of it. Say there was a big hole in the road and someone fell in it. Under behavioural safety, the conclusions as to the cause of the accident would be that the fault of the accident lay with the injured person, who should have been looking where they were going and paying more attention; should have perhaps arranged for better lighting so they could see the hole; and should have been wearing a bubble wrap overcoat and padded underpants to prevent injury just in case they fell down a hole.

Our position is of course ... FILL THE DAMN HOLE!!!!!

In short, the intention was to shift blame from where it belonged, with the management of safety, and onto the poor soul who got injured.

Anyway, I spoke up at the EWC meeting and said that, since this was a significant change to the safety system, under the regulations consultation was required before implementation, and that any such changes were subject to our agreement. There followed a big debate, and other EWC members supported the Grangemouth position. Many of the company reps also argued that further discussions were needed, and that the presenter of the behavioural safety slides should take more time, and talk to site reps before implementation – or not.

The presenter of the proposal was furious, and did not do a good job of hiding it. He came to the site a few months later, after the controversy had rumbled on for a while, to meet our committee to discuss and amend the proposals. The programme, which was his baby, was quite rightly changed significantly, much to his annoyance.

The architect of this safety initiative, and the presenter at the meeting, was one Tony Traynor, who was later selected to officiate at the hearing of my appeal against dismissal. Unsurprisingly, the appeal was denied!

The politics of the workhouse

In 2010 Ineos decided to move its headquarters to Switzerland, in order to save on tax. The company website estimated the potential savings as being 'around €450m between now and 2014'. Pages 68–9 give some examples of press coverage of this tax relocation.

There is lots more coverage of this kind that you can pick up on line. But the bones of it are that, having enjoyed tax relief on the debt they had saddled us with, Ineos was now on the move to Switzerland.

The cuttings give you some idea of the kind of organisation we were dealing with. And yet as a union we still helped them when they wanted to apply for government funds to assist their companies, and undertook a great deal of political work on their behalf.

One of the key events I want to tell you about in this book is the story of my mate, colleague and comrade, Stevie Deans. Stevie was our Unite branch secretary at the site, as well as my vice convener. In 2013 he was suspended by Ineos on the grounds that he (and we as officials of Unite) had wrongly been engaged in political activity during working hours.

Chapter five describes the exact circumstances that led to Stevie

MEDIA REPORTS ON THE INEOS HQ RELOCATION

Debt-laden chemicals group Ineos has confirmed it is going ahead with plans to move its headquarters from the UK to Switzerland in the hope of saving £100m a year in tax.

Britain's biggest private company incited the ire of trade unions last month when it said it wanted to follow in the footsteps of a number of major companies who have relocated their tax base away from the UK in recent years.

The company said that it had received the consent of its lenders to move its headquarters and following an internal review the decision had been finalised. Its lenders include Royal Bank of Scotland and Lloyds Banking Group, both bailed out with billions of taxpayers' money.

Ineos, which is saddled with £6bn debt after an aggressive acquisition spree to buy up parts of ICI and BP, estimates the move could save it around €450m (£395m) between now and 2014.

Guardian, 11 April 2010

One of Britain's richest business men is moving to Switzerland and taking his business with him in order to escape the government's new tax regime. Jim Ratcliffe, chairman of the troubled chemicals resigning from Ineos, in October 2013. For now though, I want to deal with this particular aspect of the allegations made against him – that he had misused company time and resources for political purposes.

It is astounding, bizarre and almost unbelievable that Ineos has claimed that it was not appropriate for us as trade union representatives to be engaged in political activity during work hours. In fact politics with a big and small 'p' were engrained in everything we did as management and union bodies on site. The best way I can put it is to say that we were up to our necks in political work and to some extent in cahoots with the company. This is because part of our role as union leaders was to do everything we could to ensure the wellbeing of our members and to preserve their jobs, which often meant

---

group Ineos, is relocating the business to Europe in the hope of saving as much as £100m a year in tax.

Ineos, which is Britain's biggest private company, is £6bn in debt thanks to an aggressive acquisitions policy that has seen it buy up chemicals businesses cast off by other players in the market – including ICI and BP – and has been badly affected by the recession.

Now Ratcliffe and other senior executives have decided to leave Britain, and believe by relocating to Switzerland they will save almost £400m in tax by 2014.

Ironically, the move has the support of two of Ineos's biggest creditors, the banks RBS and Lloyds, both of which were bailed out by the government and are therefore partly responsible for Labour's decision to increase taxes in the first place.

The news comes as a blow to Gordon Brown, who has been criticised by the private sector for increasing National Insurance contributions and has been accused of making Britain a less than attractive location to do business. According to Ineos, the new tax legislation will result in 'significant levels of additional tax'.

In 2007 Ratcliffe was 10th on the Sunday Times Rich List, with a fortune of £3.3bn. The following year his wealth had fallen to £2.3bn and he is now said to be worth a meagre £150m.

The Week, April 2010

supporting management in their efforts to promote the company, whether or not we privately agreed with what they were doing. And of course this kind of support was often directly political – it could include asking our local Labour MP for support, or organising union support for oil industry lobbies.

A great deal of the political work we undertook on behalf of the business was difficult for us, and cut across our best instincts in terms of political ideology. But we always tried to remember the game we were in. Our job in this context was not to drive forward any personal crusade and reform the world. Our job was to adopt whatever stance would improve and secure the lot of the members who had elected us and put their trust in us.

Let me give you a few examples of the dilemmas we faced in pursuing this goal – the same dilemmas that are probably faced by principled union representatives the world over.

After their tax relocation, the company spoke to us about the need to secure alternative feedstock so that they had enough to supply the factory with its needs. They wanted a new tank because gas production in the North Sea was declining and they needed the capacity to receive more feedstock from elsewhere. The plan was to bring gas from the USA in ships and store it in a massive new tank. (Incidentally this US gas was ethane – a cheaper, shale-based, product.)

They told us they were aiming to get a £9 million grant from the Scottish government to assist in this. They also wanted the UK government to underwrite loans, so that they could borrow lots of money and have significantly reduced interest payments over the period.

They told us that some of the finance they were applying for was available only for 'infrastructure' projects, and that they were pleading for a very broad and liberal interpretation of the criteria to be applied in suggesting that a feed tank for a plant was infrastructure for the country.

This was quite plainly a commercial venture to make money for Ineos – a big, but nevertheless everyday part of the plant – like any other part. In my opinion, this was clearly a drive to harvest financial assistance from us, the tax-payers and full-time residents of the UK, and to get us to bankroll the commercial project of building their ethane tank.

Gordon Grant himself confided in us that they were going to ask to have the tank defined as 'infrastructure', because only projects categorised as such could be afforded public assistance of this kind. As I understand it, if a project is built to benefit all the citizens of an area or country, or to genuinely support industry and jobs in difficulty, this kind of application is acceptable – but in my opinion this was not the case at Grangemouth.

My view is that there should be an inquiry into the whole portrayal of this tank as infrastructure, and the willingness of government bodies to go along with it. Tax-payers need to know who was complicit in the process. There is no inference of fraud or illegality in all this, but you have to question how the whole system always feels weighted to the benefit of the wealth-laden gaffer.

It was interesting to hear James Arthur Ratcliffe (JAR) when he appeared on the TV conveying yet another one of his fascinating, insightful and educational addresses to the nation, and asserting that this 'infrastructure' project was the best thing since sliced bread. The tank project was no more an infrastructure project than it was a fully filled-out tax return from Switzerland.

What sticks in my mind is the gloating way Gordon Grant told us about this, and the inference that they were so clever that they could successfully put forward this position and get the support of both governments and the people. He was right though. They did.

I also find it very surprising that other good employers and companies are not screaming the house down over this subsidised project, and asking why they had not been similarly favoured.

Anyway, Ineos was asking us, through Gordon Grant and Calum Maclean, to work with them politically to secure this funding, and to present the case in the way they wanted.

My first reaction was to ask why Ineos was not prepared to fund the project and pay interest like every other business in the country. The proposed investment was a good one and was projected to make a fortune once completed. Why was Ineos not willing to pay up like everyone else? The answer given was that they could invest where they liked, and Jim was not prepared to invest in Grangemouth unless the risk was carried by the government. We could easily have a ten-day seminar on this, reflecting on the transition from nationalised industry to the point at which we had now arrived – but it would drive you nuts.

Anyway, I told Gordon Grant at a subsequent meeting – after consulting our representatives and having some soak time to get used to the idea and take the sharp edges of my screaming instincts – that we would do what we could to help. This was on the basis that it would secure the jobs of our members and allow them to enjoy good conditions while supporting the community and the economy.

Was this the right thing to do? I am not sure now, given that employees' terms and conditions have been so savagely attacked since then, and that the site has seen massive plant closures and job losses.

The bottom line was, though, that our members' wishes were paramount as always, and we, on balance, thought it was our only option and the most responsible thing to do.

I told Gordon that it choked me to think that someone could take off to Switzerland to avoid tax and yet be here with the begging bowl to scrounge from the Scottish and UK tax-payer. Ratcliffe was asking for every assistance but was not asked to accept any conditions. There were no demands by the government for future investment or job security or reasonable treatment of workers or any other criteria. Gordon agreed – and then he told me that it was even worse than that. Because Ineos had upped sticks and moved to Switzerland they were now categorised as a foreign investor, so they would also reap all the preferential benefits from this angle as well!

Friends, we have well and truly lost the plot.

The wages of sin is death (Romans 6:23) ... but the wages of Ineos are worse!

One other thing that happened around 2008 was that Gordon Grant told us that Ineos had realised that it could be about to default on the covenant conditions attached to its massive loan. My understanding is that Ineos Capital, as part of its agreement with the banks, had been given financial targets that it was required to meet. But, according to Calum Maclean, the company was furious when it was forced to pay the banks extra money when it asked for a covenant waiver. My understanding is also that this was not a question of a default on payments: it was an issue about the performance of the company, and the confidence of the banks – or not. Calum Maclean told us that he felt that the banks had taken advantage of their circumstances, and had made hay on the backs of the company's misfortune. Taking financial advantage of a temporary unfortunate situation ... Fancy that!

To cut a long story short, political activity for Stevie Deans and me was not some tolerated add-on to our site work, and nor was it an incidental by-product of our duties. No. It was a 100-per-cent integral part of our role, and was not only known about and specifically approved by the company: it was actively encouraged. We worked hand in hand with all levels of Ineos management on many political issues, with the blessing and encouragement of the company.

Every month we met on site with Michael Connarty, the then Labour MP for Linlithgow and East Falkirk, to discuss site issues and challenges facing the business. We also discussed our union concerns and agenda. We make no apology for that – that is the role of elected, recognised and legally protected trade union representatives.

The company also asked us to participate in a political campaign to get access to a pipeline at Mossmoran petrochemical plant in Fife. (The kingdom of Fife, not the grade one referee). The companies on that site were at the time considering whether to allow Ineos to connect to the pipe so that they could have feedstock delivered directly to Grangemouth. Gary Haywood, a company CEO, asked me to convene a meeting with our local MP, which he then participated in alongside Gordon Grant. The idea was for us to give support for Michael to lobby to gain access to the pipeline – something he most certainly did. The last we heard of this story was when Ineos told us they were making their customary threats towards the Mossmoran companies, saying the company would take legal action if they did not allow them to draw from the well. There is correspondence relating to all this, and there was also interaction with the Scottish parliamentary structures on the issue. It would be interesting to see all the email traffic about the companies at Mossmoran.

Another political campaign the company encouraged us to get involved with, and fed us information on, concerned the issue of gas emissions from the site. A European directive set out the permitted levels of SOx and NOx that could be emitted from the site, and these were expressed in terms of the average amount allowed over an hour. However, the UK interpretation was that the time frame for measuring emissions should be reduced to fifteen minutes. This decision meant that the site had virtually no leeway, given the short period of measurement, so that, essentially, the emissions permitted were zero. This placed our factory at a significant disadvantage when compared to installations in continental Europe. The direct result of this was that our fuel sources were restricted for fear of breaching the control levels. The site was forced to use more expensive fuel gas to fire furnaces, instead of the more affordable fuel oil. Naturally we took the case up as it was to the benefit of members, and we raised the issue within the Labour groups at Westminster and Holyrood. Stevie Deans did much of this work and travelled to a number of meetings, often in his own time, to act on behalf of the members – and was briefed and encouraged by Ineos managers.

A further issue in which we were involved centred on tax liabilities related to shipping oil-based products. Our main brief on this came from the commercial manager for the refinery, Andrew Gardner. He met us and briefed us on the problem, as well as sending us emails on the subject. He asked us to highlight the disadvantage to Ineos if we had the opportunity, and to engage our political contacts. The bones of the issue are these. If a ship was travelling laden with fuel from the spot market, say from Rotterdam, the product would be measured and metered when it was offloaded at the UK port. It was then only the offloaded cargo that would be subject to taxation. The reason this is important is that a small but significant portion of every cargo would be lost in transit, through evaporation or tiny leaks into the atmosphere, so that the amount that was taxed would be slightly smaller on arrival. In contrast, when a cargo travelled by sea from one UK installation to another, the cargo was metered when it was going on to the ship. This meant that the tax applicable was on the whole cargo and not on the amount that was actually delivered. The difference here is pennies per barrel, but the margin on a barrel was also often expressed in pennies. So this practice once again placed us at a disadvantage, and acted as an incentive to imports. Once again, we found ourselves up to our necks in collusion with the company to lobby on this.

Yet another issue was the carbon floor price, which is basically an EU tax on the use of carbon-based fuels, designed to reduce emissions. Such fuel use is inevitable in refining and chemical manufacture, and it also affects the bulk of heavy energy users in all sectors. The United Kingdom Petroleum Industry Association (UKPIA), which is the employers' federation representing refineries in Britain, argued that this tax placed EU refineries at a disadvantage compared with non-EU countries that were not subject to these costs. They accordingly set out the case for tackling this cost and published papers and political briefing notes. The view was that this was a potentially crippling burden, given reduced profit margins on petrochemical products. Guess what? The company's commercial manager and refinery manager sent us briefing papers on all this to keep us in the loop ... You get the picture.

There was also an issue involving the European Emission Trading Scheme. It was projected that alterations to its third phase (to be implemented from 2013) would place an additional tax burden of around £75 million on UK refiners as compared with non-EU installations. Once again the company requested us to raise the matter with Michael Connarty, and with our various political contacts.

There is lots more to come on all this, but please reflect here for a moment on the company assertion that they were surprised to learn that Stevie had been engaged in political work during company time.

We were deeply involved politically – with the full consent, support, encouragement and, above all, knowledge of the company. To suggest otherwise is quite outrageous.

Let me continue to outline for you some more of the work we did, often because of the difficulties faced by the oil industry as a whole. It is difficult to pin down a time when the oil industry moved from being awash with money and very much in demand to the position we are in today, but it is of note that in the late 1970s the UK needed eighteen oil refineries whereas in 2015 we had seven, and it is possible that this number could reduce still further.

For this reason, in conjunction with the National Oil Refining Co-ordinating Committee (NORCC), a lay member committee involving senior representatives from Unite in all our UK refineries, our site initiated a process that sought to highlight the difficulties facing the industry, and to devise a campaign to save jobs, and to lobby for sustainable trading conditions and improvements to members' terms, conditions and job security. The NORCC is a non-constitutional body of Unite members and has been in existence for many years – and it should be noted that at this point Ineos were only too happy to give us time off to attend this committee: in fact they encouraged our participation in it.

By non-constitutional I mean that the committee was funded from branches on a shoe-string, and we have met everywhere from the dining room tables of guesthouses to the back rooms of pubs and all points between. The committee has seen the loss of a number of refineries over the years, worked through the disgraceful attempt to derecognise unions across the industry, and witnessed the migration

of ownership of most of the sites from major employers to other organisations. Additionally there have been the difficulties associated with
reduced demand for petrol in particular, the unhelpful configuration
of some plants that meant they were set up to make more petrol than
in-demand diesel, increased environmental demands and lack of
government intervention or clarity of direction in support of manufacturing. All this added to the industry's woes.

One of the NORCC plans was to engage with employers at our
individual sites and to request meetings to share our ideas and
resources, and agree the best way forward.

At our site in Grangemouth management were very supportive of
this proposal, but suggested that it would look better if our union reps
met the industry representative bodies i.e. UKPIA and the Chemical
Industry Association. This was because the company thought that if
we made open, joint and direct representation to government as
employers and unions in the same room, it could be dismissed as
simply a case of the company driving the campaign for its own selfish
company interests, with us as simply a front (as if!). They thought it
would be better to place a buffer layer between them and us. We saw
the sense of that, even if we thought this elaborate arrangement was
perhaps unnecessary, and so set up a number of meetings with the
suggested organisations, with assistance from our Unite departments
such as research, political, education, media and communications.

We then held a meeting with Chris Hunt, director general of
UKPIA, at which we discussed the dynamics of the industry and how
we could best work industrially and politically to protect and preserve
the remaining refineries. At the beginning of the meeting Chris could
not resist a dig at Unite general secretary Len McCluskey right off the
bat, over the threat of possible industrial action by tanker drivers
belonging to Unite. We reminded Chris that there were always issues
on the horizon and that there were real difficulties in that sector,
which was why our members were unhappy, but suggested we should
concentrate on the matter at hand – and this was accepted. But just on
the tankers for a minute. This is another sector where our members
have over the years been moved from employment with majors to
contractors, with all the insecurity, reduction in terms and fragmented
pension arrangements that involves. It was ironic that Chris should
raise this issue, given that he was effectively the shop steward for the
industry that had consciously moved in this direction.

Anyway, one of the things Chris told us was that UKPIA had been trying to secure an adjournment debate in the UK parliament for a long time, so that the challenges facing the oil industry could be highlighted to MPs, but that it had not so far been successful. Our fantastic political department representatives at the meeting said that they might be able to explore the possibility with Labour MPs. It was therefore with some pride in our union that I was able to phone Chris within days to say that the debate had been secured and was scheduled for a couple of weeks' time.

Chris was genuinely delighted and surprised with this, and we jointly set about making the event a success. Ineos sent briefs to me and I was tied in with communication across the sector. We also met our MP Michael Connarty, who was, once again, immensely helpful and enthusiastic. Our union wrote to every MP in the Labour group, and our senior members in the individual refineries wrote to and contacted the MPs in constituencies where the sites were located. This included MPs from the Labour, Liberal Democrat and Conservative parties. We also encouraged individual Ineos employee union members in constituencies surrounding the sites to contact their MPs and ask them to participate. All this political work on company time and on company computer systems and email was done with the full knowledge, encouragement and consent of Ineos.

We briefed Michael Connarty on all this, both from our own knowledge and from the extensive information provided by Ineos to assist with this political work. It is probably important to stress that all this political work was carried out in company time. There was no complaint from Ineos or any other refining company as we opened doors and provided influence with MPs, and a platform that on their own they could only have dreamed of.

Even the member for Falkirk West (slugger Eric Joyce) was encouraged to attend and was given a point to make by Michael, which he delivered pretty much as required. The companies had also briefed their political contacts, and the event went very well: the issues were highlighted and everyone was now better briefed and aware.

A few years later, at my tribunal hearing, the solicitor acting for Ineos described our political work as 'a few cheese and wines'. I do not think this event could be described as a cheese and wine evening – or, as Prince Charles is fond of saying, 'a lunch, a launch and a logo'. This was a serious political intervention set up and facilitated by Unite the Union and jointly worked on by employers and our union.

Another of the many meetings we facilitated (during this political activity in company time) was a two-day event entitled 'Refining our Future', at Unite's training and conference centre at Esher Place in Surrey. This was attended by refinery union representatives, European Union representatives, and colleagues from the United Steelworkers, who are our partner union in the states, to give us a comparative international perspective. We also invited Tom Greatrex, shadow minister for energy and Labour MP for Rutherglen and Hamilton West, whose attendance for the whole event provided a tremendous opportunity to explore the issues. And the employers' federations also attended as our guests. We had brilliant support for the event from our political and research departments, led by Steve Hart and Simon Dubbins respectively, and from our assistant general secretary Tony Burke and national officer Linda McCulloch. These brothers and sisters took the two days out to attend as well as doing a raft of work before and after the event to support our purpose.

I chaired this meeting over two days, and there is no doubt that this moved the agenda forward politically for us. In the months following the meeting Unite published *Refining Our Future: A Unite strategy for the future of the UK Oil Refining Sector*, a document that set out our position in support of the industry, as well as our objectives to support and enhance the lot of our members.

I have to confess right enough that there may well have been cheese and wine served to our guests during dinner in the evening.

Our own Stevie Deans also presented our case for the industry to Labour groups in both the Westminster and Scottish Parliaments – once more with the full knowledge and support and encouragement of Ineos.

Our campaign has continued, and been funded and resourced by our union, to this day. In May 2014, even though by then I had been sacked for carrying out legitimate union functions, I still participated in a meeting of NORCC representatives in Glasgow to continue this work and do all I could to support our industry.

In 2010 I was elected national vice chair of our union, and around the same time Stevie Deans was elected as the chair of the Scottish region. When Calum Maclean met us soon after these elections in a routine gathering he made some, in my view, very notable and important offers and statements. After making a joke when one of the secretaries offered us tea, asking her if there were any china cups since they were in the presence of the vice chair, he offered Stevie and I congratulations and said words to the effect that if there was anything the company could do, to let them know. Time off would not be a problem. This was a good thing for the company and management would support us.

This is important. These were not glib statements. They were serious points made by someone who, perhaps genuinely at that time, supported the positions we held and wanted to be helpful. Not surprisingly, given some of the work we had done in supporting the company and industry, he clearly saw potential advantages, useful contacts and access opportunities for the company. For a long time afterwards he was as good as his word, and we did not have any problems with requests for time off or use of company facilities or systems. This continued, as offered, right up until the time that Ineos executed its plot against us in 2013 – the plot designed to attack our union, and force the UK and Scottish governments to subsidise the site financially.

It would seem that this willingness on the part of Ineos to encourage and assist trades unions in campaigning for political objectives was not confined to Grangemouth. For example I had a briefing from a councillor who was a union representative at another Ineos site, who had been extensively briefed and asked for advice regarding site issues like planning.

The bottom line is we were afforded unlimited time off for industrial, union and political work. This included time off to attend conferences, including Labour Party ones. Management knew full well we were involved in all aspects of the role of senior union representatives, and we had the use of company email systems as the company had participated in these communications. The reason I want to draw your attention specifically to the use of emails in this company-sponsored and supported political campaigning was that the use of company email systems was one of the central accusations made against Stevie when they moved to discipline him.

'Another shift closer to the big sleep'

Ian Buchanan, one of my mates in the plant, used to say this at the end of every shift. It was his idea of a joke. But life on-site over this time made this comment seem only too close to the truth.

After the arrival of Ineos, industrial relations were launched on a downward spiral, and I want to outline here some of the problems we had, and to identify some of the major fault lines and examples of company incompetence. I also want to touch on some of the significant contributions to good practice and harmony made by our union.

Something that has always stuck with me was a comment made by union colleagues when I visited a BP refinery in Chicago at the invitation of the company around 2001, to meet union reps and compare the way we worked. When I asked how many HR people they had they told me that the numbers were a fraction of ours. According to the Chicago union guys you didn't need all that wasteful resource if you had good and robust agreements and if people stuck to them. That insight came back to haunt me during the Ineos years. Our HR department was dreadful. The number of times agreements were broken, and the amount of time and energy expended in sorting out the ensuing mess, was staggering. This was not all down to utter incompetence, although this was a major factor.

The HR department were constantly trying to eat away at employees' conditions. So members would complain to us when the HR people had detrimentally 'interpreted' our agreements. When this happened we would typically raise it with HR, and then, when they refused to comply, we would end up taking it higher. In every such case, without exception, the existing conditions were secured, but only after huge amounts of negative energy and effort.

My constant concern was that some of our members would just accept what they were told by HR, and so lose out on their agreed entitlements. My opinion is that this was the hope of HR, and that any small benefit that could be stripped from our members was seen as a victory by these people.

Their pet cause was denying reclaimed holidays to those who had been unable to take the time off because they had been off sick when the holidays were due. In 2013, after Ratcliffe and Ineos had threatened to close the entire site unless they got their way, they finally settled this vindictive score and forced through a change that meant that holiday reclaim following a period of sickness was reduced for everyone.

It's funny how sickness absence has gone up since 2013. Employees are actually having more time off now following this draconian move. But I'm sure the two things are unrelated.

This is just one example of the daily war of attrition between the people whose starting point was that everyone in a boiler suit was lazy, on the make and beneath them, and our union. Not everyone in the department was like this, of course, and we did have some friends in there. I can even remember when the HR department was viewed as an honest broker, and the advisors were seen to be there to help everyone and facilitate consensus. No more. One such professional was Amy Smith who, under the BP regime, was known to be excellent, knowledgeable in her field, and, above all, fair. Sadly, Amy passed away recently. She will be sorely missed by all who knew her.

It was usually Gordon Grant, as the site director, who ended up having to sort out the latest mess created by HR. The truth is, for a long time we had a pretty good working relationship with Gordon. Sure, we had our differences, but – as the chair of my interim tribunal hearing later pointed out – that is something that sometimes happens in the game played by unions and management.

Anyway most of the HR moves to break our agreements or deny our members what they were due eventually ended up with Gordon Grant. It felt as if he had to negotiate every little thing with the advisers in his own department. Only Gordon was able to force the issue when needed. However the reporting and authority structure was obviously chaotic.

There were also many occasions when the company would ask us to help when they had a problem. One example of this occurred during a major overhaul programme. The company had treated our contract maintenance workers very badly, and they had been placed in accommodation that was cramped, dirty and unhygienic. Management had also set up a system whereby workers had to go through a local time-keeping checkpoint that resembled a cattle grid. In addition there had been a number of safety and IR problems.

The contract workers were, quite understandably, very angry and upset at the disrespectful way they were being treated, and had walked off the job on a number of occasions. The atmosphere was very tense and relationships between workers and managers were exceptionally bad. Gordon Grant and his fellow managers were at a loss as to what should be done. So Gordon asked us to help, as in-house union representatives, by addressing the contract workers and seeking a solution and way forward.

Such company ineptitude and incompetence when out of their comfort zone was fairly typical – and it was often their own failings that had created the problem in the first place.

Stevie Deans, Ian Proudlove and I, together with some of our senior stewards, made recommendations to sort the situation out, including the provision of contractor workplace representatives who would be on hand to defuse problems at source and before they escalated. We also secured decent conditions and enhanced safety cover for contractors.

The thing that Gordon and the management team most feared was meeting the angry workers, and so they asked us to do that for them. It is quite incredible that they were incapable of dealing with this, but we were more than willing to meet with the honourable people working on the overhaul. Predictably, progress was then made and the necessary improvements implemented.

The overhaul went well after that, and a fortune was saved by the company as a result of our intervention. The safety performance also improved dramatically.

This is just one example of the continuing assistance we gave to the company over the years.

The depressing thing about all this is that we always had difficulty in convincing successive overhaul managers to adopt the best practice we had devised and implemented over the years. These individuals seemed to bring only their short-term memories to the table.

We also worked well with a few of the HR advisors, and we designed and ran equality courses for them, based on material supplied by Diana Holland, Unite's equality director. A couple of HR advisors actually came to Unite's equality rep training sessions, and we used the training in a few situations where shifts and areas requested it.

On another occasion our intervention led to an improvement in the company's safety regime. This came about when we realised that there had been three cases of cancer in one area and on one shift. The illnesses were different, and there was no obvious link, but I asked for an investigation to be conducted in any case. Whether there was a link or not, it was important to put our members' minds at rest. There was an initial reluctance from the company to do this, but they did eventually agree to it. I asked an old colleague of mine, Professor Andrew Watterson, who is an epidemiologist and expert in occupational hygiene at Stirling University, to look at the cases. This ultimately led to our team visiting all the shifts in all the areas of the refinery to gather information about safety concerns, including discussing such delicate matters as absolute compliance with safety measures. The reason this could be delicate is that it is undeniably true that some corners were cut at times by our troops while on the job – though this was done from a genuine and honourable desire to get the job done, and we are not talking about serious breaches of procedure. But our Unite team wanted to ensure that everyone was as safe as humanly possible at all times. Following this work we then conducted training sessions with the company, which led to a real step change in its safety culture and performance.

I mention this example partly in response to the later accusations that I used safety for political reasons. The company may have chosen not to believe it, but my concern actually was for the safety of our members and the plant.

I think the fact that Gordon stuck to our agreements and honoured the letter and spirit of them – and that we could normally work together to find an acceptable solution as problems arose – was the main reason that he was unceremoniously dumped from this role at the time of the plot against us. It seems to me that the last thing Ineos wanted as they rolled out their company-instigated conflict in 2103 was any hint of constructive dialogue or engagement.

When Gordon was the site manager we had sound working methods and always attempted to find our way through difficulties. Gordon was a seeker of solutions and deal-maker at heart – like us. But the splits and cracks running through the company organisation, and the dreadful lack of accurate communications between the site and Jim Ratcliffe, were at the very heart of the calamitous situation that later arose – and are currently at play – in every aspect of the management of the site.

There are many failings in the Ineos organisation that have taken the site to the place it is in now. However, if I was asked to identify the one that was most at play, the key and fundamental issue, the clincher and the most deadly deficiency, it would be the failure to tell Jim Ratcliffe about all the problems that were going on at the site. The problem with yes men is that they constantly say yes.

This was not because of malicious intent on the part of Gordon and his team. They just lacked the backbone to stand up to Ratcliffe.

During the dispute and in his threats to close the site in 2013, Jim Ratcliffe asserted, in the press and in company communications, that we had repeatedly threatened strike action. One example given by

Calum Maclean was that we had threatened such action during the pay negotiations in 2012/2013, over 0.1 per cent. This is, of course nonsense. The truth is that we had a mandate to press for wages to keep pace with the RPI, and we were short by that margin on the offer. Our take was that it was achievable, and we held out for it in continued discussions. Nothing more. We were right in our assessment and we did get the full RPI figure. I make no apology for that, but I deny utterly that we threatened strike action at any stage. This example, and the assertion that we had threatened action at the drop of a hat over the years, got us thinking. We were baffled as to where this idea had come from and how Ratcliffe could be so wrong.

My view about how this came about can be illustrated by what I believe – after much reflection – must have happened in the 2012/13 negotiations. It is my belief that Gordon Grant was up for the deal on RPI, but did not have the courage or conviction to tell Jim that this was the right thing to do to seal the deal. Instead he went to Ineos Capital and told them that we had made the threat, so that he could move things on without looking as if he was siding with us. If I am right about this, you can understand how a man like Jim – whom I imagine would not take kindly to what he thought were threats from us – could go right off the deep end, and resolve to embark on the disastrous and revengeful path that he has taken.

I shudder when I think about the negative and destructive energy this probably created in the mind of Ratcliffe. I bet such idiotic stories went down a treat in the high cycling trails of the Alps though.

This failure of communication is the central flaw in the system. And this is how we ended up on strike in 2008: no one had told Jim the facts. They kept telling him that everything was under control because that was the last instruction they had been given, and they were too afraid to go back and lay down the true position.

I wonder if our Jim will ever read this. I am willing to bet if he does that he will be saying to himself that this account sounds very credible, and that he has been well and truly done over by his own team. The blame for what happened, though, lies with Ratcliffe himself and his attitude and behaviour towards others. It is this attitude that drives such spineless conduct: the majority of his managers lacked the necessary courage to challenge him.

We did however end up with a mandate to ballot for industrial action in 2011-12, but this was caused by a different management weakness. When Calum MacLean had shown up to discuss wages with us he had acted in a most peculiar fashion. He had immediately embarked on a ridiculous monologue, in which he told us that there would be no pay rise, and that our bonus for the next year would be taken off us and put into the pension pot. According to Calum, that was it: there would be no more discussion and the company was implementing this position right away.

I asked a very straightforward question, as to whether or not this marked the end of the internal negotiation process. Other negotiators will know why I asked this. If there was to be no more discussion or negotiation, then the only place we could take the offer was to the members, for their position and action. Gordon later told us that the voice in his head was crying out, say no, say no, say no.

But Calum said ... Yes.

We therefore held an emergency stewards' meeting the next day and a mass meeting the week after, where the members consented to an immediate ballot for action. To quote Jim Ratcliffe in ill-advised gloating mode after the 2013 dispute, they 'reversed in a millisecond'. The company backed down immediately, and gave us a pay rise plus an enhanced bonus etc.

Gordon told us at the time that Calum was used to commercial negotiations but was not so hot on union-management ones. Quite an understatement.

You can see, though, given my previous comments, how this might have been reported back to Ratcliffe, and how it could have added to his unjustified anger at what he would have seen as our impertinence in challenging his authority, and added to his resolve to silence our union.

The China syndrome

In July 2011, PetroChina, a state-owned Chinese oil and gas company, completed its deal with Ineos to buy a 50 per cent stake in our refinery for a reported $1 billion. The talks had started at least a year before. We were supportive of the deal pretty much right away because it meant we had a credible organisation involved again after quite some time. We knew PetroChina had technical knowledge and the kind of finances needed to own a refinery and chemical complex. We had reservations, of course, but on balance it felt right for our members.

The considerable difficulty for us was that the change would require new commercial entities to be set up, TUPE transfers, subdivision of our pension schemes and a hundred and one other complications. Our stewards were rightly very concerned that it implied the division of the membership into two bargaining units – those in the refinery and associated plants and those in the chemicals and associated plants. However we talked it through and got to the position that this was, on balance, the best way forward. It is worth noting that Ineos later took devastating advantage of the weakness this created by dividing our members into those at immediate risk of unemployment and those at risk further down the line. This action was even more disgusting given that they had been falling over themselves to accommodate and work with us when they wanted to make the PetroChina deal happen.

We jointly devised an umbrella agreement and facility agreement with the company. This agreement meant that the site would indeed be split into separate legal entities, and, technically, our members would be in two bargaining units. But in every practical sense we would continue to have single-table bargaining and cross-site representation. This compromise offered the best of both worlds. The company secured the advantages of continuing to operate essentially as one site while still selling off part of the refinery and harvesting $1 billion from the sale. On the other hand we kept our collective, and retained consistency and equality of terms for all members and representation as one body.

Regional Secretary Pat Rafferty was our officer at the time, and he worked his socks off – to conclude an agreement to help us, but also help the company secure the much-needed investment. It makes me angry to hear the derogatory comments the company subsequently made about Pat, given that they were falling over themselves with praise for him at the time.

Calum Maclean and Gordon Grant led for the company in discussions with us over many weeks, including weekends and late evenings (for us), and, as noted, Pat also gave generously of his time to advise and assist with closing out the agreements.

One weekend, Ian P, Stevie D and I had a meeting with Calum and Gordon at about 10am. They had been with a delegation from PetroChina the night before at a local hotel, and when we arrived they were – how can I best say this? – absolutely hammered, smashed, blootered, wasted, squiffy, wrecked, pie-eyed, plastered, paralytic. In short, as drunk as Lords. The smell of drink was unbelievable. I asked for a recess right away so that our team could decide what best to do in this delicate situation. The best way I can describe the scene is by referring to the episode of *Dad's Army* when Captain Mainwaring's brother comes to stay and he is staggering about the place complete with bed head and a shirt that looked as if he had slept in a hedge.

Calum was the worst, and was talking nonsense while clapping and wringing his hands. He asked if anyone wanted a drink – 'a soft drink'. What other kind of drink would we be having at our work on a weekend morning?

We should have called security really, and insisted on the same kind of substance-abuse test that so many of our members have been subjected to over the years. But to do that did not feel right, given our normal position on such matters and our general dislike of substance-abuse testing. So we said nothing, kept the agenda light and got out of there as soon as possible. I guess we were also a bit taken aback by this situation, and were thinking about the bigger picture – not least how important the outcome of the talks would be to our members.

When I raised the question of this inebriation with Gordon during the following week, he told me what had happened. They had been having a dinner with colleagues from PetroChina, and the proceedings had descended into a whisky-swilling session with calls for shots of malt to be downed one after the other. Gordon had tried to say that the tradition was to slowly sip the 'mystical barley bree', but they were having none of it. The session had gone on well into the night, and this is how they had ended up in the state they were in.

Now we are not members of the temperance movement – and it actually sounds like a fine way to pass an evening – but this was at a time of life or death for the site, and not really appropriate or professional behaviour.

We will take no lessons on professional conduct from Calum or Gordon.

They were absolutely desperate to get the PetroChina deal done, and we could have taken advantage of that big time. If we had demanded that quails' eggs were served in the canteen they would have agreed to it. It was all sweetness and light as they closed in on the $1 billion, but we did not try to take advantage. We simply asked for the agreement and facilities to ensure we had collective equality in line with the current arrangements. Thank goodness the deal with PetroChina went through. Since it did, the refinery has used a credit facility underwritten by PetroChina to cover costs. I am convinced that without the competence and financial clout of the Chinese company the refinery would be in very serious jeopardy by now.

Apparently there was some concern from PetroChina about the pension scheme deficit that Ineos had allowed to accumulate, and Calum asked to speak to us about that. They suggested, and we agreed, that an additional payment should be made to the scheme to reduce the deficit. In the end it was agreed that £15 million would be put into the schemes every year as part of the deal, in order to reduce the short-fall. We were very welcoming of this measure, even though it was not before time.

In the fullness of time, and during the lead up to the calamitous events at the site in 2013, the fact that the company were having to pay this £15 million was cast up repeatedly, even though they had enthusiastically agreed to pay this sum at the time of the PetroChina deal. We must remember that this yearly payment of £15 million was put in place in the context of the injection of $1 billion from PetroChina. That figure was peanuts in the scheme of things – but keep in mind the parable of the apple and the dinner money.

Once again our union had acted with nothing but moderation and good sense, and the deal was completed with a liberal measure of assistance and cooperation from us.

One of our Unite senior officers recently said to me, as an intended compliment, that ours was like an old-fashioned combative branch; he told me that his view was that this was why the company took the discriminatory and outrageous action they did – because they could not control us. I am grateful for the sentiment intended, but this was not the story at all. In reality, Ineos has worked hard to portray us as a militant, inflexible branch who were resistant to change – and this thinking kind of plays into that. But it is not the case. Our branch was the most democratic and pragmatic body you could imagine. I believe that when history judges us it will not be our union that is found to be inflexible and aggressive: I believe that title will belong to Jim Arthur Ratcliffe and his disciples.

The only things certain are death and … well actually just death….

One other delicious treat for your mind concerns Gordon Grant and Ian Fyfe. Please bear in mind when you read this story that these guys went hell for leather to destroy our pension arrangements during the 2013 plot. Gordon was even on the telly saying that the company's proposed 'survival plan' – actually it was more like a 'destructive suicide plan' – was vital, and that our pensions were not affordable. Here's what happened. The HM tax folks were fixin' to reduce the amount of the lifetime allowance you could have in your pension pot. If you were over the new limit you would have to pay tax on it (perish the very thought!). However, in common with a raft of other regulations, there was a loophole provided for the Great and the Good: you could apply for protection against paying the excise man on the cash you had accrued above the limit before the change came into force. In other words, the little lambs could avoid said tax. The non-taxable allowance was being reduced to the paltry level of £1.25 million. Gordon was in the frame for this poverty-ridden retirement. He told us all about this. I swear I am not making this up. You could not concoct this even with the most vivid imagination.

The plan was to file for protection, but the forms and stuff were apparently complicated and not for the faint-hearted. In Gordon's words, 'Ian Fyfe is spending half his working life sorting out the tax for me and the other managers'. I keep thinking about the *Shawshank Redemption*, where Andy Dufresne, played by Tim Robbins, spends all his time doing the tax returns for the prison guards. But take a moment to think about this. Firstly Gordon Grant's pension pot was so enormous he was over the limit, and his pension would therefore be colossal. Nevertheless his view was that our pensions, a fraction of his, were far too generous. Secondly, he was taking advantage of the tax loophole, as was his right – but what about the poor Chancellor? And thirdly, Ian Fyfe (who you may recall was a Grade One referee) was using up company time on non-work-related tax avoidance schemes, yet had plenty to say when Stevie Deans was undertaking legitimate political work under our facility agreement. How revealing is that murky, grubby little business?

The Falkirk Labour Party affair

THE BONES OF the story are as follows. In 2012 sitting Labour MP Eric Joyce announced that he would not seek re-election in Falkirk at the 2015 election. Stevie Deans became chair of the town's Labour Party not long after that – though well before any selection contest for the replacement Labour candidate. Karie Murphy, a former State Registered Nurse and longstanding Labour Party and trade union activist, having made it known in 2013 that she would like to be selected for the seat, then proceeded to campaign for her selection, in absolute accordance with Labour's selection rules and those concerning the recruitment of new party members. Stevie Deans proceeded in the same way. Elements in the Labour Party who resented the success of Karie's honourable campaign then cried foul and made accusations of ballot-rigging and dishonesty. Incredibly, the national party leadership went on to hand information about the selection to the police and made a formal complaint against Karie and Stevie, both of whom were suspended by the party. Karie subsequently relinquished her candidacy in the interests of unity. Karie and Steve were cleared of any wrongdoing by the police and the party and were subsequently reinstated to full membership.

To date, no apology to Stevie or Karie has been received from the Labour Party.

Ineos chose to turn this row into an industrial relations issue within the site, since no opportunity to attack the union has ever been passed over by them. Our efforts to defend Stevie against disciplinary action then became the issue that they picked on as the trigger for the showdown they had been planning for a long time.

For the union there were real industrial and political reasons for campaigning to select such a fine candidate as Karie, but the main and critical driver for us, and Stevie in particular, was the desire to have an MP we could work with in the neighbouring constituency to the site. We wanted someone who would represent the interests of the site, many of whose workers lived in Falkirk, and someone who would be more engaged in the challenges of the industrial and social landscape facing our members than in occupying their time, as did sitting MP Joyce, by exacting extreme violence on Tory MPs in the Strangers Bar in the 'Big Hoose'. Or rolling about on the floor of Edinburgh Airport with officers of the East Lothian constabulary, as astonished travellers looked on while he roared out such gems as 'do you know who I am?'; 'I will take the lot of you'; 'your feet will never touch the ground'; 'I was a major in the Army you know'; 'I want my f****n phone', etc, etc ...

Incidentally, Gordon Grant also appraised us of an incident one weekend when our Eric had crashed his car near the site in Grangemouth and showed up at the gatehouse smelling of strong drink and clearly intoxicated. We had a bit of a laugh about it at the time, to be honest, but the serious point is that the Falkirk constituency needed a new and committed representative. There was no real need for a drink-sodden brawler in the political trenches of Falkirk.

Karie on at your convenience

Let me set the story out from my own perspective rather than that of friends and comrades. It is important to me that I just tell you what I saw and experienced, and outline where I was personally involved and where I was not.

Stevie Deans is, like Ian P, a big mate of mine. Stevie is very organised and tough and he brought this to our team. He was from the chemical side of the Grangemouth fence originally, so we had been thrown together under the BP reorganisation. Stevie is exceptionally hard-working, and all for noble intent. He was involved in everything, including the parish council, the school board, community group and the Labour Party, and held a host of positions in our union including chair of the Scottish region.

I will tell you the truth, and Stevie would bear this out, that I questioned his decision to accept the chair of the Falkirk Labour Party constituency when the opportunity presented itself. My misgivings centred on the additional work and commitment involved in this role. I do not intend to comment much on the underlying workings and personalities involved in this little fiefdom. Suffice it to say that some big personalities were deeply ensconced in a self-interested, scampi-in-a-basket approach to local politics. It was obvious to me that negotiating a way through the self-preservation instincts of some of these individuals would be a drain on energy before any progress could be made on policy or the pursuit of badly needed positive change.

My mate was resolved to go ahead with it, so I set aside my nervousness and offered support where I could. We agreed it would be best for our branch business to be fire-walled, and kept completely separate from any decision-making in Stevie's new role. I also wanted to refrain from interfering as I lived in a different parliamentary constituency. To be clear, as branch convener I was resolving to keep my nose out of this portfolio.

This was many months before any discussion took place on candidates to replace the disgraced Eric Joyce, Falkirk's answer to Mike Tyson and Ollie Reed combined. The much-publicised myth that Stevie was parachuted into the chair by union barons to support a run for a Unite candidate is total and utter nonsense. There was no such thought or intention. Stevie and I shared an office and we also shared our thinking on most things. I can clarify once and for all that the candidate selection did not feature in Stevie's decision to take on the role as chair of the constituency.

It is also important to point out that Stevie set about trying to improve the constituency right away, as I would have expected, given my knowledge of the man. He did recruit members – as we all do – from friends, some family members and other acquaintances. Of course he did. This was part of his role – and the best laugh of all this is that the party sent him a letter congratulating him on his recruiting success! Remember well, all this recruitment was way before any candidate selection process.

The majority of people who joined while Stevie was chair were not Unite members, although some were. In any case they were all good folks who were up for change. It was extremely disappointing that these new members were later made to feel so unwelcome in the party and accused of being stooges signed up to fix a ballot. In many ways the approach to our Falkirk recruits could be seen as a forerunner of the response to Corbyn supporters in the Labour Party leadership election of 2015.

The issue of candidate selection did eventually arise some time after

Stevie took up his post, and it was evident that, as usual, moves were being made by Labour Party apparatchiks to push forward a pre-selected candidate. This seemed to be the well-rehearsed and indeed historic way of things as far as I could see. Loyalty, probably misplaced loyalty, to the party that I have been a member of for many years prevents me from saying too much about specific individuals, but let's get real. How do you think MPs usually get selected to stand in any of the UK mainstream political parties? Perhaps through a transparent democratic process where members in the constituency proceed unmolested to consider the finest candidate, listen to the manifestos and vote for the most qualified and thoroughly good egg?

Don't make me laugh!

Karie Murphy decided to stand, and accordingly took what is apparently a most bizarre and unconventional approach in seeking to secure support. She came to us and our community with policies and an agenda, and said she wanted to represent working-class people. She set out objectives to improve the lot of workers, and to secure good jobs and underpin the industrial manufacturing base while securing and improving public services. Outrageous and just about unheard of!

One characteristic that made Karie stand out from many of the MPs you will see on the green benches of parliament was that she had the life experience of actually having had a job. She had worked in public service in our NHS hospitals, helping people in their time of need.

Karie consulted Stevie and others in the constituency to see if there was any level of support for this radical approach. When her pitch was warmly received, she spoke to other people, like me, because she would not even consider standing unless there was some level of industrial consent for her to do so.

I asked our HR manager, Helen Stewart, if it would be OK to use our Ineos conference room to hold a meeting where Karie would address union leaders from across the district on her vision, and seek guidance on a potential campaign for the nomination. Helen gave us permission both to set this meeting up and to use the Ineos facility.

Let me repeat this at least one more time. Ineos, in the person of our HR manager, knew that we were meeting in company time. Ineos not only knew the purpose of the meeting, they also gave express permission for the meeting – not surprisingly, given that it was indus-trially important to the constituency and, potentially, to the site.

Ineos had never had any qualms about asking for our intervention in the political world. It had done so many times, as I have previously described. The political work and industrial intervention of Falkirk and Linlithgow MP Michael Connarty had previously been really helpful to us and the company, in equal measure. The idea that unions and companies would jointly ask MPs for help and guidance was not exactly revolutionary. It would be beneficial for Ineos to have a credible MP with an interest in the site and the jobs it provided in the neighbouring constituency to Grangemouth. One who was sober and not accustomed to being led away in handcuffs would be a considerable improvement.

It was me that convened this meeting at the Ineos conference room, not Stevie. And it was me who asked the HR manager for permission to hold the meeting and arranged it. Although we were fire-walling the Unite branch from Falkirk constituency business, this event was different. The context of this meeting was industrial as well as political. The hope was that an MP in the neighbouring constituency to the factory would be able to take forward issues affecting our workplace as well as other manufacturing sites around the Forth Valley, in the interests of employers and employees alike, and this made it absolutely appropriate for me to arrange it.

The meeting was excellent. It was attended by many Unite conveners from the major workplaces around Falkirk and also, as expressly permitted by Ineos, a good few of our own branch shop stewards, who were released from work that day to come to the meeting. Karie set out her position, and it was delightfully refreshing. So much so that some of the stewards asked Karie if they could join the party, and enquired as to whether they could convey her message to others, so that a popular movement could be built towards her vision. This inevitably led to other members who worked at Ineos joining the party: they were workmates of those who had been enthused. But this was simply a side effect of the meeting, and it is important to say that recruitment to the party arising from the meeting was not confined to the Falkirk constituency. The expansion in membership took place across quite a number of seats.

A voice in the wilderness calling for progressive political direction was embraced by 'ordinary' working people, and we were amazed at how members reacted. They wanted to be part of this. They wanted to see change and someone speaking out for them for a change. They wanted fairness in the workplace; they wanted secure employment;

they wanted fair taxation; they wanted good public services; and they wanted to be on the front foot and firmly on the side of the angels.

This is why people joined the party. There is no mystery or dirty little agenda. People got behind a candidate who had their values. For our part, we thought the party wanted new members on the basis of political belief. There was no sense that the party was full up and not open to new members.

The reaction of the Labour leadership at that time to a candidate setting out a sound agenda and vision, and the consequent membership increases it led to, was a sign that the party had real problems.

The desperately sad and awful truth is that Karie and other good activists had well and truly upset the Westminster-based selection apple cart, and dared to pursue democratically based local support for change in the constituency. The furious reaction that this impertinence ignited from the comfortably ensconced party grandees was every bit as shocking as it was depressing. Looking back at this now, after the election of Jeremy Corbyn as Labour leader, I can see many parallels in the reactions from the Labour parliamentary establishment to his election.

How can we hope to effect real and radical change, the kind of change that can prevent the greedy harvesting of public money to build private empires in concert with vigorous tax avoidance? Change to prevent disastrous events of the kind that happened at Grangemouth? We must surely value enhanced participation, broader membership and local people selecting their own representatives. My hope is that the Labour Party is now moving in this direction.

Another thing we asked Helen for was that Karie could have the occasional use of a small side room next to the union office at the site, for administrative purposes. Helen said this would be fine but she wanted to check with Gordon. She then came back to us and told us it was not an issue.

Later on the company threw up its arms in horror that Stevie had used the company email system during some of the unlimited time and resources and facilities Calum had offered us (see p102). But, to repeat, we had express permission to be engaged in meetings about the Falkirk constituency selection, and express permission to invite Karie to the site. In any case it is custom and practice for senior union representatives to undertake political work as part of their role. Ask any union rep, in any major organisation, anywhere in the UK.

All our and Karie's actions were very much in line with our union's political strategy. The thrust of that strategy is that policy comes first, and candidates aspiring to become MPs should be considered for selection with that in mind – not the other way round. Our strategy has often been described as 'reclaiming the party', and it is understandable that some people in the party establishment found this threatening to the status quo, and the safe ground they thought they were occupying.

They were right to feel threatened in seeking to maintain this situation. I believe that in not embracing radical change in priorities and focus, the party risked becoming marginalised. It was struggling to peep out of the murky shadows of the middle political ground. Its political comfort zone facilitated the objectives of bad employers, and the spivs and speculators who have been allowed to make the UK more unequal and more unfair, disadvantaging working people, the disabled, the elderly and the sick. The current Labour leadership has moved out of this comfort zone, and in doing so attracted a similarly angry reaction. The outcome of the current battle to reverse this decision will make a huge difference to our members.

The only effective answer to organized greed is organized labour

Thomas Donahue (AFL-CIO)

One of the other areas we were working on at this time, again with the full knowledge of the company, was our organising strategy – basically a drive to recruit and organise members. I mention this here because in the course of this drive we set about organising the security guards, and our completely appropriate actions in doing so were later used against Ian Proudlove, Stevie and me, when we were criticised by the company for 'talking harshly' to a security manager.

We worked hard on the drive to increase membership in all sections of the site, but, just as importantly, we worked to put organisation in place in the shape of representatives and committees. We achieved 100 per cent membership of the bargaining units at Ineos, and brought employees like shift supervisors and laboratory staff into the unit. We had recruited many traditional staff members to our union, including engineers, admin staff, safety advisors, planners and quite senior line managers. We had also worked with our contractors and been involved in inductions to the plant, encouraging union membership. We had also assisted in recruiting 100 per cent of technicians in an independent power station that services the site, and had achieved collective bargaining and equal pay for those members.

The security guards had previously been in-house employees, but had long since been contracted out and were now far worse off their colleagues who had remained on the Ineos payroll. Anyway, we set up a meeting with them in our conference room (this may sound like a broken record, but all with the knowledge and express consent of Ineos). Before the meeting started we could see a supervisor from the security company lurking outside our building, noting which security guards were going in.

During the meeting, as we were being told about the usual raft of issues, including wages, other terms and a ridiculous situation concerning holidays, one of our members from the contractor cleaning company came up to tell us that the supervisor had asked her to tell the members that the security manager would be 'dealing with this in the morning'. Our brilliant Unite officer Scott Foley, who was at the meeting, was aghast. I told the attendees that they were there as my guests and with the permission of Ineos; and that they had every right to be at this out-of-hours meeting, and if they were challenged they should refer complaints from anyone involved to me.

Because of this I called HR manager Helen Stewart first thing the next day and warned her to expect problems. Sure enough, at about one minute past nine that morning the members were on the phone telling me they had been reprimanded and that their explanation that I had invited them to this authorised meeting had been rejected.

I called Helen again and said that Stevie, Ian Proudlove and I would drop down to the security gate and clear this up with the security manager Ian Duncan, who worked for Securitas. She agreed it would help.

I sometimes wonder if some guys are called 'Big Ears' or something at school and then embark on a lifelong campaign to exact revenge on everyone they can.

Anyway we went to see Ian Duncan, the security manager, and he was extremely hostile and did not accept our explanation. After ten minutes or so we left, and referred the matter to Ineos. That was the last we heard of all this until the beginning of the execution stage of the company plot in 2013.

Lies, damn lies and Ineos statements

But let me elaborate further on the preposterous story of the alleged takeover of Falkirk constituency by our union.

Sections of the media had been stoking the story of the Falkirk candidate selection for many months – and they appeared to have been briefed both on the internal workings of the company and internal issues relating to the party. Briefed, but inaccurately briefed, of course.

Stories were beginning to appear about the recruitment of Unite members at Ineos to the Labour Party. It was implied that this was a contrived strategy to stack the constituency using our membership base. As I have set out, this was not the case, but I knew the minute that the name of Ineos was used in the press in connection with this that there would be problems.

Some of the bingo and scampi-in-a-basket politicians, as well as the pugilistic sitting MP, spoke to the press and appeared on TV at every opportunity, stoking the flames of the row by alleging sinister connections such as the fact that Stevie worked at Ineos and employees had become party members from there.

The fact that Ineos members had every right to join the party, and, given the mismanagement of the site over the decades, would quite naturally be looking for a political change to improve things, was never highlighted in the media coverage. Some people just wanted to draw negative conclusions from what happened. Some also hoped it would remove the scary threat of positive change and the threat to their own embedded and comfy positions.

But the mention of Ineos's name presented opportunities for the company to attack and discriminate against our representatives and our union in a way I think they would never have dreamt of in a million years. The Falkirk Labour Party controversy was obviously not part of the original November plot, as it had not even been thought of when Ineos first started its plotting at Grangemouth. It was when the Labour Party, in a knee-jerk response to all the press coverage, made the ridiculous decisions just outlined – and it really gives me no pleasure at all to say this – that it made possible the assault on Steve and, ultimately, the attack on our members.

My thinking on the Labour Party at that time was not that it was in any way rotten to the core – i.e. all the fantastic people and politicians who make up the party and take forward an excellent agenda are not rotten by any measure – but that some elements are rotten AT the core, and that some people involved in our party would have better fitted elsewhere in the political world.

The Labour Party 'investigation' and subsequent report into alleged malpractice by Unite was, quite simply, farcical and embarrassing, but it was also very damaging in a number of ways. It damaged the new membership who had wanted change in the Falkirk party, many of whom subsequently abandoned their membership. It also damaged the party in terms of the more general membership. Those who understood the situation remain critical of the actions of the party leadership at that time. The report was not a report at all: when it finally surfaced it was nothing more than a collection of ill-founded allegations, with not a shred of evidence of any wrongdoing.

The worst of it was that there was no right to reply to the smear campaign against us. The newspapers were full of nonsense, saying that there was reason to believe that there had been naughtiness, but absolutely no facts were presented at all. This flies in the face of any kind of justice, far less natural justice. It is unbelievable that Stevie and Karie were suspended by the party on the back of this cringe-worthy report.

In May 2015 I attended a meeting of Unite activists from one of our leading banks. Stevie and I had been asked to go along and talk about the Grangemouth and Ineos events. Now I thought I knew pretty much everything there is to know about what had happened regarding Falkirk, but in Stevie's contribution he highlighted something I had either missed or forgotten about.

There were audible gasps from the assembled company when Stevie reminded us that during the entire Labour Party 'inquiry' – and while he and Karie Murphy were suspended from membership – not one person from the party had asked either of them for a comment, or interviewed them formally over the allegations made against them in the lead up to the 'report' being produced.

Yet the police were contacted by our party and given this report and urged to take action on the grounds of criminality. From which planet did our leaders hail? Reporting members to the police for running an election campaign and recruiting new members? It is a joke. What on earth were they thinking?

At the same event Stevie described how our union had provided him with a contact for criminal legal representation, as it was thought that the police could arrive at his home at any time and that he could be arrested. He and his wife had the contacts put on their phones on speed dial, and they lived with this dreadful situation for months. I don't mind telling you that it is actually quite hard to write about this.

Incredibly, this farce led directly to a review of the whole relationship between the unions and the Labour Party. Lord Collins of Highbury conducted the review, urged on by sections of the party who would not even know what an actual workplace looked like.

Ray Collins had previously worked for Unite for a long time, and his story was pretty interesting. He had started work in the mailroom of the Transport & General Workers' Union (which merged with Amicus in 2007 to create Unite), and worked his way up to national officer and then assistant general secretary. Ray was AGS when I was elected to the TGWU executive council, and was always helpful to me. He became general secretary of the Labour Party in 2008. I always thought Ray was creative in positioning things to get to his desired outcome – if I can be a bit euphemistic for a moment.

Anyway Ray had been asked to conduct the review, and as a result he made a number of recommendations, including that affiliation fees from unions to the party should only be accepted on an individual basis rather than by block; that union members should have to consent individually to this affiliation; and that only affiliated members would have the right to vote in matters relating to the Labour Party on an individual basis. There were also recommendations about candidate selection, and other references to one member one vote.

I think there were some big positives in the wake of the review, by the way. Len McCluskey's positioning has been movement-leading in a way, because he has said that members should be more personally involved in decision-making over issues like picking the party leader or over party policy. The expected reaction from some people within the party was total resistance to any change suggested by Unite, and a rift in the relationship between the union and the party. I have no doubt that some of these people were hoping that this would happen.

However, the moves subsequently initiated by Len have given momentum to more positive relationships. The massive reduction in automatic funding and greater emphasis on conscious engagement can only improve our political relationship with members and will free up union finance for set-piece political imperatives.

The starkest irony in all this is that I don't think Corbyn would have been elected but for the changes instigated on the back of Falkirk!

It's a pity these positives arose by accident and because of astute moves by our general secretary. The decisions made by the Labour Party concerning the Falkirk constituency itself were absolutely disastrous for our members and for Stevie Deans, and very damaging to the party itself at the time.

Individual Labour party members were brilliant during the whole Falkirk and Grangemouth affair, however, including some MPs and MSPs, and we are eternally grateful for their superb support.

The current leadership in Westminster are looking to renew the links between the unions and the party, and we welcome this. Indeed we believe that the Falkirk events contributed to the rule change that allowed registered supporters to vote in the leadership contest – it was seen as a way of reducing dangerous union influence!

In complimenting Labour politicians, I also want to compliment MSPs from the SNP at Holyrood as well as ordinary SNP members who were nothing but supportive and helpful to us in 2013 and I thank them for that.

I am not a member of the SNP, I remain a committed member of Labour, but I, and many of our stewards, were very impressed by the work of the nationalists and their attempts to help us resolve the difficulties at the site. My thanks go to SNP cabinet minister John Swinney in particular, but I am grateful for the positioning of the nationalist party during 2013.

The overall situation has caused people to question whether the UK political landscape is recoverable, and I am being very open with you when I say that many of our members and our stewards have been won over to the argument for independence. Those who went on the No campaign trail need to take note of the impact of all this. People are sick of the perceived London-driven agenda, and, worse still, many Labour members felt for a long time that our party was firmly in the corner of the gaffer rather than the workforce.

Workers subject to the kind of disgraceful treatment permitted at Grangemouth want to support a party which speaks openly and publicly for them without fear or reluctance.

One of the many ironies of this story is that in the end Labour lost the Falkirk constituency at the May 2015 election, in the SNP landslide.

Countdown to disaster: the plot against Stevie

The following is a timeline detailing as best I can the company's actions against Stevie Deans: how they used the political situation, the media coverage and the interference from on high within the Labour Party to inflame issues at the site by accusing Stevie of wrongfully using company time and email systems. In a series of opportunistic actions, Ineos moved to discipline Stevie and thus create a situation where our branch would have to act to protect him and ultimately take industrial action, after all attempts by us had failed to defuse and resolve the situation.

I will try to explain how the unjust accusations against Stevie were used to assist in the company plot to secure funding from taxpayers; to secure underwritten loans from the UK government; and to elicit reduced feedstock prices from BP. The allegations were also used to impose brutal cuts to the terms and pensions of the employees at the site.

After reading this account you may conclude, as I have, that the treatment of Stevie by the company, which ultimately ended in his departure from his job, was nothing less than disgraceful. The disciplinary process against Stevie was deeply flawed. Far from being a simple and robust inquiry to look into ill-founded accusations from individuals in the Labour Party, it became an opportunistic attack against the fabric, structures and very existence of our union.

Because of the sheer volume of meetings and all the things that took place, the odd date in this account may be slightly wrong. But the most important thing is to give an accurate account of what happened in 2013; the exact sequence of events is of secondary importance. I am very clear on the actual events.

Mid-June to early July

Media speculation about the Falkirk constituency Labour Party was intensifying. The papers were full of reports of alleged wrongdoing and conspiracy theories. The truth was that Unite's political strategy was proving to be a spectacular success in Falkirk and that every action taken by Stevie was within party rules, within our company rules and facility agreement, and in every circumstance in line with the law.

It was unfortunate that the name of the company was used in press coverage. We were aware that this was not helpful or desirable, but the name was dragged in by individuals who were in opposition to our political strategy. The same individuals made complaints about specific recruits to the party, and made assertions that they had been recruited from our company and without their knowledge. An important point here is that the individuals named had not made a complaint. It is also vitally important to remember that none of the new members cited as being in question were either Unite members or employees of Ineos. None!

9 July

Stevie was approached by HR manager Helen Stewart and asked to participate in a 'formal discussion' with the company. The proposal was for Stevie to be interviewed by the HR manager, and for another HR professional to take a statement. Stevie was informed that this would be recorded and would form part of an investigation into breaches of the law, breaches of party rules and misuse of company systems.

It so happened that Howard Beckett, head of the legal department at Unite, and Pat Rafferty, our regional secretary, were on site that day. The reason for this was that a legal response to the ridiculous and libellous accusations made by the Labour Party against Stevie was being prepared by the union. Eventually Stevie was exonerated in relation to all these allegations, as I have already made clear, but at that time the assertions were still being made.

Our officers spoke directly to the company and voiced concerns over the proposed disciplinary action against Stevie. But there were no facts to speak of, and there was insufficient time available to us to rebut the outrageous and fanciful assertions about ballot-rigging, and about the use of company time and systems to do so.

It was accepted by the company management on site that the process had been premature. It was agreed that Stevie and our regional secretary would meet the company in a week's time to discuss the situation, and it was hoped that by that time the matter would be cleared up. This, as events showed, proved not to be the case. It took much longer than that to secure retractions and findings of fact (all of which supported our position).

It was acknowledged at the time that the only reason for company involvement was that it had been named in the press. Once it had been clearly established in the media that the company had had no part in the alleged plot to 'pack' the constituency with our members, we worked hard to remove the company name from any statements we made as a union. It is an unfortunate fact, however, that the company name continued to come up in regurgitated reports for some time after this. The main point here is that the company action against Stevie began on the basis of a false premise, and as a result of inaccurate and maliciously placed information from individuals who felt threatened by our effective and proper political strategy.

16 July

The site board met Jim Ratcliffe. My reason for pointing this meeting out is that I am convinced that very few decisions about the treatment of Stevie or the developing company plot were made at the site. You will see that key turning points in the decision-making process involve the direct intervention of Ineos Capital and Ratcliffe himself.

17 July

Stevie and our regional secretary met Gordon Grant and Ian Fyfe. Our expectation of the meeting was that it was a catch up on the week's events. There was no warning that it had a more sinister purpose, and it is fair to say that the unfolding events were as unexpected as they were shocking. Perhaps this was the first serious departure by the company from the way anyone would usually be treated – unless they were being subjected to discrimination. It was unheard of for any serious meeting involving any member to take place without some sort of heads-up for the convener from the company. Although I was on holiday in the US at this time I had asked to be kept up to date. I had been in constant communication with the site during this holiday and was contactable by phone at any time. Yet no approach of any kind was made to me by the company on this issue prior to the meeting on 17 July.

At the meeting Stevie was referred to as 'Mr Stephen Deans' and treated in a very formal way. It is important for readers to know that this behaviour was unbelievable to us. Remember that we, as a joint negotiating committee, had worked on an almost daily basis with Gordon Grant, and we had been in more scrapes together than you could count – and we all knew where the bodies were buried. It may seem like a trivial point, but this conduct signalled a significant shift in the way the matter was being dealt with. But it is our understanding now, as a result of subsequent discussions, that Ineos Capital (effectively the board, led by Jim Ratcliffe) had an input into directing the course of action between 9 and 17 July.

The meeting proceeded with a very formal contribution from Gordon, culminating with a declaration that Stevie was to be suspended from work with immediate effect, and that an investigation would be carried out into his activity in work time, including his use of company computer systems.

Stevie and Pat were shocked. No warning had been given that this meeting could result in such an action. At the very least it constituted a serious departure from the process that would be used for any other employee.

A vitally important point to take note of here was the formal communication to Stevie at this meeting about how the disciplinary process would be conducted. It was stated that Ian Fyfe would have sole responsibility for carrying out an investigation, and at the end of it he alone would draw up a report and make a recommendation to Gordon Grant on whether or not it was appropriate to move to a formal disciplinary hearing. If this was the case then Gordon alone would conduct and chair the disciplinary hearing and reach conclusions on any action required.

This specific part of the process was entirely in line with company procedure, and the way in which every employee in all of the many cases in which we had been involved would be treated. However it was far from the way in which events were to unfold.

At the end of the meeting Gordon informed Stevie that the company were also going to publicise his suspension and name him on the company intranet. Stevie protested, and pointed out that this was in contravention of the agreed disciplinary process. This is another key point, as there can be no grounds for saying that the company did not know from the beginning that it was flouting agreed procedure.

The site process states very clearly that confidentiality must be maintained at every stage of the site disciplinary procedure. This is crystal clear, and it is inconceivable that anyone could have failed to understand this key point. To broadcast such information to around 1500 people was perhaps the most blatant procedural act of discrimination against Stevie.

Stevie was also informed by letter that he was not to conduct any business as a trustee of the pension fund. This instruction by the company was completely inappropriate, given the independent nature of that role and the representative nature of the work. Trustees are elected from members, and we therefore questioned the right of the company to take this action. In time both boards of trustees – two boards were created when the site was split – wrote to the company formally voicing their concerns.

Stevie left the meeting and returned to our office to collect some personal belongings prior to leaving the site. He was followed over by Ian Fyfe, who confiscated his laptop computer there and then. Stevie was then, shamefully, escorted from the premises.

The communication telling all and sundry that Stevie had been suspended from work was indeed posted on the intranet and remained there for a period of time.

I would say that, considering all the accusations of misuse of the company computer systems that were flying around, and talk of compliance with the internet and disciplinary processes, this was by far the most outrageous abuse of the system that occurred during the dispute. In posting Stevie's name on the intranet, a coach and horses had been driven through just about every company rule and procedure. The bitter irony was that it was Stevie that was being accused of breaching company rules!

When Stevie called me in the US to tell me what had happened I called Gordon Grant to ask what on earth was going on, and why our well established and agreed processes had not been followed. I also protested about the posting on the intranet and the process being followed. Gordon was apologetic, but said that Ineos Capital had insisted Stevie was suspended and that he and Ian Fyfe had been asked to investigate Stevie's activities. I was obviously unhappy at this, but I asked for a meeting with Gordon when I got back and he agreed. Later, in his sworn statement at my tribunal, Gordon stated that I was beyond anger on the call. This was a disgraceful misrepresentation, as my wife, who was there at the time, can confirm. But bear in mind please how this portrayal of my attitude would have been received by Ratcliffe if Gordon told him the same story at the time of Stevie's suspension.

In the same call, Gordon told me that he was duty-bound to inform me that I was also under investigation, following a complaint from the security manager Ian Duncan about my behaviour and that of Stevie and Ian Proudlove in the case I told you about earlier (see p97). I actually laughed at this. What a shower!

When we later robustly defended ourselves against this nonsense, the charges were all dropped and we were entirely cleared, but I believe this was part of a cynical strategy to have a go at all of us as the senior lay representatives on site. We wrote formally to Ineos with a complaint that the accusations by Duncan were malicious and vexatious, and sought assurances that Ineos was not involved in a coordinated effort to discipline Unite stewards as part of an overall plan to attack our organisation. The company said that nothing could be further from the truth! They did not act on our complaint in any way, and we did not hear another word about it.

The case dissolved of course: the company must have realised that these allegations were too fanciful even for them to proceed with. Instead they waited for a better reason to sack me. The irony is that the allegations they ultimately used to try to sack me were even more ridiculous.

In addition to my call to Gordon, Len McCluskey also called him on the day Stevie was suspended, and asked for a message of disapproval and concern, and request for Stevie's reinstatement, to be passed directly to Ratcliffe. He also pointed out the discriminatory nature of the intranet posting and asked for it to be withdrawn. This was a very helpful intervention. Len explained that the situation was entirely unwarranted, and he raised concerns that the situation could escalate and lead to industrial relations problems.

Big Jim later said that the reason Ineos was going to proceed with the suspension, and the reason he wanted to be personally involved in the decision-making and outcome of Stevie's disciplinary (in clear contravention of Stevie's rights as an employee, in clear breach of the company's explicit procedures and against all reasonable recourse to natural justice), was that he was livid that Len had dared to send a message direct to him questioning his decision and authority. And this man was in charge of a plant which made up more than 10 per cent of Scotland's GDP!

19 July

I met Gordon at my request as soon as I returned from holiday. The meeting was an opportunity to point out all the procedural flaws in the process, and to assert that the company's actions constituted discrimination against Stevie on the grounds of trade union activity. I pointed out that there had been no fore-warning of the seriousness of the meeting on 17 July, and that management had revealed personal and very private proceedings on the intranet. I told him that it was our belief that Ineos Capital had interfered in the process. And I argued that it would be virtually impossible now for a fair process to be conducted, and that this was the principal reason why confidentiality was a vital element in the procedure.

I also told Gordon that there had been no wrongdoing, and I gave an assurance that it would be proven that no wrongdoing of any kind had taken place (this, of course, proved to be the case in time).

Gordon agreed at this meeting to reinstate Stevie given the facts and circumstances, but said that the preference of Ratcliffe was to do this after a mass meeting scheduled for 23 July. There was no mention from Gordon at this point that this reinstatement was under sufferance, and certainly no indication that the intention was to post yet another deeply discriminatory and procedure-breaking notice on the intranet.

On a personal note – I had been on holiday and trying to relax over the previous couple of weeks but that day I felt like I had never been away. I felt really uneasy, because Gordon's behaviour and the way things were unfolding told me that something unpleasant was in the post for the site.

23 July

A mass meeting that had been hastily convened went ahead at the Inchyra Hotel in Grangemouth. We initially asked to have the meeting in the canteen as usual, but the company's negative response to allowing Stevie on the site, even in the canteen, led us to withdraw the request. The meeting was attended by many hundreds of members and, given the very short notice of calling it, the response from branch members and friends of our branch was nothing short of magnificent. Len McCluskey and Pat Rafferty were present, together with other Unite officials Linda McCulloch, Jackson Cullinane and Scott Foley. Tony Woodhouse, as chair of our union, also attended. A number of contributions were made in support of Stevie and some questions taken from the floor.

The meeting was supported with a PA system and venue arrangements by our friends at 'Fair Pley', an ethical and unionised events organising outfit who have played at Unite functions for years, and assisted us with many meetings and demos, including during the Grangemouth dispute. They are led by Stephen Wright, who later penned the 'ballad of Grangemouth'.

The unanimous decision reached by the meeting was that senior stewards would have the permission of the branch to move to a ballot for industrial action if this discrimination and victimisation was not withdrawn.

The meeting took place during a holiday period, which normally makes it difficult to get a good attendance. And there was also a move by management to deny members the right to attend the meeting in company time, even though this situation was also way out of the ordinary. But despite the hurdles erected by the company and the fact that it was the holiday period, around 500 members attended.

It was a fantastic response as usual from our members.

24 July

Stevie was informed by letter that he was reinstated but only due to Unite intervention. Stevie was made to feel very unwelcome on site by this letter.

Unbelievably, the company then posted a further notice on the intranet stating that Stevie was to be reinstated but only under sufferance. This was a staggering further breach of company procedure and a clear infringement of Stevie's rights as an employee. It was in further stark contrast to any other disciplinary process we had known at Grangemouth, at any Ineos site or in our experience at any workplace.

A number of discussions took place during this period, resulting in a meeting with the company at our suggestion. We were keen to open our books, offer any assistance to the company and answer any question, and to make representations on a number of issues.

I was minded at that time that the treatment of Stevie could all be put down to poor communications or a fundamental misunderstanding. I kept waiting for the company to come back and say that it had all been a terrible mistake on its part. This is why I was keen to meet them and talk it through.

14 August

A meeting took place involving Gordon Grant, Ian Fyfe, Helen Stewart, Ian Proudlove, Stevie Deans and myself, at our request. The meeting allowed us to put forward evidence and our position on a number of matters.

We wanted to know why an informal process was not used as the first stage of the disciplinary hearings in line with every other case we had dealt with and in line with the agreed procedure.

We expressed disgust that the notices had been posted on the intranet. We stressed the importance of confidentiality, the reason for confidentiality and the impossibility of any kind of fair process given how widely the notices had been viewed. We pointed out the effect on Stevie, whose good name had been dragged through the mud, and that employees should be presumed and treated as innocent until shown otherwise.

We expressed our concern about the company rifling through confidential computer files and information held on behalf of members, and we also asked about the timing of this part of the investigation. Gordon and Ian told us that although searches had already been done, it would take weeks to download the information. We were unconvinced by this reply, given the speedy process adopted in past cases where Internet use by members was being questioned. I will describe later in the book why I think delay was important to the company as they set out to provoke a dispute in their preferred timeline.

We asked for a clear description of the process we were involved in. It was confirmed again that Ian Fyfe would investigate and Gordon Grant was to hear any case. We asked for a written description of this process, and a commitment was given to do this by Gordon. We are still waiting.

We discussed our agreement on union facilities as set out in writing. We pointed out that the agreement acknowledges that the duties of a senior steward are 'many and varied'. The agreement purposely did not define them, but committed the company to assisting and facilitating these duties. One of our duties was to be involved in Unite's political strategy as defined by our executive. Politics was very much part of our role. Time taken during the day on-site was no different from time off-site on wider trade union duties. The HR manager knew about our strategy and had full knowledge of the meeting involving Karie

Murphy and our stewards at the site. We had her permission to have this meeting.

We raised the point that, as chair of the Scottish region, it was very much part of Stevie's role to undertake union activities dictated by its policies.

We reminded Gordon that at the time of my election as vice chair of the union, Calum Maclean had offered Stevie and I unlimited time off, facilities and 'anything else you need' to perform the roles.

We presented substantial evidence to the meeting of political work carried out in company time, not only with the full knowledge of the company but also with the assistance and encouragement of key individuals on site. Examples were presented of meetings and events that our representatives had been involved in to help with project funding, environmental lobbying and promoting the chemical and refining industry.

We included details of such events as: meetings with MPs and the shadow minister for energy and our involvement with Unite in setting up an adjournment debate in parliament. We listed meetings with the Chemical Industries Association, with the UK Petroleum Institute, with the Labour groups at Westminster and Holyrood and liaison with Conservative, Liberal Democrat and SNP MPs. We also referred to our involvement in global union federations and our input into motions and the democratic processes of our union.

We presented email exchanges encouraging our political involvement in site-related taxation and legislation issues from such senior managers as Gary Haywood (CEO), Gordon Grant, Russell Mann (refinery manager), Andrew Gardner (refinery commercial manager) and others.

We said that to suggest that political work was not part of our role was inaccurate and rank hypocrisy.

A submission was made by us about use of company time, and the fact that the company gave no consideration to time taken to travel to European company meetings and pension meetings. We pointed out that, for example, evidence for medical cases was typically prepared outside work time, and that we attended NORCC meetings in our own time, sometimes while acting on information from the company. Then there was the time we spent at weekends and other unpaid hours on the PetroChina deal, when the company had been only too keen to have us involved. We submitted many other examples of occasions when we used our own time. Of course this benefited our members, but very often it also benefited the company.

We made the simple point that although we had to wade through all this work, we did not have Wi-Fi in the office. Since there was of course Wi-Fi in the senior managers' office, it had been established and well understood that, given that we had to perform all kinds of diverse duties during the day, the only option was often to use the company system.

As can be seen from this argument, and the fuller account of our political work given on pp68–79, political work was not only tolerated but encouraged by the company, and we had often colluded with them for mutually beneficial political ends. The only time there had been a problem was when the 'opportunity' presented itself for the company to take action against our representative. The hypocrisy was breathtaking.

We were thanked for our contribution and complimented by Gordon on the clarity and logic of the case. Both he and Ian said it was very helpful and would assist with the case.

26 August

We met the company with the full expectation of having a decision on Stevie and with the clear position that there was no case to answer. We were astounded to be told that Ian and Gordon were now required to make a presentation to Ineos Capital, so that it could have an input into the decision-making. Please take a moment to consider how contrary to process, unusual, inappropriate and discriminatory this was. It was explicitly reported to us by Gordon that Jim Ratcliffe now wanted to make the final decision because he was angry with Len McCluskey for phoning Gordon!

Unbelievable!

It is worth reminding ourselves of the process that had been set out by the company – that Fyfe would conduct an investigation, present his findings to Grant and then Grant would decide if any disciplinary hearing was required. Clearly this had been cast aside and any semblance of workplace justice cast aside with it.

I am convinced that the dynamic here was that Jim Ratcliffe was pressing them as local managers to find a way to escalate the situation and take action against Stevie. Gordon and Ian welcomed our contribution and the presentation of the case at this meeting because they could use it to try and divert Ratcliffe from going after Stevie. It was agreed between Gordon and myself to meet as soon as possible to arrive at what would hopefully be a just and proper outcome to this case.

28 August

We had another amazing mass meeting in the canteen, partly called because of evidence that the company was planning an anti-strike contingency plan (see pp128–30).

We think there were in the region of 650 to 700 members in attendance across both meetings that day, and the warmth and support for Stevie was palpable.

The report on the discriminatory process employed by the company was received with incredulity, and a reinforced mandate was granted to the stewards over the victimisation. There was a clear branch decision urging members to vote Yes to strike action and Yes to action short of a strike in any ballot. This was confirmed unanimously, and when the question was put to the members present there was not a single voice of opposition.

At this meeting we also renewed our mandate for permission to negotiate on pensions (although the company had walked away from the proposals we had made to discuss pensions in the previous year (see pp120–2), there were still ongoing negotiations in this area). And we were given authority to meet BP to allay any concerns they might have over the North Sea operation in the event of industrial action (for more on this see pp134–5).

Once again, our branch was simply magnificent, courageous and principled in every regard. I was very proud of them that day.

September

From September onwards, the dispute over the disciplining of Stevie was accompanied by ever increasing demands from the company for deterioration in the pay and conditions of the work force (see p141–4).

12 September

An Ineos Capital board meeting took place with Gordon in attendance. We were told openly that the issue of Stevie would be discussed and decided at this meeting. We fully expected the company to declare Stevie cleared. We had a clear indication of this likely outcome from the mouths of Gordon Grant and Ian Fyfe. An apology would have been nice regarding the unfair process Stevie had been put through, but we were not demanding it at that time.

Gordon had committed to calling me in the evening to let me know what had happened. Ironically I was on my way back from Brussels, having been at a European meeting with our global union federation with Unite assistant general secretary Tony Burke and national officer for chemicals Linda McCulloch, to talk about assistance for the industry amid cumulative environmental demands and the costs associated with them.

No call was made and it was clear that there was a problem when a text asking to meet first thing in the morning was all that was sent to me by Gordon Grant that night.

13 September

A meeting was arranged for 8.15 in the morning. In attendance were Gordon Grant, Ian Fyfe (who was a Grade One referee), Stevie Deans, Ian Proudlove and me.

Gordon Grant set out the following three points.

The outcome of the investigation had been reported to Ineos Capital on the 12th. The inquiry would not be dropped as expected, but it would now be widened and a firm of lawyers would be employed to further interrogate Stevie's files and look for evidence. The profound unfairness of this and the clear determination to uncover anything to proceed against Stevie was not lost on us. This came after many weeks of searching through Stevie's files.

It was also reported that the company intended to begin preparation for industrial action, including training scab labour to oversee the site. This scab labour was to be drawn from poor unfortunate site employees who were not union members. We pointed out that these workers often found it difficult to manage the site when we were present, never mind when we were not, but they told us they were going to do it. There was also a bit of important positioning from us as a union branch. We said we would help BP with continued production and provide safety cover in the event of any industrial action. We meant to do this – it was a genuine offer.

The third point – out of the blue – was that, although they had rebuffed our earlier attempts to discuss pensions as part of a considered package of reforms, they now wanted to start formal discussions on pensions, with immediate effect. We had, of course, already signalled our willingness to engage in a discussion about pensions, but the timing of the proposed meeting was quite sinister. They told us they wanted to meet to discuss the issue during the following week. But I had already notified the company that the Unite executive was scheduled to meet that week. The EC meets four times a year and these dates were notified to the company months in advance. The reply was that they expected to meet on the following Monday regardless of the commitments they had given on time off. I pointed out that this was not the best context for constructive discussions and that the company position felt vindictive. However, we were eager not to present any more opportunities for disciplinary action so we agreed the date of the meeting.

One of the most disappointing aspects of missing the Executive was that I had moved an emergency motion at the annual TUC conference the week before on helicopter safety given recent fatalities offshore, and one of the scheduled executive council reports was on this issue and how we should proceed as a union. There was also a very important debate about the Falkirk Constituency Labour Party, and reports on assisting heavy energy users like our own workplace. I believe the timing of the meeting with management represented a very significant act of aggression from the company and a deliberate escalation.

The dynamics of the dispute

Let me make this crystal clear. Gordon and I had worked on all sorts over the years and we were naturally in regular contact about Stevie's suspension. The union were fully aware of the fact that Gordon and the other site management had been trying to make this disciplinary go away from day one. They knew how unfair as well as destructive this could be. I believe that part of the problem was that Gordon was, once more, telling us one thing and JAR another. In our various discussions with Ian Fyfe and Gordon Grant it would have been impossible to reach any other conclusion than that there was no case to answer.

The evidence had been pored over for many weeks. Our conviction was that the individuals tasked with carrying out this process had been strongly minded to recommend that any disciplinary action was neither appropriate nor warranted.

But JAR was clearly insisting on a strategy that he had decided in advance, and the site managers were trying to look as if they were following his orders. However they were also trying to get to a point where the only possible outcome would be to drop these charges. At various stages Gordon and Ian Fyfe told me this. I challenge either of them to deny it. The truth is that Gordon repeatedly said that he was trying to get to the 'right answer', and to persuade Ineos Capital that there was no case to answer. Separately, Ian Fyfe said the same thing.

In one of the many conversations I had with Gordon over this period, I asked outright where we were. This was not in any way unusual by the way. As union folks will know, it is regular practice to have such informal conversations. Gordon replied with words to the effect that 'there has been no murder committed according to Ian, so not too much to worry about'.

What evidently happened was that Ian and Gordon reported their findings to JAR and he told them that it was the wrong answer and they should think again. Don't take my word for it, glance at the evidence – it is obvious that this is what happened.

It was obvious throughout this process that, following discussions between Grangemouth managers and Ineos Capital, the mood had constantly changed. The company and Ratcliffe himself continually interfered with the process and gave directions to move the goalposts.

This can be seen in Ratcliffe becoming involved in what was supposed to be a site-based investigation conducted by Ian Fyfe and Gordon Grant; in the continuous prolonging of a process initially expected to last a few weeks; and – the clincher – in the sudden introduction of completely new industrial relations issues once they had decided to escalate the dispute into a full scale attack on the union.

A further note on communications

I want to mention here a notable email communication that was sent out during these proceedings by an employee who supported the company position. This employee was not disciplined for her unauthorised use of the intranet but instead was complimented by Ratcliffe. In fact our response to her intervention was cited by JAR as one of the reasons he did not seek a negotiated settlement over all the issues arising from the events on site in 2013. Here is what he said in an article in the *Telegraph*:

> During the dispute, a female employee in accounting, who was worried by the union drumbeat, expressed concern about her job and confirmed that the business was in financial difficulty (she prepared the figures each month) in an email that she put out across the site. She received rude anonymous phone calls, with the phone being slammed down.
>
> This small incident was much discussed in Ineos. It upset many of us that a lady in our company, a mother of three, was unable to express her views and concerns freely. It played a part, ultimately, in our resolve not to accept a solution for the site that did not bring with it changes on many fronts, but most importantly, in attitude and working practices.

> *Daily Telegraph*, 2 November 2013

What actually happened was that this employee, Nicola Butler, who was not a member of our union, sent out an unauthorised email in contravention to the IT policy. She sent it to the distribution list created, owned and used by Stevie and me to communicate with our union members. It was sent during the voting period for our ballot and heavily criticised our union. Nicola had set out on a frolic of her own (maybe???) to tell our members, in this company-procedure-breaking communication, all about her personal view on life. The email was totally inappropriate and broke the IT policy in a way Stevie's actions did not.

The email intimated that if union members exercised their democratic right and voted to take industrial action in support of Stevie, we would all lose our jobs and the whole town would be destroyed, and we would never again be able to go for days out with our families or go on holidays. Think about the message here: that we should abandon Stevie to the wolves – Stevie who had worked tirelessly so people like Nicola could have days off and the money to look after their families. To me, the note was actually shameful.

The first I knew about the email was when our steward who was responsible for communications, who happened to be in the office at the time, told me that a note had been sent to our list and proceeded to read it out.

The very first words out of my mouth were to ask her to get a note out straight away to our members, telling them not to respond in any way.

The next thing to happen was that Steven Boyle – who had by now been brought in to replace Helen Stewart in HR, as part of the plot – called the office. In his usual blustering and breathless manner he said he had seen the email and was mortified. He would get hold of the person responsible and make sure it did not happen again. I was not best pleased at what had happened, but agreed with him that he should have a quiet word to ensure there would be no repetition, rather than make a big deal of it.

I also told him we were putting a note out to members asking for restraint, and that at that very moment our steward was signalling that it was already out.

Not one reply was made from our members to this individual, and if there were any people who made rude comments to her on the phone, as alleged by Ratcliffe, it was against our specific request not to do so.

The implication from Ratcliffe in the *Telegraph* was that our union had orchestrated rude comments to this woman. I deny that and invite him to either produce evidence in support of this smear or to withdraw his insulting comments.

It is very frustrating when people like Nicola – who had gained time and time again over the years due to our influence – take such selfish and inappropriate actions. But it would do us no good to have a go at her.

But read the statement – the breathtaking statement – from Ratcliffe: 'It played a part, ultimately, in our resolve not to accept a solution for the site that did not bring with it changes on many fronts'. A spurious and unauthorised personal note sent out by a panicking employee, and a false insinuation about the reaction of other employees, had apparently led to a personal agenda to drive home destructive changes at the site, and to threaten the industrial complex that provided a massive chunk of the GDP of Scotland.

This is insanity however you view it. Is Ratcliffe really saying that he made decisions about our members' terms and conditions, and planned to enforce destructive changes, because of allegations that people were rude on the phone to an employee? If that is the case, how can such an organisation have been allowed to have this national asset in their control? How can there be any level of confidence in the competence of JAR, or his capacity for making rational decisions? Read it again: 'It played a part, ultimately, in our resolve not to accept a solution for the site that did not bring with it changes on many fronts' … 'It played a part, ultimately, in our resolve not to accept a solution for the site that did not bring with it changes on many fronts'.

Abandon hope all ye who enter here!

Postscript

In a subsequent disciplinary hearing Ian Fyfe trotted out a lot of tripe saying that Stevie had sent out 1000 emails relating to his role as chair of the Falkirk constituency. I wanted to know why the figure was so low. Our friend Nicola Butler, who had predicted we would never have holidays or be able to take the kids to Blair Drummond Safari Park if we voted for strike action, had sent out over 1000 in one go.

There was also some utter rubbish talked about the content of Stevie's emails – an attempt to say that some light-hearted comments in the emails constituted serious disciplinary breaches.

When we came out of this shameful show trial we both knew Stevie was going to be sacked. It was sickening.

CHAPTER SIX

The build-up of the plot

I HAVE BEEN MENTIONING the company's plot against the union throughout the book. The Falkirk Labour Party events merely gave them a good excuse to get things going. The date scheduled for putting the plot into action was November 2013. But before then there were many indicators that something was afoot.

Ominous signs

In hindsight, the company's response to our negotiations at the beginning of 2013 was clearly a part of the plot.

In the last quarter of 2012 we had been approaching the annual pay review, and we had been having a very difficult but mature and business-like consultation with our members. Some of our stewards, including our senior team, were concerned about the site and the way it was being managed. We were also concerned about the way the company finances were being presented. We were mindful that the pension scheme had been allowed to fall into a pretty significant deficit. We were also mindful, as previously noted, that the company had not carried over our share of the BP-administered pension surplus at the time of the company sale. We were aware that investment decisions regarding the pension funding had not gone to plan, and we would have had every right to take the view that the difficulties facing the pension scheme were something for which the company was responsible, and that we, therefore, would not assist in resolving them.

The decision we took as a union was not to adopt that position.

No. In 2012 we had agreed to a difficult discussion on potential detrimental changes to the pension scheme.

The bottom line was that the scheme was indeed in deficit. We also considered the fact that pension provision had generally been

Mark Lyon in 2008. (*Gerry McCann 2008*)

Picketing during the 2008 pensions dispute. (*Gerry McCann 2008*)

Mass meeting during the dispute. (*Gerry McCann 2008*)

Mass walkout during the 2008 dispute. (*Copyright PA Images*)

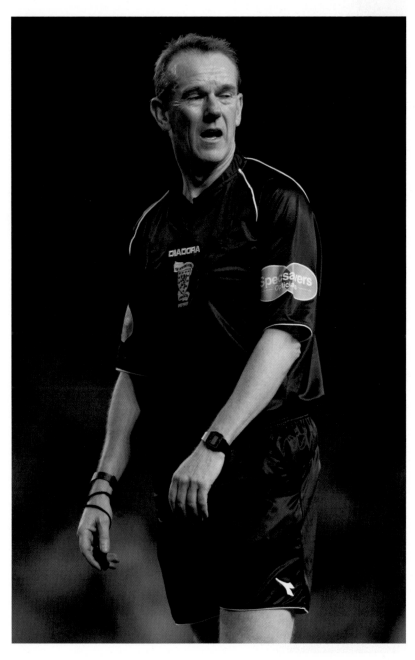

Referee Ian Fyfe in 2005. (*Copyright PA Images*)

Jim Ratcliffe (left) and Calum Maclean in 2008.
(*Copyright PA Images*)

Jim Ratcliffe's yacht *Hampshire II* in 2013.
(*Daily Record/Paul Chappells 2013*)

Karie Murphy in 2015. (*Mark Harvey 2015*)

Stevie Deans (left) and Mark Lyon in 2013.
(*Jeff J Mitchell/Getty Images*)

The ethane tank in 2016. (*Mark Lyon 2016*)

allowed to decrease across the UK chemical and oil sectors. While there is not one shred of criticism intended of our fellow union reps, as this is unquestionably a bosses-led industrial agenda, it is a fact that many schemes across the sectors had closed to new entrants or closed entirely.

This, I guess, is a bit like the environmental debate. As a country or industry we can continue with a principled position and apply standards way in excess of other countries, BUT, once our industry is closed as a result, the production will shift to the nations with less rigorous compliance demands. It's not a very good argument and it makes you feel very uncomfortable, but often pragmatism comes above principle. It is one of the prices you pay for effective union representation.

Just as with the environmental argument, we felt that we were a bit out of line with other pensions in the industry. This had the potential to make us less competitive in the rotten race-to-the-bottom capitalist system. We wanted to adopt a position in the negotiations that would enable the company to succeed, and allow it to continue to provide secure employment for as many people as possible, and to invest in the site.

Our stewards were therefore authorised by our members to approach the company to see if sensible changes could be made to pensions to bring us more into line with other schemes. Obviously we were not offering to hand over the scheme without some protection, and we were proud once again of our members' stance that we must not sell new entrants down the river. There would undoubtedly be changes, but we wanted to be able to look such members in the eye and have a credible position as to how we had protected their pensions as much as possible.

The site management were taken aback at this position, but pleased all the same, and talks took place over the next few months. Maybe there was an element of premonition underlying all this. Maybe it is possible to sense when malignant intent towards you is gathering pace. I certainly felt uneasy at the time, but this was not the reason we approached the company.

Eventually we arrived at a point in discussions when we thought we could make substantial moves to reduce the cost of pensions, while at the same time not being concerned about showing our faces at a mass meeting, or when welcoming new employees to our branch.

The bones of it were that the scheme would close to new entrants, but such employees would have an enhanced pension when compared to the standard defined contribution Ineos scheme. Crucially, there would also be assurances about site investment in the form of the proposed feed tank, and some measures which would bring people into the full-time Ineos contract, rather than remain as agency workers or contractors. We wanted some of these concessions before agreeing a deal over the scheme. Part of the agreement would be that apprentices who were on college contracts but felt very much part of our team would be put on Ineos contracts. A substantial wage offer would clearly also be tied into the deal as a sensible softener for the dramatic change we were proposing, and in consideration of the enormous financial savings the company would enjoy forever as a result of the change.

This conciliatory move by us is pretty unconventional you will agree, and flies right in the face of the absolute and idiotic and insulting nonsense JAR insists on continuing to spout about our union.

So, at the beginning of 2013 we thought we had proposals to take back to members. Site management had said that they were delighted with the package, which would secure investment and take us all forward. But at this stage something then happened outside the site.

A meeting had been convened in our union conference room with the management team: we thought we were getting together to nail some of the finer points, and prepare to go out to the members for their agreement, with the good news story about intent on investment. I was really excited by this I don't mind telling you, as the site is very dear to me – as are our members and the community I was brought up in. For me, the prospect of long-term security for the factory was the biggest prize.

I knew something was not quite right when the company showed up at the meeting. They were grim-faced and clearly very uncomfortable. I asked right out if everything was OK with the deal, and Gordon said, not really. I can still remember clearly the words he used. He said 'it's not enough'. He told us Ineos Capital had come back after all these months of negotiations and were now saying they wanted 'more' if they were to invest at the site.

I have to confess that there was a big argument and I was really shocked. I asked if this was the parable of the apple and the dinner money all over again. When would enough be enough? Why could the site not just have a good news story for a change, and have invest-ment without blackmail? Why was the investment being use as a battering ram to make changes when it was a project that would ultimately make Ineos a fortune, and why could we not all share in this success?

Our team was disgusted – and Gordon Grant later tried to smear my name in his sworn statement in the run-up to my tribunal by saying that I had sworn in the meeting. (Gordon, and others, signed prepared statements supporting Ineos in advance of my tribunal hearing after I had been unfairly dismissed later on in this story. I say 'signed' the statements, as it is unclear to me who actually prepared them.) There is not one lie in this book so I will confess that I did swear at the meeting. However I will qualify that by saying that industrial language was an everyday feature of our meetings, including from Helen, Gordon and everyone else in the union and management teams.

Gordon also stated that I had said words to the effect that they should just shut the site down then. This *is* a lie – and I utterly reject and deny it. The site was very important to me and I would never make such a ridiculous remark.

There was a period of uncomfortable silence in the following days, and Gordon tried to turn the tables by saying in an email to me that he had been unhappy with my behaviour in the meeting. I replied saying that we were not in the boy scouts, and that the real issue was the company betrayal of the deal.

However, life had to go on, and so I made yet another conciliatory move to try and get things back on track. The issue of wages was still outstanding despite the company walking away from the pension talks, and we would have to try to resolve that.

I was also still hoping that something could be done to move all the issues forward, so I asked if I could meet CEO Calum Maclean to see if I could persuade the company to get back round the table on all the issues – investment, pensions and wages. Gordon came back to me and asked if we could do a teleconference with Calum. This was on the day that we had a mass meeting arranged for the afternoon, to update members on our concerns over what had happened. Up to this point our senior team had kept the disappointing actions of the company to ourselves, in the hope that we could salvage the situation and, in so doing, spare our members.

Anyway, we participated in the discussion, and this is where the events took the most sinister of turns. Calum came on all friendly but was perceptibly nervous. Gordon and Helen were in Gordon's office on the phone, and Ian and Stevie and I were in the union office. I kicked off after the usual pleasantries by saying that we were confused and disappointed by the company stance. I reminded Calum what was on offer and suggested the possibility of re-opening talks. Our mass meeting was that afternoon and there was still time to revise our message, put a holding position in place and get back round the table.

At the time his response was quite pleasing to us, if not a bit surprising, especially to Gordon, as he soon after told us. But when I think back now, its message and intent are chilling.

Calum told us that perhaps the time was not right for all this. He said that we needed to concentrate on the investment strategy, and in the meantime put the pensions into the long grass. They didn't want to get into all that right now, but might come back to it in the years to come. He wanted us to agree to leave it for the time being.

I was surprised, given his previous stance on zero pay rises, but told him I was OK with that. We wanted to be fully involved in the investment proposals, and would help any way we could. I also raised the small matter of the wage deal. Calum said words to the effect that we could probably do something up to, but no more than, RPI. I immediately said that's fine, RPI it is. (Gordon's assessment of Calum's negotiating skills were not that far off the mark.)

Calum proposed that we talked to Gordon over the following week or so and put a deal together. I reminded him that we had a mass meeting in two hours. What about meeting now? He agreed, and we met Gordon and Helen in their office about half an hour later. They were gobsmacked by what had been agreed, and it was very obvious that Calum's position had taken them by surprise every bit as much as it had us.

There was a tiny lighter moment when, after telling them, if I remember rightly, that the RPI figure was 2.9 per cent, we realised when we retired so they could write up the deal that RPI was actually 0.1 per cent less than that. When we reconvened I said that the 2.9 was no longer acceptable and we wanted to revise our claim. Gordon looked worried, until I said it was actually 2.8 we wanted, and he just rolled up and threw a slice of paper he had prepared on RPI over his shoulder and on to the floor.

We took the position to members and they were understandably pleased and supportive. We also took the step of refreshing our mandate to talk about pension revision at any time with the company.

This is a critical passage for me because I can see now that this was the first time Ineos had begun to execute the plot. I realise now that the company had decided not to do a sensible compromise deal with us on pension terms at that time because they preferred to force a strike on their terms in November 2013, when they could threaten us with the total closure of the site, with all the inevitable devastation to our people and the community of Grangemouth that this would involve.

Financial tricks

A very important part of the plot was to portray the finances of the site in the worst possible light. This would then become the excuse both for exacting subsidies from government and for undermining wages and conditions.

The industry standard reporting measure for credible chemical companies was called EBITDA (Earnings before interest, tax, depreciation and amortisation), but the company had moved away from that model and instead adopted a simple cash model of accounting. This meant it included its investment in things like the KG Cracker plant (which is capable of processing the ethane gas arriving from the US) as a cost that appeared in its bottom-line financial result for the year in which the expense occurred – i.e. as a one-off payment to be subtracted from a single year's profits, rather than gradually subtracted from profits over time, as is the norm. Multinational organisations on the world stage would typically take such an investment and write it down over twenty years or so, placing the interest payments and servicing of loans as a deduction from the bottom-line profit over that period, rather than a one-off deduction.

It is different if you are running a whelk stall, where you may set out your accounts by including such investments as whelks, brine, vinegar, containers, wee wooden forks and plastic containers. Take the cost of all of that off the cash from seafood-loving punters over the counter and hey presto … The bottom line.

But you can't run an international chemical and refining business in that fashion.

The company also claimed that the ongoing cost of pensions was about 65 per cent of the wage bill at the site. Once again this is nonsense. The way they worked that out was to take the actual cost of paying in for existing working members, and to add to that the cost of providing pensions to retired members and deceased members' dependants, as well as the £15 million extra payment agreed during the PetroChina deal. They then divided this total by the payroll of employees who were on site, and arrived at the figure of 65 per cent. It was preposterous. An accurate reflection of the 'ongoing' cost of pensions to existing members would simply be the total amount of conventional contributions they were paying in to the fund. Neither the £15 million exceptional payments should have been included in the calculation, nor the cost of pensions that were actually being paid to retired employees from the existing pension fund.

During the later stages of execution of the plot we made a genuine offer, direct from our general secretary, to bring in an expert on accounts to examine the books forensically, at our own expense, so we could see what the actual financial picture was. Needless to say this

'NEGATIVE EARNINGS'

Ineos has supported its claims of 'financial distress' with evidence from its auditor, PwC.

This showed negative earnings of £110m between 2010 and this year, and capital expenditure of £468m. This has been described as a loss of £579m.

However, Unite asked Richard Murphy, an accountant and tax campaigner, to assess the claims, and to find out more about Ineos' finances.

He concluded that the claim of a £579m 'loss' is misleading, as it includes capital spending and is cash flow.

Mr Murphy admitted that it is hard to find which parts of the Ineos business cover operations at Grangemouth.

But his assessment of the company called Ineos Chemicals Grangemouth Ltd suggests that the company has added special one-was rejected out of hand, and at one of the excruciating and tedious 'town hall meetings' they organised (company propaganda meetings to you and me), Calum told the poor souls assembled that there was no way the likes of Mark Lyon would be looking at the company's books. What did they have to hide?

Another important point to make here is that an organisation that is begging for money from the UK tax-payer should be flatly refused any such assistance until every aspect of its financial affairs has been laid bare before the public and forensically examined.

After our offer was refused we decided to engage the services of chartered accountant Richard Murphy, a long-standing and active member of the Tax Justice Network, to examine the available information. Below is an excerpt from an article on the BBC site, posted on 17 October 2013. It gives a very different picture of the site's finances.

The company continues to claim that the site is a distressed business. Make your own mind up friends. My belief is that this constituted the well laid groundwork for the intended plot.

You don't have to be a professor of accountancy to spot this. It's just like the gentle art of animal husbandry ... You don't need to be a vet to identify bullshit.

off measures to make the accounts look bad, including the write-off in valuation of the petro-chemical plant.

Mr Murphy says a deferred tax allowance of £117m implies that the company expects to make around £500m in profits over several years.

His assessment says the pension fund gained £7m, sales grew 50% and operating profit grew by 56%.

Unite says the findings 'blow a hole' in the Ineos financial claims. Pat Rafferty, regional secretary of Unite, commented: 'We believe the company is using fancy accounting tricks to pull the wool over the country's eyes and treat us with contempt.

'The company gives the impression it is broke and it may need to close the Grangemouth site, but we believe this is just a ploy to justify attacking its workforce and to demand government handouts'.

BBC 17.10.2013

To cap it all, at the end of September Ineos decided to write down the value of the Grangemouth chemical business in the company accounts from around £400 million to zero. I still find it unbelievable that a company could legally devalue an asset in this way: it seems such a blatant manipulation of the books.

Forward planning for strike breaking

The next important evidence to present – and the next strand of the devious plot – is the company's advance planning for a dispute.

INFO – EXTREMELY CONFIDENTIAL.

Cannot disclose reproduce etc (unless by O&P board member).

Operation Plan for I.A.

Objectives during s/down or s/by mode.

No Accidents
No Incidents
No Environmental
Maintain Kinneil Ops
Maintain Fuel Supplies
C2 P/Line Op's

Notice Period for IA
7 or 14 Days
Timing/Potential Duration of IA
Nov 2013

1st Pass 24th August to allow consolidation into O&P and Ops Plan

Actions:
Define shutdown and stand-by plans for all plants and unit operations respecting any sequencing, dependencies (utilities

I received the words set out below on slides left on my desk by an anonymous source on 22 August 2013. At first I thought it was a joke. Alas, it was not a joke at all. I say 'words' because the information on the slides was hand-written rather than printed off. Our informant was probably a senior and concerned manager who did not want to leave a trail on the computer system. The slides showed that the company had been preparing for industrial action for some time. Our hope at first was that there was some misunderstanding, but our suspicions were later confirmed.

requirements) to ensure safe shutdown and stand-by without compromising basis of safety plus.

Define sufficient resources and capability to effect shutdown plan to achieve the defined stand-by state before labour is withdrawn (7 or 14 days).

Define sufficient resources and capability to sustain the defined stand-by state for an indefinite period of time (resource will need to be trained and deemed competent) plus identify who in current teams would be potentially available during this stand-by state.

Define training requirements for identify resources to be trained and deemed competent during stand-by.

Define adequate availability of all plant, equipment and machinery to prepare and execute the defined shutdown and stand-by plan. This will require a capability to effect repairs, maintenance and inspections on said plant, equipment and machinery i.e. technically competent resource, with the necessary tools/equipment and with a means to access (e.g. scaffold) and lift (e.g. crane) as necessary.

Define safety critical operations e.g. equipment in commission, plant tours, fire watch.

Identify the emergency scenarios for the stand-by mode

Identify the required safe systems of work; control of work (e.g. PTW, hotwork and confined space entry etc), management of change/ modifications.

Define sampling requirements during stand-by mode.

There you have it. The company was not seeking to agree change with us, or progress investment with the workforce as partners. No. They were planning for industrial action ('I.A.' in the slides) and were working towards provoking it in November, as I have already stated.

The sides showed that the company were asking their site management team to make the necessary preparations for their desired action, and to submit a 'first pass' plan on what needed to be put in place to enable the stoppage by 24 August. The text of the slides shows that they were considering how to shut down the plants, and were preparing for the possibility that the strike would take place over a sustained period of time.

This was in the event of action that we had neither talked about nor contemplated. An employers' strike!

I immediately arranged a meeting with Gordon Grant, with the full expectation that there had been a big misunderstanding, or that someone was making mischief. He was genuinely and visibly shocked and flustered when I asked about the plot. He asked how much I knew. I had not shown him the slides for obvious reasons. I had made a point of leaving them in a safe location, and I certainly did not have them with me.

Gordon managed to utter some, less than credible, explanation, along the lines that it could just be contingency planning in case there was action. This was not in any way believable, and I left the office very concerned at his reaction.

One of the most sinister parts of the plot was that they were planning to bring in scab labour. We had always maintained that if ever we were forced, reluctantly, to take industrial action, we would provide full cover on the plants, with expert operators and maintenance technicians, and that we would bring the plants down to hot standby (a situation where the plants would not produce but would be kept safely hot and rotating fluids). This was the stated and preferred option from the HSE, as confirmed in meetings we had with them where they told us they had said as much to Ineos.

To be clear, this was an offer we had made both prior to and during the dispute. But it was rejected by the company, who preferred to take the posturing decision to recklessly crash the units down to cold in a matter of hours, in order to intimidate our members and make it possible to make the move to threaten permanent closure. We had made explicit this offer on a number of occasions, although we were also saying that we would not work alongside scabs. It was quite reasonable for us to offer full cover without pay during a dispute, but with the small caveat that there would be no scabs, since there would be no need for any.

You see, Ineos did not want our members safely overseeing the equipment because, while the plants were being safely maintained on warm standby by our members, it would be impossible to make threats to destroy the site and lock us out. Our offer did not play well with their plot.

Later JAR was to be heard spouting yet more opinions, this time as a suggestion to the Carr Review of the law governing industrial

---

OTHER WORDS OF ADVICE FROM JIM

If you think that Jim's generosity in educating us all is confined to tax, economics, industrial prudence, trade union rights or other workplace issues, let me correct you. In 2014 he informed us in the *Sunday Times*: '… childhood diabetes didn't exist when I was growing up. It was an old man's disease. But now lots of kids have diabetes. They are eating so much sugar that by the time they are 16, the pancreas is giving up the ghost.'

Karen Addlington, who is the CEO of the Juvenile Diabetes Research Foundation, responded in a letter to the same paper:

> He [Ratcliffe] is badly misinformed. In fact, 97 per cent of UK childhood diabetes is type 1 diabetes, which is an autoimmune condition that cannot be prevented, and is not caused by lifestyle factors such as diet and exercise.
>
> Almost 30,000 children in the UK live with type 1 diabetes and must take insulin every day, via multiple injections or a pump, simply to stay alive. There is nothing that they or their parents could have done to avoid their condition.
>
> His words were particularly unfortunate given the number of children – and sometimes their parents – who receive comments from others who mistakenly believe they 'ate too many sweets'.

Don't know about you but I am wondering what other fields of expertise Jim will lecture us on next.

disputes, conducted by Bruce Carr QC at the request of the coalition government at that time. Ratcliffe's proposal was that notice periods should be extended for strike action to make things safer. At the time the Carr Review made no proposals to change the law, but the present government's anti-union bill proposes an extension to 14 days.

I was glad of Ratcliffe's public intervention because he had been neglecting our own education for a week or two.

For those not working in the industry, let me tell you that I think

The email exchange

From: Mark Lyon/GB/OP-EU/INEOS
To: Gary Haywood/GB/REFINING/INEOS@INEOS,
Cc: Declan Sealy/GB/OP-EU/INEOS@INEOS
Date: 02/10/2013 18:33
Subject: Question

Gary

I had it on my notes to ask a question about the new Ineos Grangemouth company that was registered on Friday. This was one of the most important qs I had and I forgot. What is the purpose of this and is there any prospect or issues around TUPE?

Thanks

Mark Lyon
Unite Convenor
Tel 01324 xxxxxx
Mob 07742 xxx

From: Gary Haywood/GB/Refining/INEOS
To: Mark Lyon/GB/OP-EU/INEOS@INEOS
Cc: Declan Sealy/GB/OP-EU/INEOS@INEOS
Date: 02/10/2013 19:40
Subject: Re: Question
Sent by: Gary Haywood

Mark - yes, Ineos Grangemouth Ltd was newly incorporated recently. It was established to facilitate bringing the O&P UK business back to the UK so we could secure financing for the

the decision to bring these units down to cold in preference to keeping them hot and safe was the most dangerous deliberate act I have ever seen in my thirty-three years of working in the industry.

Company trickery

Around this time I was contacted by a friend who told me that Ineos had very recently set up a new business and placed the chemicals assets

Ethane tank investment at Grangemouth (via the UK guarantee scheme we've mentioned). There are no TUPE implications for this new company, as it does not have any employees or trading activity.

Cheers,
Gary

Gary Haywood
INEOS Olefins & Polymers UK CEO

Ph +41 (0)21 xxx xxxx
Mob +41 (0)799 xxx
Email gary.haywood@ineos.com

From: Mark Lyon/GB/OP-EU/INEOS
To: Gary Haywood/GB/REFINING/INEOS@INEOS,
Cc: Declan Sealy/GB/OP-EU/INEOS@INEOS
Date: 03/10/2013 10:36
Subject: Re: Question

Thanks Gary

You will forgive us for still having concerns and anxiety around this. The advice we have had from our people is that the usual reason for such a move is to harbour assets, limit liability or protect against bankruptcy.

Thanks for the reply anyway.

Mark Lyon
Unite Convenor
Tel 01324 xxxxxx
Mob 07742 xxx

in it. This was clearly a third element of the plot against the site. I wrote to the CEO of the chemicals business at that time, a guy called Gary Haywood (you may remember that he was also heavily involved in the political work we all did on company time), and asked him for an explanation.

I asked him what was happening and why the new company had been set up. I also asserted that setting up such a company was a business move commonly used to limit liability if closure were planned. The email exchange is on pp132–3. The only change I have made to the actual emails is to remove phone numbers, but I have also reversed the order the mail was sent to make it easier to read.

The separate company was set up in secret: none of us had been told about it. But the reason given was to provide a vehicle for investment money from the government for the tank. Give us a break!

It is clear to me that the intention was to prepare the way for threats to close the site. Note the dates of the emails. This exchange took place from 2 to 3 October – twenty days before Ineos announced it was closing the site, and before the rejection of the company's 'survival plan' by the majority of our members that was given as the reason for closure by Ratcliffe.

The BP steam pipeline

The fourth element of the plot was to begin to build a pipeline to provide steam to the BP site in Grangemouth from a third-party power station, by-passing Ineos. To explain, the BP site relied on the Ineos power station for steam, and would have to close down if we did not provide it from the Ineos site. This is what had happened in 2008 during our pension strike. The whole of North Sea oil production had to be shut down at that time until the strike was over. The pipeline was designed to take away any threat we could make to close the North Sea, even though we had undertaken not to do so.

Stevie Deans, Ian Proudlove and I still laugh about a meeting we had during the strike in 2008 with the then Labour business secretary John Hutton. He told us that we should be grateful that he did not bring the troops in. We enquired how petrol could be produced using armoured tanks and bazookas. Even more amusingly, he told us he was a socialist!

In 2013 our offer on safety cover was identical to that in 2008: we had volunteered to provide cover in the event of a strike and we had repeatedly restated that commitment.

Of course, as previously stated, this agreement would have meant that our members would be operating the plant during any strike, and that would have taken away Ineos's ability to close the plant down and lock our members out.

Again, Ineos obviously did not want our members in safe control of the plants, given their intention to threaten closure. That is why they rejected our offer of safety cover without pay.

The planned project to build the steam pipeline had come to our attention when an engineer was quoted as saying that Ineos was building a strike-breaking pipeline direct to BP. They were also planning to build new gates as a separate Ineos entrance for our members who worked within the BP site, so that they could not picket the BP gates without being accused of secondary action.

Remember, there was absolutely no threat of strike at this time.

When confronted, the company said it was just a precaution, and that BP were demanding the security of supply it provided. This is partly true, as borne out in talks we held with BP about the measures it needed to deal with the problem that was Ineos. But the clincher that this was part of the Ineos plot was the fact that the pipeline had become the absolute priority for the site above other projects and overhauls – this was reported to us by managers on parts of the plant from which resources had been taken. The drop dead date for completion? … November!

When JAR came to the site during the dispute, just before they crashed the units down, the main area he visited was the strike-breaking pipeline, and it was reported to us that he was furious at the lack of progress. The line was not even finished by the end of 2013. Classic mismanagement again.

The big deal for JAR was to avoid any costs if BP claimed for loss of production or took legal action in the event of a strike. There was no need for him to worry, of course, because we had offered to provide steam as well as fuel for the public. But, as you by now know, this did not fit with the plot.

Another important element in the story to mention here is the potential knock-on effect for BP of the threat Ineos made during the dispute to close the KG chemical plant (the cracking plant that processes the gas that comes ashore with crude oil from the North Sea). BP needs to dispose of the gas to allow the liquid oil to flow, and Ineos needs it to feed KG and hence the other chemical plants on site. In threatening to close KG and the chemicals plant permanently, Ineos was effectively threatening to also close the North Sea, and thus to hold the country to ransom (unlike us). The only alternative would have been to allow BP to burn off the gas in flares, which would have been an environmental disaster. Imagine the loss to the Treasury if the North Sea and all its revenue was lost for any length of time.

As I have already mentioned, in recent years the volume of gas from the North Sea has declined, and this is why Ineos wanted to build their massive tank to store gas shipped from America. Once it is built, I guess the next step will be to threaten BP not to take the North Sea gas unless they match the price of the cheap shale-based American gas. I have been told that Ineos managed to re-negotiate the gas price from BP at the end of 2013, reducing the price drastically, on the back of its general threat to close the plants down: if the KG cracker plant had been closed BP would have had nowhere to dispose of the gas, so it had little option but to give in to the Ineos demands.

As a result of what has happened, BP are now looking to build their own power station which will mean they can use the North Sea gas without being held over a barrel by Ineos and can supply their own power and steam. Perhaps it will become known as the Ineos employer's strike-breaking power station?

Other elements of the plot

In further evidence of their planned timing of the plot, the company eventually pushed back the date of its 'investigation outcome' concerning Stevie until 25 October, and were desperately pleading with us to sit on our hands until the bogus process had been completed on this timescale. Add to 25 October the seven days minimum notice for taking strike action (the legal minimum) and where are we? … November 2013.

Another part of the forward planning for the plot was that Ineos had set up contracts with jetty operating agencies – as reported to us by local management. This was clearly in preparation for the sustained strike the company was instigating – and, once more, this was prior to any announcement of strike action.

Another indication that they were planning the strike for November was that the refinery had a big overhaul programme planned which was scheduled to be completed by … November.

It is also well-known that demand for products from the chemical business and its profit margins tend to slow down at that time of year. So there would be no better time to crash the units and threaten our members with permanent closure.

What's more, Ineos also conspired to put a clause into the disgraceful union agreement that it eventually forced on our members to the effect that it could reject our representatives if they had a disciplinary record. And then … guess what? They made me subject to such proceedings. What were the chances?

My opinion is that JAR had been seething since the ill-advised pension debacle he had instigated in 2008, and in which he failed so spectacularly. This was almost too much for a man who answers to no one and does not like opposition in any form. This is a man who broods. And this is certainly what he did until the opportunity presented itself to make capital out of the false allegations about the Falkirk Constituency Labour Party. This was the chance to turn what could have been a great and positive news story about a union agreement to enhance site security and investment into a chance to further his personal agenda.

The trap was therefore set.

One of the criticisms we have encountered is: why did we walk into it? No one has analysed this more than me friends, and I do sometimes wonder if we could have pulled a better stroke. But the only real decision before us once Ineos decided on a showdown was whether to capitulate and be immediately driven into the dirt or to stand up and fight and seek support from the political and industrial world.

'but facts are the chiels that winna ding' – *Robert Burns*

Business and government

In some ways all these commercial shenanigans are fair game in the rotten, unfettered capitalist system we live in. But surely the case for public control and ownership must at least begin to arise given all this crazy behaviour at our site – when national security of supply and revenues were placed at risk by Ineos. The company could have just about brought the country to its knees.

But in the absence of moves to greater public ownership, I at least think the issue of wealthy industrialists lobbying government is an area that needs to be looked at. In our meetings with Calum Maclean he was always boasting about how influential Ratcliffe was, and how

---

MEETINGS BETWEEN THE SCOTTISH GOVERNMENT AND INEOS MANAGEMENT JULY 2013 TO JANUARY 2016

(information supplied by Scottish Information Commissioner to Tommy Kane MSP)

18 July 2013 Meeting between Alex Salmond, then First Minister, and Calum McLean and Gordon Grant.

10 September Meeting between Alex Salmond, then First Minister, and Calum Maclean and Gordon Grant.

17 October Meeting between Alex Salmond, then First Minister, and Calum Maclean & Gordon Grant.

25 October Meeting between Alex Salmond, then First Minister, and Jim Ratcliffe.

2014

31 January Alex Salmond, then First Minister, met Jim Ratcliffe and Calum Maclean.

23 April John Ireland, and other Scottish Government Officials, met Gordon Grant.

5 June Ian Mitchell and other officials met with representatives of the unconventional oil and gas industry, including Tom Pickering, Director of Ineos Upstream, to talk them through the proposed changes to the unconventional oil and gas policies in the revised Scottish Planning Policy.

9 July Ineos (Gordon Grant & Andrew Gardner) attended an Energy Resilience Workshop in AQ.

July Meeting between Marianne Cook, a Scottish Government official, and Ineos representatives concerning business rates.

dialogue would be taking place with ministers (presumably on company time?). It seems that business 'leaders' enjoy a disproportionate hearing from influential politicians as compared to other stakeholders like employees and their representatives. An example of this is the list of meetings between the Scottish government and Ineos managers below.

22 August Ross Baird, a Scottish Government official, met with David East of Ineos communications team to plan for their participation at SG lead Critical Infrastructure Resilience Conference in October.

9&10 October Critical Infrastructure Resilience Conference, which was attended by Ineos representatives (Gordon Grant & Andrew Gardner) and Scottish government officials and included a visit for delegates to see Grangemouth.

14 October Meeting between John Ireland, a Scottish Government official, and Tom Crotty of Ineos.

30 October Meeting between Jonathan Guthrie, a Scottish Government official, and John McNally, Ineos to discuss heat and energy requirements for the wider Grangemouth area and what proportion of that total requirement Ineos account for.

25 November Meeting between Mr Ewing and Mr Swinney and Tom Crotty and Tom Pickering of Ineos.

15 December Meeting between Scottish Government officials and Andrew Gardner at the Grangemouth refinery.

(The meeting agenda was:

Draft Agenda from INEOS/Petroineos side ...

1. Petroineos Business Update
2. INEOS O&P UK Business Update
3. INEOS Upstream and onshore shale exploration
4. INEOS Upstream – offshore)

2016

28 January Meeting between First Minister Nicola Sturgeon and Jim Ratcliffe of Ineos.

The main attention Stevie Deans got from Prime Minister David Cameron was when he called him a rogue trade unionist who almost closed the Grangemouth site. This assault was launched from the dispatch box in the House of Commons. Stevie, somewhat jokingly, describes this as a badge of honour he will take to his grave.

One of the quirks of the legal system in our country is that MPs who make statements in parliament cannot be legally challenged outside it. David Cameron was directly invited by our union to repeat the claims he had made about Stevie outside parliament, and Unite contemplated instigating proceedings if he did. Needless to say Cameron declined to do so.

CHAPTER 7

The execution of the plot begins

A climate of fear

FROM THE BEGINNING of September Ineos had begun to escalate the dispute. We were not only dealing with the issue of Stevie's treatment, but with a raft of proposed changes to our pay and conditions, including a renewed demand to close the pension scheme to new entrants, though continuing with a revised defined benefit scheme for current employees (for their first attempt at this see p53). They sent out notifications about these proposed changes by email. Their communications were going out to members and employees like messages of doom, and were helping create a climate of fear. But when Len McCluskey and Pat Rafferty publicly commented about this 'culture of fear' at the Grangemouth site, Ineos launched a High Court claim for defamation. Our union made a stout legal defence, however, and refused to accept that the comments were either untrue or defamatory. In early 2014 Ineos backed down and discontinued the action. Estimates at the time were that, pleasingly, the cost to the company was in the region of £100,000.

Ineos escalate the dispute

When our industrial action ballot result over the treatment of Stevie had come back overwhelmingly in favour of action, at the beginning of September, I had phoned Gordon right away – at his request – to let him know the result. In the same call I also told him that I also would welcome a – totally separate – discussion on pensions and terms and investment. My desire, as always, was to avoid conflict and a damaging strike at the plant. I think he was taken aback by this response, but he thanked me and a meeting was set up for the following week.

The conversation with Gordon was at the back end of one week and we were summoned to a meeting at the beginning of the next.

My theory is that my response to Gordon indicating that we were still willing to talk constructively on an agreed way forward meant the company was no longer certain it would be able to manufacture the strike they wanted in November. But I also firmly believe that JAR lost the plot over the weekend at the very cheek of our members in standing up against him and returning such a fabulous result in the ballot.

I am convinced that the proposed changes to terms and conditions that JAR had already sent out to our members in the previous week were drastically and provocatively changed over the weekend, when he heard about our ballot result. Those that were issued after the weekend were unbelievable, a litany of disgrace.

The attacks were dressed up, however, as cuts that were absolutely necessary if the company was to be able to survive financially. It is clear to me that Ratcliffe also wanted to make absolutely certain that the changes put forward could never be acceptable to us, as accepting them would have avoided the strike he so desperately wanted to instigate.

The attacks on our members' conditions in the proposals are summarised below. They included the cut to the allowance shift workers got for the inconvenience of working unsociable hours. (The number of HR and senior managers on these shifts was of course nil.) Then they wanted to cut the starting rates for employees working under collective agreements by many thousands of pounds a year. (The number of HR and senior managers working under collective agreements was also nil.) They also wanted to cut overtime rates, abnormal conditions payments and the right to have a minimum four hours of overtime if asked to work late, or shifts out of the normal rota. (Needless to say, none of this impacted on HR or senior managers.) In addition they now proposed to shut the pension scheme to everyone, including existing employees, in order to satisfy the desire to settle old scores from 2008.

There were also a raft of attacks that had little or no significant financial benefit for the business. As I have previously argued, in my opinion, the company had set out to provoke the dispute, and, more importantly, to punish our members for daring to stand up to Ratcliffe in 2008 and beyond. Let me tell you about them.

They wanted to reduce drastically the conditions that I would describe as the security package – conditions that offered employees peace of mind in the event of redundancy or illness.

They proposed to slash the redundancy terms, destroying the comfort this safety net provided (though they also told us there would be no need for redundancies). This assurance is laughable looking back now, given the number of people choosing to leave the site and the ongoing struggle they have to keep people in Grangemouth.

(In fact the main question we were being asked as a union at this time by members was how they could leave employment without working their notice periods. We had repeatedly warned Ineos that our members would leave the site in their droves if they tried to impose such dreadful and detrimental changes to conditions but they would not listen. The mass exodus of experienced and skilled workers had begun.)

They proposed to slash sickness benefits for employees who were suffering with a disease or condition that meant they were unable to work long-term. The numbers of people so afflicted are mercifully low, so where is the 'business imperative' in this move? They also wanted to cut the entitlement of the sick to reclaim lost holidays on returning to work after their period of forced absence, in line with their HR dogma.

During my time as a senior union representative I have supported and represented quite a few members who have been unfortunate enough to contract illnesses that are serious enough to keep them from work for extended periods. I remember the good people, some of whom were terminally ill, who knew that, although they were ill, they or their children would not go hungry or be turned out of their homes. They knew they could fall back on financial agreements that our union had negotiated. It was proposed that this security would be destroyed by these industrial heroes. How proud they must have been.

A whole raft of cynical anti-union measures were also demanded, including the loss of office space for stewards, the loss of time off work for conveners to undertake their union roles, the refusal to recognise any workable sized IR committee, and the loss of time off to complete union duties in support of the members. However, the most dangerous, unnecessary, and troubling proposals concerned the destruction of vital trade union safety structures at the site – and these wouldn't have saved a penny.

Unite's safety structures were second to none, and these safeguards are necessary because the factory is home to all kinds of hazards, including radioactivity, toxic and corrosive chemicals, explosive substances and flammable liquids and gases in massive quantities. In short, the site at Grangemouth has the potential for many employees and members of the public to be seriously injured, maimed or killed if these hazards are not managed properly.

Our Unite safety representatives were a vital element of the safety system. The sixty or so volunteers, who reported problems and attended many meetings in order to prevent potentially devastating accidents were to be swept away as part of the company's politically-driven agenda. I offer this explanation because there certainly was no financial imperative to do this. The proposal was to replace our existing facility for sixty-four reps with three, and to discontinue most of the ways we engaged with the company and consulted on safety.

Our representatives were well-trained by our union and the STUC and devoted to the task of keeping everyone safe. The site's safety record was above average for the industry, and this was due in no small part to the efforts of our representatives. As I mentioned earlier, there were major accidents and fatalities on the site in 1987, and we have since then worked hard as a union to avoid such incidents in future.

These attacks on our members were announced directly to the membership, and only afterwards did we meet to hear it first-hand from the company. We warned management (both then and later) that this type of authoritarian conduct would drive our members to the other plentiful employment opportunities in the industry and impact dramatically on safety. Since the beginning of 2014 approaching 50 per cent of technicians have left some departments of the company and moved elsewhere, and much more of that is still to come. The safety performance has also been deplorable since that date, and the HSE's failure to act adequately is also worthy of critical note.-

In 2014 I met with the HSE, along with Pat Rafferty, Patrick McGuire from Thompsons Solicitors and a number of Safety Reps from the site. We presented information from the company's own systems showing safety incidents and widespread cases of operating hazardous equipment without sufficient competent people in post. The HSE inspectors said they had insufficient information to act, which we found incredible, given what was at stake.

It almost goes without saying that the bulk of the vindictive and totally unnecessary cuts to terms are aimed not at senior managers but at our members. The people who generate the wealth, the people who operate under-invested in and hazardous equipment day in and day out, the people who work on Christmas days and other holidays and miss precious family occasions because they are at work. These are the fine people disproportionally targeted by these industrial buccaneers.

The side-lining of Gordon Grant

When we arrived at the meeting at which these draconian demands were revealed, a familiar face was there beside Gordon. One Declan Sealy. Now, friends, it is not always a good idea to be over critical, but I do have to tell you a few things about Sealy. Firstly let me explain that he had been brought in to bring a more 'robust' style to the management in their dealings with the union! This is a matter of record, and was contained in the tribunal papers relating to my case and submitted by Ineos. What a joke!

Sealy was often the victim of ridicule even from his own colleagues for his behaviour and failure to grasp the most basic information. He also had a reputation, conveyed to us by site managers, who I will be happy to name on request, for bullying contract companies. Among our members he was known as Sideshow Dec, after Sideshow Bob from the Simpsons, on account of his unfeasibly large feet. He was also known as Big MENSA – though some have argued that he would be given a run for his money on quiz night by a single cell amoeba. He was also a guy with zero relevant IR experience.

This is the man they had selected to bring in to sit across the table from us. The only qualification he had that we could observe was that he was able to be very offensive and abrupt, and was willing to do anything he was instructed to do without question.

He was given a brief before every meeting and told to stick to it. If the agenda moved even slightly off message he became lost, and would look frantically to Ian Fyfe or whoever else was there to rescue him.

Stevie once asked him: 'Is that your script Declan?'. To which he replied indignantly: 'No it is not'. Stevie then pointed out that it quite clearly had emblazoned across the top of the page the date and the word 'SCRIPT'.

If it was not so serious all this would be hilarious.

Declan obviously had taken his inspiration right out of the *Readers Digest* book of negotiations. You know – that stuff about arriving last and leaving last and opening with an aggressive scene-setter, and continually returning to the contrived mantra. It was awful, and it was obvious that he had been put up to this crackpot behaviour. He would arrive and immediately embark on a long monologue of nonsense, reading straight from his pre-prepared pages. He would say things like: 'You need to listen, you have killed jobs, you have driven the site to near destruction, this is a distressed business' – all that kind of stuff.

We used to ignore all this and then ask him such questions as: 'Declan, could you maybe give us a briefing on the dynamisation policy of the pension scheme, and while you are at it tell us about how the investment portfolio of the scheme may measure up in all the credible scenarios, including high, medium and low risk?'

His other ploy was to take us out of the boardroom upstairs and put us in this inferior meeting room downstairs. As with the 2008 pensions dispute, the company had set up a bogus parallel 'consultation' with hand-picked and unelected 'independent representatives' of the work-force to try and justify their actions and get the feedback they wanted. These people met the company upstairs in the boardroom. Sealy thought this would upset us because of the loss of status. We gave not a jot about that. If you give us an iPad, a pencil and a pot of coffee, we can operate anywhere.

There was an issue, however, with the breadth of the table. The one downstairs was very narrow compared to the one in the boardroom. Sealy must have been told to sit right across from me, so that he could project his very toughest Paddington Bear hard stare. (He may have wondered why our team was always looking at each other and suppressing a chuckle when he did. I was not chuckling. I had to look directly at the big lummox.)

Gordon had been replaced by Sealy prior to the meeting – slapped down and utterly humiliated. But he stuck around for months after-wards rather than exiting with his massive pension and his dignity intact. I met him at the bottom of the stairs in the main management building just after he had been side-lined and we shared a joke about Sealy being at the helm. He said he was not happy at being taken out, but told me that Calum had said he would probably bring him back in later. This must have been intended for after the plot had landed. I said to Gordon that the company's behaviour over employees' terms and conditions, and the introduction of big MENSA, would end up in a strike, not least because of Sealy's attitude, and he agreed with me. This was a sad way for Gordon to end his career. I wish he had gone at that point, and disassociated himself from what was going on.

The guns are trained on me

Round about this time I attended Unite's quarterly national sector meeting in London. We had leave to attend these meetings from the company as part of our facilities agreement and had notified the HR manager well in advance. On the same day we had also been invited to meet John Swinney, a senior member of the Scottish Government at the parliament building, and Stevie had also notified the HR manager and cleared this meeting.

We went to the meeting at Holyrood with our regional secretary Pat Rafferty and some other stewards, and while we were there we bumped into Tom Crotty, an Ineos director who has featured before in this story. Tom was obviously engaged in political campaigning in work time, just like us. We exchanged pleasantries and thought no more about it.

We had some history with Tom from 2008 when he had been the industrial front man for Ineos during the pension dispute. But since 2008 he had been moved in the Ineos organisation to a role more involved with public relations and political campaigning (on company time).

Anyway, we travelled on to London to attend the Unite sector meeting, and then I received a call from Steven Boyle. If you remember, Steven had by now replaced Helen Stewart in the HR role. Steven had been in HR before, but he had been moved out a couple of years previously and sent to work in the stores with big MENSA. Join the dots comrades … Join the dots!

Steven sounded all breathless and bumbling, telling me that he was only the messenger, but that Calum Maclean had gone berserk when he heard that I was in the Scottish Parliament and was demanding I return to the site for a meeting with him at lunchtime the next day.

I pointed out to Steven that we had clearance to be at the meetings. We had arrangements and accommodation booked, I had work to do in the meeting, and it was totally unreasonable to ask me to return to the site at such short notice. Steven agreed with all of that, but said that Calum was going crazy and insisting I go back.

There followed about a half dozen calls right up to early evening. Pat advised me to go back. I agreed to do that on the grounds that we knew they were looking for any excuse to sack me. When I let them know I would return Ian Fyfe (who is a Grade One Referee) sent me a text, beginning '*Mark, I'm sorry we are having to do this … 2 options …* [Then he sets out flight options, and offers, unusually, to have me picked up from the airport]. Obviously Ian was feeling a bit guilty.

Later Steven lied in his sworn statement for my tribunal hearing when he said that they had done all they could to dissuade me from attending the meeting. This is not true. The text message from Ian gives you something of a sense of the discomfort being felt among site managers – and the split between them and Calum.

The division between site management and Ineos is also well illustrated by their response to another of JAR's rants that we had become so accustomed to. I had picked up this rant from the troops, who kept Google alerts to automatically get any news articles sent to them about the company and JAR. In this one our man was talking down the site and saying it would close etc. This was actually a strand of the plot if you think about it – warming up everybody for the false representation that the site was on its last legs. I wrote to Ian asking if he had seen the article and he wrote back saying that he just had, and that it was not good. I replied saying it was the politics of the madhouse, and his reply was '*yes, I agree, a bottle of wine at home awaiting*'. Hardly shows managerial unity does it? The head of HR agreeing that the actions of big JAR amounted to the politics of the madhouse. My, my!

As I recorded earlier, I had already been warned by the previous Unite joint general secretaries that I had better watch my back. I had also been warned by Len McCluskey and Pat Rafferty in recent weeks that they had seen this type of situation before: it was likely that Ineos would move to sack Stevie and then come after me. This was why Pat had advised me to return to Grangemouth.

Most of our senior Unite team from Grangemouth were in London at the quarterly national sector meeting, but our senior steward for equality was on site so I asked her to come to the meeting with me as a witness. She had not been involved in a meeting like this before – and, quite frankly, I have not been in many myself. I had never been spoken to like that before in any exchange with the company and it was difficult to keep my temper – but I did. I have inhabited this planet for over fifty years now, and I have never allowed anyone to talk to me in that way before or since. It still troubles me that I allowed this to happen: there is something very basic and inhuman about being treated in this way. The legal proceedings since have gone some way towards dealing with the behaviour of these individuals, but let me tell you most solemnly that there is no way we are squared up. There is still outstanding personal business to be completed on this.

The meeting was sickening and appalling. I was personally insulted by Maclean and Sealy. Amongst the vitriol and insults I was told that I would not be permitted any time to attend meetings offsite, and threats were made about how they would be watching me. Our equality steward was utterly shocked and visibly upset after the meeting. In the dark days of the illness I was later to suffer after being unfairly dismissed from my job, for which the company was responsible, I have often returned in my mind to that day.

From that day on I was not allowed to attend any meetings off-site. When I asked to take holidays in order to attend meetings, or even just to get a day off and take some rest, I was denied. I was treated completely differently in this regard to every other employee on the site. This is one of the ways in which they discriminated against me on trade union grounds, but by no means the only one.

I felt that I had done nothing more than represent the wishes of the membership of our branch, and that I had acted at all times in the best interests of the site. And yet these characters thought it was acceptable to treat me in this appalling manner.

Things deteriorate further

The company now embarked on a series of propaganda meetings with employees, setting out all their misleading financial information, threatening our members that they would be out of work if they did not agree to the company terms, and generally putting themselves about.

At one such meeting one of our stewards – a well-respected and admired sister of our union – asked Sealy a question, and since his answer was not adequate she quite rightly came back and asked it again. Sealy then became very aggressive and demanded her name, which he wrote down in an attempt to intimidate her. The woman was pretty upset when she later told me about it and I therefore challenged

Sealy about it. He tried to concoct a story that he had only wanted to take her name so that he could get back to her. This is nonsense, but it gives you an insight to the character of this big bold man.

At another meeting with our members Sealy told them I was a Marxist, that there was no place for the likes of me here, and that I belonged in North Korea or Cuba.

This was all part of the plan to get rid of me of course, and our legal team took careful note of this occurrence. But it is clear that this tripe did not come from him; these was were not his words. If you had asked him to comment on the philosophical and practical application of Marxism in the twenty-first century he would probably have replied that he liked Harpo the best. These words had obviously been first heard in a more discreet location, uttered by more devious and secretive folks, and Sealy was simply parroting this to the audience of our Unite members. What a clown. By the way, put me down for Cuba rather than North Korea if anyone is asking.

At the beginning of October we had started our overtime ban, in line with the overwhelming mandate the members had delivered in the postal ballot. (JAR had been spouting again in July as part of his unasked-for input into the Carr Review, arguing that a majority of eligible members needed to vote for action before it would be deemed lawful. It now appears that members of the current government were listening. Anyway, there was no issue in our ballot; the members were solidly behind resisting the victimisation of Stevie and had voted accordingly. Our ballots were way above any threshold being proposed either by JAR or by the present government in its 2015 industrial relations bill.)

JAR had also been banging on about how we had advised our members not to attend meetings with the company during this time. This is not true. I have emails I sent to members encouraging them to go and have their say. It would be tempting to say that JAR is simply lying about all this to make us look bad, and to support the case to take away the already weak protections that working people have. However I also go back to my earlier theory that Ratcliffe was being falsely briefed from the site with negative reports about us. He then, predictably, goes off like a three-penny whiz bang and embarks on these lunatic monologues. More worryingly, important decisions are made based on this nonsense to attack our members and representatives.

Of course, we had insisted that during the overtime ban, all core production, maintenance and safety jobs were covered, and that every emergency service would be exempt from the industrial action. We even allowed safety training to go ahead, even though this could have, strictly speaking, been delayed for a few weeks. We also invited the company to put forward any other requests for cover, and they did ask us for quite a few.

Not one request they made was denied by us.

In line with the strike in 2008, we acted with great responsibility and with strict regard to our safety responsibilities and commitments.

Our reason for increasing industrial action incrementally and in such a measured and carefully controlled way was the hope that the company would see sense and stop victimising Stevie without us having to take more serious action in the form of strikes. Our overwhelming desire was to avoid a strike, but, as we know now, the company was all the time hell-bent on driving us out the door as part of their plot.

It is a matter of great regret that the company, in the absence of any industrial action, has not found itself able to continue to follow our lead on cover since the turn of 2013 and the end of the dispute. For extended periods, plants containing highly flammable, toxic and explosive substances were run with fewer operators than specified necessary by the detailed risk assessments carried out and agreed by the company and the unions, due to the number of competent people who had left the site, and the determination of the company to run the plants despite this issue.

Anyway, the meetings between us and the company continued, and the conduct of Sealy – and when there Maclean – continued to be disgraceful. Their attitude to Stevie and me was particularly offensive. Maclean did have the grace to apologise on one occasion, when he had called Stevie thick and asked if he was able to understand the information they were giving us. The problem was, of course, not that we were too thick to understand the information, but that the information they were giving us was nonsense.

In fact, we were able to predict that Sealy's behaviour would always be even worse when Calum or one of the other CEOs attended the meetings. He used to show off like a kid who had learned to ride his bike – a lost soul, fathoms out of his depth, but eager to please … It was tiresome, an embarrassment, and utterly beneath contempt.

Around this time a number of small and very disciplined demonstrations were arranged in defence of Stevie Deans. These legitimate expressions of disgust at the conduct of Ineos and solidarity with Stevie were, in the main, conducted at Ineos premises, but a small number were organised near the homes of very senior managers who had been instrumental in the disgraceful treatment of Stevie.

Much was made of these orderly and silent protests, and a concerted effort was made by the company to portray them as a mob of baying maniacs threatening the homes and family of the poor managers.

Nothing could be further from the truth.

The well-natured and passive demonstrations were conducted in the broad vicinity of the homes of some of these managers. They were conducted in total silence. They never at any time took place in direct sight of the homes. The demonstrations did not face or look into the homes. Participants even refrained from smoking in a mark of respect for the residential nature of the sites.

The action was merely designed to impart a comparatively tiny and insignificant flavour of the horrific impact that had been visited on Stevie and his wife and his children through the actions of individual managers. If they had multiplied the very mild discomfort they felt a thousandfold they would still be nowhere near how Stevie felt.

If these dignified protests provoked even a hint of remorse and shame from the likes of JAR, Sealy, Grant, Fyfe, Maclean and co, then the efforts will have been worthwhile.

Unfortunately, rather than being influenced by these events and others to examine his conscience, Ratcliffe tried to use distorted accounts of what had happened in his efforts to influence the Carr Review, mentioned earlier. He called for even more draconian restrictions on working people's ability to defend themselves at work and make it easier for employers like himself to drive through unfair industrial relations agendas without resistance. (We were always puzzled about why – given that JAR was so fond of boasting about the industrial relations harmony that existed across his vast empire – he should want to carry on this persistent crusade for restrictions on the legal activities of trade unions.)

Of course, most credible and switched-on employer and union organisations, including Unite, refused to engage in this farcical and politicised 'review', and in the end it closed down before making any proposals for changes to the law. (Unfortunately the current government shares many of Ratcliffe's views on industrial relations, and many of his ideas seem to have found their way into the Trade Union Bill passing through parliament at the time this book went to press.)

The demonstrations in support of our brother and comrade should be viewed by Unite members with tremendous pride, and as a mark of great respect to Stevie and his loved ones.

The employer's strike

We met the company on 9 and 10 October to discuss Stevie's situation. Please remember that the dispute and ballot had nothing to do with the company's effort to attack our terms and conditions: it was all about the discrimination against our branch secretary. The company had seen the opportunity to build this into their plot after the Falkirk fiasco. This had involved bringing the plot forward a little, but they were OK with that, given that all the elements were pretty much in place – with the exception, of course, of the 'strike-breaking pipeline' designed to keep the North Sea in operation through the BP terminal if we went on strike.

The meeting was predictably unproductive. They told us that Stevie's disciplinary was going ahead since the 'investigation' conducted by Fyfe had concluded it was necessary. Effectively, they told us they would do as they please, and that the hearing was happening. This was despite the overwhelming evidence in support of Stevie's case, and the corruption of the process, and despite the fact that Gordon had recommended to JAR that there was no case to answer and had been told to think again.

We left that meeting knowing that Stevie was to be sacked at the hearing. This was now certain, and we were sure that this was being done on the express instruction of JAR.

What were we to do? No, really, what were we to do? We called an emergency meeting of our site Unite team. We knew the company were spoiling for a fight and were determined to cause a strike; we knew that Stevie was about to be sacked and we had a massive mandate to move to strike action in the event they moved to dismiss him. We had conducted mass meeting after mass meeting to consult members, and the enormous assemblies had given us the mandate. At the most recent meeting we had explained that things could move very quickly, and that strike action might, regrettably, become unavoidable. We knew the company were planning to instigate the strike in November. In reality, the only choice we had was to move the date forward in the hope that this would pre-empt the plot, giving us a chance to get management back round the table and prevent the actual action taking place.

This was a risk, but a calculated risk – a difficult option in the midst of very few other available options.

We could have done nothing and let Stevie be sacked, ignoring the clear will and mandate of the members.

We could have waited until the company's chosen time for the strike as set out in the plot.

We had tried reason. We had tried to negotiate and insist that Stevie was treated like every other employee.

We notified the company on 11 October that strike action would begin in a week's time.

I notified the company by hand-delivered letter, and our regional office notified management by email. It was only ten minutes or so before Sealy called me and asked if the strike was going ahead.

I told him that the situation was as the notification said, but also told him that no action had taken place yet. There was still time to discuss the issues. I reminded him that our offer to give 100 per cent safety cover also still stood, and to keep the plants on hot standby throughout (you will remember that the HSE had stated a preference for this plant condition and so had we on safety grounds).

I asked him a very clear question. I asked if they wanted to meet to try and avoid the strike.

He replied: no.

The call was only a few seconds, although I had anticipated a longer conversation and had prepared a list of things to say.

I just want here to express gratitude for the backing of our general secretary, national officers, assistant general secretary, Linda McCulloch and Scott Foley, our regional secretary, our stewards and reps and our magnificent branch members. They had backed us all the way. Whatever decision we made, we knew we would continue to have that support. There was never any doubt in our minds about that as we had taken the difficult decision to press forward.

On Monday 14 October the company started bringing the units down to cold as quickly as they possibly could, using their pre-prepared procedures, in an act designed to 'out strike the strike' and put pressure on our members.

The site was brought down safely, but only because of the sheer professionalism and expertise of our members. The HSE recommendation was rejected. Our offer to give safety cover was rejected. And the offer to give 100 per cent cover by our technicians, including both process and maintenance staff, was also rejected.

One of the key elements of the plot was to have the plants cold so that they could lock us out and amplify the threat to close the site permanently, partly so that they could squeeze money out of the organisations on their hit list.

Stevie and I had spent the previous weekend at the plant talking to our members, who were obviously concerned, but were resolved and supportive of the branch mandate.

We urged the company to come to ACAS to try and resolve the dispute, and, despite the company's initial reluctance, the SNP-led Scottish government did some excellent work and eventually persuaded them to attend.

I have probably over-used the word disgrace, but the company's conduct at ACAS was disgraceful in a way that was beyond belief. Sealy was later daft enough to admit that they showed up at the ACAS meeting with the attitude that they had us on the run and had taken us to a place we had never been before. This comment was made in an ill-advised and triumphalist film commissioned by Ineos after the dispute called *The Battle for Grangemouth*, in order to try to show how clever they had been. It can still be viewed on YouTube. Anyway, Sealy's comment confirmed that there had been no intention at any time to resolve this dispute. They had crashed the units to intimidate our members and place the factory in their desired condition to fully enact the plot.

You should have a look at the *Battle for Grangemouth* (though the film was berated in the press for its content and tone). Check out the acting … Sir John Gielgud it ain't. But the film will give you a look at some of the main players in this pageant – Grant, The Referee, Maclean, Gordon Milne (see below) and big MENSA and the rest all feature in this thespian feast for the eyes and ears!

We were at ACAS on 14 and 15 October. The first thing the company did in their efforts to derail the proceedings was to demand that Stevie left, on the bogus argument that he was involved in the terms of the dispute. We – and Stevie to his enormous credit – agreed to withdraw to take away the excuse for Ineos to sabotage the talks.

Calum Maclean and Gary Haywood (who you may recall had been the refining CEO at an earlier point in our story, when he had been heavily involved in giving us briefings so that we could do political work on company time) attended on day one, and on day two it was Maclean and Sealy

Remember, this was not our first venture into industrial relations: we knew they would walk out of the talks at the drop of a hat because they were hell bent on strike action. We proceeded on that basis, and tried not to give any hostages to fortune that would allow them off the hook. This is why we tried our level best to accommodate them within the terms of any agreement to hold them in and hold them to account.

It was not our confirmed intention at the time, but looking back it seems as if the pattern was that they would make demands and we would not rule anything out, in order to try and reach an agreement. We proposed that the manufacturing plants on site should be immediately restarted, and that we should get into very intense and serious talks to try and resolve the dispute. In response they wanted a guarantee that we would not strike again until the end of the year if this happened, and we agreed – much to their frustration.

Then they said they wanted an agreement whereby we would only strike for a maximum of a few days in any set period. I genuinely can't remember the exact terms – but again we agreed.

They said they wanted to proceed with the hearing for Stevie, and we agreed to that, with the condition that this would be in parallel to the formal talks with a view to resolution. Again, much to their frustration, they did not have the excuse to walk out. I was there with Ian Proudlove from the site and Pat Rafferty and Peter Welsh from the Glasgow Unite office

We suggested that ACAS should be involved in any talks on resolution of the dispute and they messed about with that, but they were unable to refuse.

A package was more or less put together, and we began to look forward to getting the plants back up to a safe condition and resuming talks to resolve the dispute. Obviously this was not their agenda. They wanted to have us 'on the run'.

Every response from the company took ages at the ACAS meetings. We were able to consider proposals and give a response in good time.

But every time something fresh came on the agenda they told us they had to talk directly with JAR, and this sometimes took hours. Whether this was just part of their stalling tactics, or whether they had to actually check on every line with Big Jim, it was an appalling way of behaving given the seriousness of the situation and the continuing damage to the site.

I would like to tell you it was at the eleventh hour, but actually it was about the eighteenth hour when the most absurd of the many unbelievable occurrences unfolded.

The ACAS officer came to see us and said that Ineos now had a fresh list of demands, and that these items were, in their words, 'walking away issues if not agreed to in full'.

One of the demands was that we would accept and never question their version of the company accounts and site finances. The other was that Pat Rafferty would have to write a letter of apology to Jim Ratcliffe because we had questioned his authority. The economy of Scotland now hinged on us saying sorry and getting behind financial accounts we did not agree with.

Just how big is this guy's ego? Of course the reason for these demands was that there was no way on earth we could agree to them, and they could then walk away in line with their objective since the start.

We responded with alternative proposals, and once again they had to call JAR to be told what to do next.

We passed the time waiting for this response by downloading such melodies as 'Who's sorry now' and 'Sorry seems to be the hardest word' on our phones, and doing impersonations of Father Jack saying sorry to Bishop Brennan in the excellent *Father Ted* – 'We're sooo sarry' ... Now that was sarcasm! Check it out on YouTube when you are looking up the *Battle for Grangemouth*.

In our defence, it was the early hours of the morning and we had been messed about by them for hours and hours. I think we were a bit delirious. I think there may have also been a medley of show tunes, but I may have just imagined that.

The ACAS officer eventually brought grim news, though; he came to tell us that Maclean and Sealy were leaving. All the work we had done and all the accommodations we had made had come to nought. The company had finally wriggled out of the process and kept their plot on track.

Predictably, they put out a misleading and inaccurate press release criticising and blaming us.

We had discussed the options in the event that talks broke down and had extensively canvassed our members and stewards over the weekend. The plants were cold and shut down and the company was refusing to start them again. The only credible option was to suggest to our members at a mass meeting scheduled for the 16 October that we withdraw the notice to strike, since the employer was on strike anyway.

We attended the meeting next day and put the options to the floor. There was a big debate, but the near unanimous decision was to withdraw the notice, since any financial penalty from loss of production was already on the company, since they were refusing to start up the plants. Our members' other concern was that poorly-trained scab labour would be brought in to try to control these massive and hazardous plants, and that someone might be killed.

There has been some criticism of this decision within sections of the union movement, and some speculation that it was the full-time officers of the union who called the action off. This was not the case. The members had considered all the aspects, had been briefed and advised by us, and had reached their own conclusion.

The bravest, most selfless and principled man in the room was Stevie Deans, who knew he was effectively signing his own death warrant. Stevie gave words of comfort to the members. He was very clear that this was the only possible action, given the way we knew the company were behaving. Privately we talked more, of course: Stevie's first priority remained, not himself, but the members and the site he valued so much.

The meeting must have been attended by about 700 members. We were supported once more by officers at all levels of the union, but the decision was, quite rightly, in the hands of the troops.

CHAPTER 8

The company move in for the kill

W<small>E HAD DECIDED</small> at the mass meeting to hold an ad hoc gathering on the steps of the canteen on the following day, Thursday
17 October, to brief members on any developments – just to touch
base with them given the situation. The company knew we were
having this meeting because we had made no secret of it. We were
only going to meet outside for a brief time and then disperse.

The meeting was scheduled for 4pm, and at 3.37pm I got an email
from Steven Boyle saying that we did not have permission to hold a
meeting, and that we should not do so. This was obviously a last-
minute attempt to derail our gathering, but it turned out brilliantly for
us. Word was almost instantly passed to everyone, as these things
often work out, and the members streamed across the main road in
their hundreds to a bit of public ground across from the main offices.
The spectacle was excellent, and it helped to foster a spirit of camara-
derie. Our meeting went ahead despite their best efforts to stop it.

In the event we had something major to discuss at the mass
meeting, because Calum Maclean had met us earlier that same day
and had moved on with the next phase of their plot. We had met
him at the request of the company, and the best way I can explain
the tone of the session was that Maclean venomously spat out what
he had to say. He told us that the terms they had put before us at the
meeting at the beginning of October would now be rolled out, and
the minimum 'consultation' period of 45 days would end at the
beginning of December. Every clause would be implemented, and
all the employees would be given the choice to sign up to the new
deal or be sacked. They would be given notice and dismissed at the
end of that period, without redundancy, if they had not signed up.
They would be 'consulted' on the pensions issue for 60 days, and
then the changes demanded by management on this issue would also
be implemented.

This treatment of our members was just dreadful. This was a work-force of varying experience and service, but a highly skilled group of workers that had been loyal to the company but were now being treated like dirt.

We had already made what I consider to be a very reasonable offer to sign a 'transition agreement' that meant we would help the company cut costs and secure investment, but it also stipulated that we would all benefit when the predicted substantial profits were made. We had tried to co-operate with the company because of our assumed joint interest in securing the future of the site. But Ineos at no point had any interest in such co-operation.

Maclean also announced that, in spite of the 45-day 'consultation' period, members would be urged to sign up to the new conditions by Monday 21 October – only a few days later – and the company would

---

Workers at Grangemouth overwhelmingly rejected a 'D-Day' ultimatum on new terms and conditions as owners Ineos sought to provoke unrest.

More than 1000 workers at the plant rejected the sign or be sacked threat from Ineos at a meeting yesterday.

Unite slammed the ultimatum as 'blackmail' by the company who have shut down the facility despite the union calling off a planned strike.

First Minister Alex Salmond cut short his attendance at the first day of the SNP conference in Perth to hold talks with the company and Unite yesterday.

In letters sent to workers Ineos threatened to walk away from Grangemouth if employees did not accept new conditions including ending their final salary pension scheme.

Unite said staff have been told to accept the new terms and conditions by 6pm on Monday, which amounts to a 'sign or be sacked' ultimatum.

Unite Scottish secretary Pat Rafferty said they are considering legal action.

He said: 'This is cynical blackmail from a company that is putting a gun to the heads of its loyal workforce to slash pay, pensions and jobs.'

Workers will now stage a 'daylight vigil' outside Ineos headquarters until fresh talks begin on Monday.

then 'review' the decisions made by individuals on Tuesday 29 October.

If people bent to the will of the company within this ludicrous timescale they would be given a lump sum and receive an 11 per cent contribution to their pensions in the Ineos scheme. If they did not bend to the will of the company, they would get no such lump sum and receive only a 9 per cent pension contribution.

Technically there was a 45 day consultation period, but the company wanted people to sign up almost immediately. If they refused to be treated in this way and insisted on having their say in the 'consultation' period, they would be severely financially penalised.

Once again, the members made their feelings known at our meeting, and the unanimous decision was that we would stick to our principles and refuse to be blackmailed. I was very proud that day

---

The plant remains shut down despite Unite calling off a planned two-day strike.

Addressing members at the plant, Unite convener and vice-chairman Mark Lyon said 'the Dickensian workforce had better than what we are facing here'.

He said: 'We are urging members not to sign this plan by the sign-or-die date on Monday to enable us to try and negotiate a more favourable decision.'

Manufacturing technician Sara Grant has been at Grangemouth for more than seven years.

She said: 'There is definitely a lot of anger among the workers now, without a doubt. At the end of the day, Ineos are holding their workforce to ransom for one person's gain.'

Ineos chairman Calum MacLean said: 'This is D-Day for Grangemouth.

'The site is safely closed whilst we consult the workforce. If we can get the changes we want, the company have committed to investment which will help secure its long-term survival.'

Ineos tipped the union into a strike threat by suspending trade union convener Stephen Deans, who was involved in the row over the selection of a Labour candidate in Falkirk.

Daily Record, 18 October 2013

because people were clearly upset and worried by the actions of JAR and his chums, but they were strong in the face of this aggression and resolved to stick together and resist.

The other decision taken by the meeting was to hold a daylight vigil over the weekend in the run up to this deadline. The reasons for this were that we were no longer staging the planned strike about Stevie, but we wanted to show our unity and resolve and continue to protest at his treatment.

The extract from the *Daily Record* on pp 160–1 captures the story in a few lines.

Consent forms were issued to everyone at the plant to sign up to the plan. Members had suggested collecting the forms in the union office rather than hand them to the company – or binning them as a show of collective resistance.

The forms just flooded into us, and everywhere we went we collected them in.

We had a big demonstration on Sunday 20 October outside the plant, with excellent speakers, including Pat Rafferty, Grahame Smith from the STUC, Michael Connarty MP and Tony Burke, our assistant general secretary. The demonstration and rally were massive despite the rain, and it was great when our tanker drivers' branch marched across the Bo'ness Road to join us, led by the bagpipes of course. Unite executive council chair Tony Woodhouse was also in attendance again, and this gave the troops a big boost.

The tanker drivers were true friends to us during all this. The leadership of good comrades like Gary and Alan Lamont and Tam Conroy was most welcome. Their support and solidarity was incredible over this time, and so was the backing of our Grangemouth Hub. This is an organisation involving colleagues in Unite from all sectors who meet to compare employers and plan campaigns against those who impose inferior terms and conditions. After a brief pause at the end of 2013, the hub commission is once more operational (see p215).

Similarly our Unite friends at BP, like Cliff Bowen and Colin McKay, were always supportive, and are also valued members of the commission.

The deadline had been set for 6pm on the Monday for forms to be in. Just after 6pm Pat Rafferty and our Unite officer Scott Foley took the enormous box of forms out of the office to report to the press that company threats, intimidation and blackmail had failed, and that the vast majority of members had voted No by passing the forms to us.

The company announced that it had lots of consent forms in as well … Aye right!

The true costs of the company's actions

The members had spoken and the company should have recognised this for what it was: a sign that their employees were disgusted by their treatment. Any management worth their salt would have paused and reflected that their foolish and brash assault on the workforce would come back to bite them if they proceeded with it.

The right thing to do would have been to accept the voice of the troops and take up our offer to sit down and agree a sensible compromise, one that would, without doubt, involve change. The company needed to take our members with them and make them part of the future.

We warned Maclean then and many times after that they were heading for disaster. Perhaps they felt strong at that moment, but their actions have since prompted the departure of about 50 per cent of our members, with many more to follow. It is difficult these days to find anyone at the site who is not looking for a job.

Management found themselves in 2014 in a state of panic and disarray as they tried desperately to keep and recruit people. They said at the time of this 'consultation' that there was no plan B. What a joke. They were on plan double Z by then. In order to keep staff they have had to award retention bonuses and change terms and conditions; they have had to ask retired folk, some of whom have been away from the plant for years, to come back, and they have had to beg people to stay on. They have been humbled by all this. But at the time they were full of themselves, talking loud, and ruling the roost.

They are not talking so loud now.

Our members have 'sacked' them time and time again, as they have moved to the plentiful and welcoming job market. As part of the continuing decline of the site Ineos have had to close a massive plant called the G4 cracker at least a year earlier than they had planned, because of lack of people to work in it. The disastrous decision to smash and grab our members' terms and conditions has in the end cost them much more than the cost of leaving the terms alone would have done – and it will continue to do so.

As a result of their high-handed actions and misguided media strategy they have made the atmosphere at the site so toxic that it is extremely difficult to attract people from some professions to go and work in Grangemouth, especially if they are already working for a sensible and credible employer in the petrochemical sector.

What incompetence, what poor decision making, and what an absolute mess!

Another line spat out by Maclean during the dispute was that the company did not care who left – and the more that left the better. He claimed that they would just close the plants if needed, while they retrained people. None of this has happened of course. They are running plants every day with below the necessary core numbers of operators. They are using trainees as operators, and occasionally running the nerve centre of the main chemical cracker without key specialists. It is a disaster in the post, and I believe the lives of many people are in mortal peril.

The regulators have been notified of this problem by our union, but at the time of writing they have yet to issue any enforcement notices to prevent this practice.

Gordon Milne, who is one of the Ineos 'Ratcliffetes' and a very senior manager in the Grangemouth chemicals business, at one point was claiming in team meetings that the Health and Safety Executive had been complimentary about the safety on site. (If this is true there should be a public enquiry.) But by February 2015, the same Gordon Milne was sending out a note to employees saying that the company had 'a very poor safety performance' and urging people to 'get a grip'. There was a very troubling incident where lack of proper control of work led to someone cutting through a pipeline which was still in service. Fortunately the pipe did not contain flammable or toxic substances, but the incident is none the less very worrying. There was also an incident where there was a gas leak so serious that the main road through Grangemouth had to be shut and the children in nearby nurseries had to be kept inside with the windows closed for fear there would be an explosion.

The safety issues have arisen not just from a lack of trained staff on the site as a whole, but also from the reduction in union safety representation at the site. Just to remind you, we had an agreement for 64 safety representatives, and actually had about 50 or so in place at the time of the plot. There were dozens of safety committees and structures, as you would expect in such a dangerous place. The proposals destroyed all that and axed all our well-trained and vigilant safety representatives, save three.

This is just madness. There is no other way to describe it, and it has directly led to the steep decline in safety performance now evident at the site. The reason given by Declan Sealy for attacking our union structures was that I had personally used safety as a political weapon, and had studied the subject to this end. About five years of study by distance learning, arduous exams and assignments, weekends spent studying and a programme of continuous professional development – all to help me coordinate this army of 50 collaborative people in a safety-related political attack on the company. Are they absolutely and utterly bonkers?

Anyway, Ratcliffe and his mob, with the sword of Damocles hanging above our heads, met on 22 October to consider their employees' response. On 23 October management set up a meeting in the canteen to report back to employees. The smug and smiling Maclean then announced that the company was shutting the chemicals plants, that the refinery was likely follow, and that the receivers would be in as early as the Friday.

The keystone of the plot had been laid, and one of the most contemptible acts I know of in modern industrial relations had been committed.

Our people returned from the meeting understandably despondent and very alarmed at the suddenness of the announcement and the shocking content of the presentation. Some of them were in tears of despair as they considered the impact on their wives, husbands, partners and children.

This was exactly the reaction the company had cynically intended.

This move by Ineos was designed to cut right to the heart of human frailty. The fact that the company was prepared to go to such lengths to threaten the livelihoods of our members in order to get its way is still a source of sickening disbelief to me.

It was Gandhi who said that the worst form of violence is poverty.

The union's response

I immediately called a meeting of the stewards, who had been consulting the members all morning and early afternoon, to decide what to do.

I will be blunt with you here and tell you that I did not think, and still do not think, that the company had any intention of closing the plant if we had held our nerve. Knowing what we all know about its plotting, it is evident they had sought to bring matters to this point, and it might have been an option to call their bluff.

In reality, though, it was not really an option, given the unrelenting pressure exerted by Ineos on our members, and in the context of the potential political and economic impact on the site and the town of Grangemouth if I was wrong and the plants were closed.

The other very serious consideration was that we were not dealing with the type of employer that we were used to. This company was run by one man, and he had the power to take the hit and refuse to go ahead – even with the fabulously lucrative investment that would be paid for by government grants and loan guarantees – just to prove how right he always was.

This could never have happened under public ownership. In fact, this could never have happened under a sensible board of directors – such a board wouldn't dream of acting in this cavalier fashion.

Perhaps the real disgrace in all this is that we have allowed these national assets to fall into the hands of such an unstable organisation.

So, in the end there was no real option other than to agree to their demands. I made the decision with the full support of every steward and with the backing of the members. We simply had to give the company all it wanted at that stage, in order to be sure of keeping the plants open. We have always tried to act in a responsible way and, given the situation we were in, there was only one possible way to go.

Refusing to hand over your wallet to a knife-wielding stick-up man may seem noble and courageous, but in the end staying alive may be the principal priority.

Retaining our organisation for future encounters was, I believe, the right thing to do.

Let me clear up one point once and for all. The decisions made throughout this dispute were taken by the members of Branch SC-126 of Unite the Union. There has speculation in some quarters that the London leadership somehow betrayed the workforce and sold us out in an agreement to accommodate Ineos. Nothing could be further from the truth, and I hope this account goes some way to setting aside such beliefs.

There was also some suggestion at the meeting that we should occupy the factory and prepare for siege conditions as they did during the Upper Clyde Shipbuilders work-in in 1971-2. This was never seriously considered, friends. This is a site with chemical substances that are toxic, corrosive, explosive and highly flammable. The site operates under very strict conditions laid down in law – and rightly so. The very thought that we would assume responsibility for the safety of members and the public and take custody of the factory was not credible. Any fleeting thought on this was almost instantly dismissed by the decision makers … our members.

On top of the concerns faced by our members, there was also deeply felt disquiet in the small business community linked to the site, mainly contractors and suppliers. This was very much in my mind as we went to meet Maclean and Sealy on the afternoon of 23 October.

On the way to the meeting we were shouted at by an HR 'professional' who swore at us, blaming us for the closure. We forgave this gullible person in time. Her conduct was really down to the company's antics.

At the meeting Maclean was full of himself. In spite of our decision, he almost said that the closure was now set in stone, but he then corrected himself and spluttered that the closure was 'in black and white and that was it'. This was the first revealing slip from this transparent fellow. In response I stated that in that case we had better get down to talking about the closure programme and what practical matters should be looked at. Maclean replied that that was it – unless there was a dramatic change. This was the second revealing giveaway. When I asked him what he meant, he said that if the plan was accepted at this stage then Jim might reconsider. This was the biggest slip of all – from the man whose competence in negotiations had been questioned by Gordon Grant.

At that very moment, and with absolute certainty, I knew the plants were staying open. But there was no cause for celebration. The closure threat may have been phoney, but the real threat and heavy price to be paid by our members was on its way.

How I would have loved to walk away from that table and refuse to discuss anything with them, to tell them we would fight and campaign for the continuance of the site without Ineos, and never have to meet with them again. I would have loved to tell them exactly what I thought, but, for all the reasons I have already described, this was not going to be possible.

They told me that if I sent a note saying that we would agree to the terms and lift any threat of action, Jim might reconsider. The transparent Sealy was positively slavering over the prospect of my sending that note.

It was agonising for me to send it, but I bit down hard and did it. My note was then released to the press by the company the following day, and we immediately instigated legal action over what was a breach of data protection law.

Surprise, surprise – the company held a meeting on Friday 25 October to announce that the plant would be kept open. We were not at the meeting, but our members reported that some folks from the staff were cheering. I guess it was a relief, but just think about it: the company's attempts to fool everyone, and the devastating cuts on the way to pensions and terms and conditions – and the victims of the plot were cheering!

WHAT INEOS TELLS US ABOUT POWER IN BRITAIN TODAY

... The closure of a community centre in Grangemouth would have required a more extensive due process, and greater transparency and accountability than was involved in the decisions to close a vital industrial facility.

Far from being a crisis for the trade union movement, this is a crisis for democracy, political and industrial democracy.

When a union, on behalf of a workforce, and an employer enter into a collective agreement it is a form of industrial democracy or, although in no sense equal, of workplace power sharing. With it comes a responsibility on both sides to negotiate to resolve differences and, on union members, a legal requirement to demonstrate through a secret ballot that there is support for any industrial action proposed if agreement cannot be reached.

It has been lost amongst the many other issues involved at Ineos that the ballot of Unite members had a turnout of 86%, exceptional by any standards, with 82% in support of strike action and 92% in support of action short of strike. Implicit in this legal requirement on the union to ballot is the expectation that the employer will recognise its outcome and the strength of feeling it demonstrates and respond accordingly.

They also reported at the meeting on 25 October that they had squeezed a better deal on raw material gas from BP, had secured a large subvention from taxpayers in Scotland, and had persuaded the UK government to underwrite the loan they needed. Add in the savage attacks on our terms and conditions and it was not a bad day at the office for Ratcliffe.

Len McCluskey dropped everything and flew north to Grangemouth. He was not, as some speculated, coming to take over the reins, or take the decision-making away from our members. He simply came to be with us and give us his support in any way he could. It was brilliant for our members to know he was there beside us.

Grahame Smith, STUC general secretary, summed up the whole situation in an excellent piece, an extract of which is reproduced below, 'What Ineos tells us about power in Britain today'

Despite voluntarily entering into a collective agreement with Unite, Ineos simply refused to negotiate at every turn, issued a take it or leave it ultimatum, and its response to the outrage of its workforce at the treatment of one of their colleagues and the rejection of its ultimatum was to shut the plant.

It has been suggested that the level of investment proposed by Ineos at Grangemouth justified its actions. The company has presented this as if Jim Ratcliffe intends to write a personal cheque for the £300m involved.

The truth is that, as is the way with private equity companies, the money will come from the markets not from earned income. As Ineos is so highly levered it needs to use earned income to pay the interest on its debt. New borrowing for Grangemouth demands the minimum of lender risk. That risk has now been transferred in large part to the Scottish and UK taxpayers and, given the sacrifice they made to keep the plant open, the workforce.

It is important to look to the future and to the success that we all know the Grangemouth facility will be. But we cannot ignore the fundamental issues thrown up in the last week about where power should lie and how the will of the people in a democracy should be exercised.

Grahame Smith, http://stucbetterway.blogspot.co.uk/, 27.10.13

The departure of Stephen Deans

On 28 October our team met to discuss Stevie's situation.

I have not said much about the external treatment of Stevie, but suffice it to say that the media speculation was intense. Stevie had reason to think that he, his house, his wife and his children were under constant scrutiny and surveillance. TV and newspapers had at times been camped out at his home. Remember he had been subject to a groundless police investigation – after being reported to them by the Labour Party, of which he had been a member for decades, and to which he had given so much service. He had also been suspended by the same party and subject to an equally groundless internal investigation. As we have seen, he had been referred to by the prime minister in the House of Commons as a 'rogue' trade unionist whose actions had almost led to the closure of the site.

Even the Dundee *Sunday Post* had been at his door – a newspaper based in the mecca of fruit preserves in the Highlands.

Ineos was continuing with its victimisation of Stevie, and the knowledge that he was about to face them again at a kangaroo court with a pre-ordained outcome was getting too much for him. He wanted out right there and then.

Perhaps his case should have gone to the tribunal. Perhaps he should have gone through the ritual humiliation of yet another bogus Ineos process and allowed himself to be sacked and therefore given himself recourse to the law.

But this was not what Stevie wanted. His main focus was on the welfare and well-being of his wife and his children, and he made up his mind not to give the company the satisfaction they craved, and to resign with immediate effect.

We all embraced as brothers at the end of the meeting when Stevie told us of his decision and left the office for the last time. I don't know why I feel so privileged, honoured and glad to have been in that meeting. Perhaps it was just that I had never before been in the presence of such dignity and high principle.

An innocent man had lost his job.

CHAPTER 9

After the strike

THE PRESS WERE relentless in their pursuit of Stevie following his resignation, and I had some real concerns for his well-being. Members were contacting me continuously to ask after him and make sure he was OK. There was even some minor criticism that we, as a branch, should have done more to help. I therefore decided to drop the members a note commenting on the treatment Stevie had received, and criticising those involved. Most importantly, I asked members to do the simple thing and send a note to him to let him know people were thinking about him and his family. An extract from the note is reproduced on pp172–3.

The members' response was wonderful, and cards galore were sent to Stevie's home. One or two members had holiday homes and these were quickly offered to give him and the family a break if they wanted one. Our Unite sector conferences also subsequently sent hundreds of post-cards wishing him the best, and when I spoke to Stevie he thanked me for sending the note out and said it had helped him to feel so much better.

It was quite appropriate and not remotely out of the ordinary for me to send communications to the members.

The company response was different. I was asked to have a 'chat' with Steven Boyle. There was no notice of any formal process, just a chat. Steven was like Declan Sealy that day – he had a script of questions which, as far as I could work out, were all the same question asked in different ways. He wanted to know who I had meant when I referred in my note to people involved in a smear campaign against Stevie. My truthful answer was that I was thinking about sections of the press, some of whom had been running inaccurate stories about Stevie for about a year. I was also referring to David Cameron for his outburst in parliament in which he had said that Stevie was a rogue trade unionist. I was also critical of some of the ill-advised comments from members of the Labour Party.

He asked me if my criticism was directed towards the company. The company had not been my focus in the communication I had sent, but his questions made me wonder where that question was coming from. I know now and will explain where it was coming from in a moment. Steven persisted, and asked me again if it was the company that I was referring to. I asked him if the company had been involved in the smear campaign I had discussed, but he said they had not – I was therefore confused as to this line of inquiry. That was how the meeting was left, but I knew full well they were lining me up.

As I mentioned earlier, a clause had been included in the newly enforced agreements saying that if an employee had a disciplinary record, management could reserve the right to refuse to recognise them as a union representative.

A coconut to the first person who can guess what happened next …

A ridiculous note went out to all employees from management, head-lined 'enough is enough' and claiming that I was putting the site in jeopardy by asking for support for Stevie and criticising his treatment.

One of the signatories to this note was Tony Traynor, who was later to oversee my appeal against dismissal, in my absence (see p184)!

Dear Brothers and Sisters

You will have seen the ongoing disgusting and horrible smear campaign against Stevie.

Members have been contacting me in numbers to express their concern for Stevie and to ask me to pass on messages of support.

Stevie is grateful for this at least. The campaign against him has been coordinated and relentless.

The criticism of his actions are unfair and unjust and he has done nothing wrong.

All his actions have been lawful, within party rules and within the facility agreements of the company.

There is a danger in being overly defensive and rebutting every accusation but the 'lead story' at the weekend was unbelievable. A family were wrongly proclaimed to have been signed to the party against their knowledge, they asked Stevie for help in correcting this, Stevie correctly asked for legal advice and passed this on. In the event the statements were not even used and the

They wrote to me soon after this meeting, telling me it was necessary to have a disciplinary hearing (did any of you guess?), and that Declan Sealy would be the chairman of it.

Sealy went through the same script as Boyle at the 'hearing', and I gave the same answers. He demanded that I withdraw the note but I replied that there was no reason to do that because it was accurate. I was within my rights to send it out and it was proper in every sense.

Scott Foley was with me as our union officer and he waded in as well: this was absolute nonsense and there was no case to answer. Sealy said, quite menacingly, that if I did not withdraw the note, it was likely the site would close, but if I did withdraw the note, this would be taken into account in my disciplinary sanction.

They were threatening to close the site and put swathes of people out of work and severely dent the Scottish economy unless my email was withdrawn. May the saints preserve us!

I took some advice from valued colleagues overnight, and the consensus was that they would sack me on the spot if I did not retract, which meant that I would not be there to try and salvage what I could from the so called consultation on the new terms and conditions.

family elected to talk directly to our legal department as they were more comfortable and they wanted to make sure the record was put right. There is no story here and I am asking where the information on all this was gathered?

Stevie and his wife and his children have been subjected to all kinds of pressure including media at their door at all hours as well as the obvious disgraceful misrepresentation of the facts in the press and on television. Whoever has instigated this are beneath contempt.

In recent days Stevie has also returned often to the abusive way he was treated in meetings while acting on your behalf over the last few weeks and I have had cause to question my own role in allowing that to happen to him and all of us at the time.

Anyone tainted with involvement in this should be ashamed of themselves.

Please drop me a message for Stevie and his family to try and help him at this desperate time.

There was also a small but real fear that they would re-activate the plot and threaten the site. The fear was that they had changed their minds about the site and were looking for someone to blame for its closure. Given their crazy and erratic behaviour, it could not be ruled out. So I agreed to issue the clarification. Needless to say I was remembering the words of Tony Woodley and Derek Simpson in 2008, when they had told me that I had better watch my back, and the warning from Len in more recent months predicting that they would set out to sack me.

I offered to attend the 'disciplinary feedback' meeting on my own because it was obvious there was no case to answer, but big MENSA told me I had better bring someone with me.

At the meeting they gave me no less than a final written warning. Boyle's face was beetroot red. It was pretty much like that all the time anyway, right enough, but he could not even look up. Sealy had a big grin on his face.

They said the reason for the final warning was that I had been instructed to retract the message by my union and had not done it of my own accord. Keep this in mind please. The mighty Engelman, Unite's barrister, subsequently had a field day with this at my tribunal hearing.

I believe there were three reasons for the company's action. One concerned the drive to give me a disciplinary record and thus debar me from holding office. The second was to prepare the groundwork for dismissing me. I did not know about the third one at the time …

It turns out that a stack of Stevie's emails had found their way from the sole custody of the company and into the hands of the newspapers. This was obviously in contravention of Stevie's rights as an employee, and against the IT policy as agreed on site. It also flew in the face of the Data Protection Act. I did not know about this situation at the time I sent my note to members talking about the smear campaign, but my members were asking how on earth the information could have ended up in the hands of the media. It is one of the enduring mysteries of the time.

The company obviously thought I had been talking about them being directly involved in handing over Stevie's emails to the papers. This is why the company had gone berserk when my note, sent out in all innocence, asked for support for Stevie. I asked Sealy during his 'investigation' into my email if the company had deliberately handed over the emails in question, to which he replied 'no comment'.

I stand by every word of that note. I hereby reinstate every word of it and set aside the forced retraction issued under duress at the time. Let me clarify one point, though, as I was not in possession of all the facts at the time. I hereby extend and expand on my assertion in the note about those responsible for treating Stevie so badly, specifically to include Ineos and in particular Jim Ratcliffe.

The 'consultation' period

I know I keep using inverted commas, but I just have to. I am going to cut this section short. We put forward good arguments against some of the cuts and alternative suggestions – all the things you would expect as representatives, on both the terms of employment and pensions. But the way Sealy behaved in the meetings, particularly when he was showing off in front of one of the CEOs, was disgraceful.

I spoke to Ian Fyfe about Sealy's behaviour after I had been off sick following one of the consultation meetings. For the first time in twenty years I had taken a day's sickness absence, because of a migraine caused by the stress of all this (particularly having to listen to a moron who I would, under normal circumstances, have put in his place in about 10 seconds. As Bill Morris used to say: 'He had delusions of mediocrity'.)

I told Fyfe that Sealy's behaviour towards me and our reps was unacceptable, and he agreed immediately and without argument. I asked him what he was going to do about it and he told me that he had tried to talk to Sealy, but it was no use and he could not control him. I reminded him that he was the HR lead for the site. This admission of weakness said it all.

When I was off work Steven Boyle sent me a very offensive email saying that he thought I had 'Man Flu'.

Another time, when Sealy was not there, our negotiating team met Fyfe and a CEO called Harry Deans, who was a strong contender for the title of most boring man in Western Europe. Harry was one of the many CEOs in this organisation, one of the band who had moved to Switzerland as part of Ratcliffe's tax avoidance measures. This was the first time we had met Harry, and he was eager to tell us that he was from Glasgow and his dad was a tradesman. Why do these people do that? Are they trying to say that they have some kind of empathy with us?

Scottish is a condition and a philosophy. There is no automatic qualification by birth Harry old son. You are about as Scottish in nature as Eric Pickles, and, given the shameful actions you have been embroiled in, the fact you breathed first in our country cuts no ice with us.

Fyfe followed one of our team out into the corridor during a break and said to him – in what could be seen as an act of treachery against Ratcliffe and once again acting as a double agent – that we should try and make the case to Harry to get concessions while Big Mensa was not there.

At the same meeting we had Boyle in to settle his old scores about the entitlement to reclaim holidays after being off sick, which I have told you about before. They wanted to change the maximum holidays you could reclaim from three to two days.

They were also taking the 'service days' off us – money paid to people who had earned an extra three days holiday a year after twenty years' service.

During this 'consultation' period I was asked to leave my office while an IT expert the company had sent over trawled through my computer searching for any reason to hang me. This was apparently because the company had received a request under the Data Protection Act to see if there was any information held on my computer on Lorraine Kane, who was one of the people cited as part of the Labour Party investigation into Falkirk. I had asserted that there was no way Lorraine had instigated this request on her own, and asked Sealy whether all this had been contrived by Media Zoo. His answer was 'no comment'. At the end of the search I asked the IT expert the question I already knew the answer to, and he told me they had found nothing. Once again, though, the bungling was not far from the surface, and I immediately informed him, and subsequently Fyfe, that he was entirely wrong. You see, when Ian Fyfe, who used to be a grade one referee, had sent me a document by email telling me I was to be investigated, he had accidentally included a number of highly sensitive and confidential papers belonging to Lorraine, including a full print off of her passport ID page and a copy of her utility bills! The email was on my computer but had not been spotted!

I am describing some of this so that you can have a flavour of atmosphere while the 'consultation' that was taking place. It was nothing but a sham and a waste of everyone's time.

Mercifully, the process came to an end. Not one proposal they had forced on the members had been altered, and everyone was forced to sign or be sacked. This was just before Christmas and most people signed, but just about everyone was already seeking work elsewhere and making plans to get out.

The collective agreements had to be signed as well, and Len had asked that a national officer should do so, as the wording in this disgraceful dossier constituted an agreement between the general union and Ineos, making it effectively a national agreement. On the day our team were on-site to do just that, I had the distasteful duty to talk to Fyfe and arrange for the papers to be handed over to us, signed and returned. Our officers had asked if we (lay members and officers) should meet the company, since we were all on site. I called Fyfe and he initially agreed, saying it was a good idea.

Later on he had obviously had his card marked, and he called to say that Jim was sick of Unite and did not want anyone meeting us. This illustrates perfectly the petty and childish way this international operation was being run – an operation on which major economies and thousands of workers were reliant.

A number of members, including myself, were at this time pursuing personal tribunal cases against the company concerning unlawful inducement to break industrial action. We believed that it had been unlawful for the company to offer a lump sum to members to accept their terms and break our democratically agreed action. To put a stop to this legal action, the company once more resorted to its favourite tactic: if we did not withdraw these cases, Jim Ratcliffe would once more review the decision to keep the plant open. We reluctantly instructed our solicitors to drop the claims, since we were not at all sure what Ratcliffe was capable of and were not prepared to take the chance, even though we felt our cases were sound. Such claims have to be progressed within tight timeframes if they are to be accepted by the Tribunal, and I feel it is a great shame, and a flaw in the judicial process, that claims like mine cannot be resurrected, given that the decision to drop the case was made under such duress.

At another meeting Sealy had asked us about our election process for branch representatives and I had supplied him with the relevant information and rule book, branch processes, etc. We had carried out elections as per the new hideous enforced agreement and entirely in line with proper branch and union procedures. We had also maintained all our safety reps and stewards, as branch reps recognised by the members, despite the reduction in those recognised by the company. I also notified the company about the identity of the three safety reps plus nine stewards. And that concluded our obligations under the agreement.

On the Monday of the week before the Christmas holidays Sealy met us again. Having started off with his usual mindless drivel, he ended by telling us we were to be evicted from our union office by Friday of the same week. He told us that if they had to move anything at the end of the week, they would throw it out and send Pat Rafferty the bill for the work involved. It would have been mildly amusing if they had sent a bill to Pat, right enough, to see his reply, but there were very serious issues involved here.

I explained to Sealy that we had decades of files and papers in the office, including very sensitive materials like death in service paperwork, fatal accident reports, disciplinary reports, grievance reports and financial papers. In short, all the very confidential paperwork found in a union office.

This was the most private information you could imagine, and we felt responsible for protecting it because it was in our custody.

We also explained that we had personal effects and all manner of stuff to shift. We cared not a jot about offices, as I previously said – give us an Ipad, a pencil and a pot of coffee and we can cover anything. But the timescale they had given us was outrageous.

In reply to our reasonable submission, Sealy aggressively said. 'Friday! Be out or the handymen will throw all your remaining stuff out.'

The plot had ended, but for me the drama was just beginning.

We are sailing

I just want to mention that while Ineos were telling us about how hard times were and while Ratcliffe was lecturing us about how our pensions were too generous, Jim Arthur himself was safely holed up on his £130 million yacht.

The *Daily Record* ran a story on 21 October 2013:

Grangemouth Crisis: Billionaire Ineos Boss lapped up sun on his £130m yacht as he drew up plans to dump 1400 Scots on the dole.

WORKERS at the Grangemouth refinery have until Monday to sign up to new terms and conditions put forward by Ineos boss Jim Ratcliffe drawn up on this floating palace in the French port of La Ciotat.

THIS is the £130million yacht where oil boss Jim Ratcliffe plotted to shaft 1400 Grangemouth workers.

I may be a simple soul but why on earth were we, the honest tax-payers, handing over our hard-earned cash to this sailor when he was flaunting such obvious material wealth? (Please don't think this is the politics of envy. Our team in Grangemouth actually had a bit of a chuckle when we first heard about the boat Ratcliffe had bought, and more than one reference was made about how most old geezers suffering a mid-life crisis just buy a sports car.)

Victimisation and discrimination (the sequel)

At the beginning of December 2013, the *Daily Record* ran a story about how, despite the draconian cuts that had been forced on employees in the name of survival, Ineos was now preparing to betray the workforce and close five operating plants at the site.

The *Record* had asked Pat Rafferty to confirm that these plants were closing and Pat had asked me if it was true. Bear in mind that the company had broadcast to every employee that they wanted to close these plants some time before, and had actually sent out a slide to all and sundry telling them about the plan. The slide had even been posted on the company intranet and was available and accessible to anyone on site.

Pat's main concern when we spoke was not the story. He was worried about the jobs that would be lost and asked me if I knew about any planned closures.

I told Pat that the proposed closure of the plants, though devastating and constituting a massive loss of employment and significant shrinkage of the site, was well-known and had been for some time. The words I used were that the story was 'old news'.

The paper ran the factual story and I thought nothing more about it.

The next day we were meeting Sealy about pensions and he was showing off again because Harry Deans CEO was there. He embarked on his script as usual, and asked if I had seen the *Record* and if I knew anything about the story.

I told him the truth about my limited involvement as set out above.

Boyle was asked to investigate this a week or two later, and I, once again, truthfully answered his questions about what had happened and responded to the ludicrous insinuation that I had done something wrong or outside my role, or said anything untrue. Just to be clear, Pat had spoken to the paper, not me, and every word he had said was true and confirmed by the company's own slides.

Why were they even talking to me?

Incidentally, the *Daily Record* article to which Pat contributed predicted the closure of five plants: the benzene plant – which closed in January 2014; the massive G4 cracker plant – which closed at the end of March 2014; the BE3 plant – which closed at the end of March 2014; the Ethanol plant – which is still running but under review of possible closure; and number one crude unit – which it is still planned to close.

Everything predicted in the *Daily Record* proved to be correct.

It is important not to minimise the closures at the site. It has been gutted, and little remains of the once proud and massive chemical site. Hundreds of jobs have been lost under the short period of Ineos's stewardship, and all the fuss and all the conflict and sacrifices made by our members were only able to save a couple of those plants when you think about it.

When the predicted closure of G4 did come about it was described by Fyfe as nothing really, and he actually said in one of the reports that this was 'an old news story'. Sound familiar? The truth is that, as I have already argued, they were forced to close G4 early because of the number of our members who had left the company. Management tried to play the early closure down, but make no mistake, the closure was a real tragedy, with many quality jobs lost and a big hole smashed through the local and national economies.

But the questions and thinly veiled accusations about the *Record* article were just one strand of a sub-plot the company were running to sack me from my job.

The other accusation was that I had objected to certain practices and management decisions in the refinery. Here is what happened.

I was invited, along with our refinery senior stewards, to our scheduled union/management meeting in December 2013. This meeting was normally quite informal and open and so it was on that day.

The company representatives asked us if we had any issues and I raised a number of points.

I told them that the idea of having only one safety rep for the refinery was not workable because we had five shifts, lots of areas and differing disciplines. My suggestion was that more were needed. *Since the meeting my suggestion has been adopted and they are looking to get more reps in place.*

I also said I was concerned about proposals to reduce the core numbers in one of the areas of the refinery, and argued that we should have a departmental meeting and 'management of change' process before any reduction. The manager for that area, Sharon Hooper, agreed with me, but was later to lie in her sworn statement about this. *Since the meeting my suggestion to have such a process has been adopted.*

Thirdly, I raised a concern on behalf of our members who were about to start working on a major overhaul, regarding altered working patterns. The local Hydrocracker manager, Umesh Dhokia, had already been down to the area concerned and floated the idea of the change to working practices, and had been told in industrial language what the company could do with their ideas. The bone of contention, as I say, concerned working patterns, and I suggested that the company review this and think again. *Since the meeting my suggestion has been adopted and the pattern worked during the maintenance event was as I had put forward.*

Fourthly, I raised a concern that the new policy on sickness absence would be very harsh on two members I had been representing over many months. The members were desperately ill, and I was concerned that they were having their pay cut so close to Christmas. The reply from management was that there was never a good time. Gawd bless us every one, eh? *Since the meeting our members have, indeed, had their pay cut, and have suffered the resultant hardship, but, as I suggested, at least one of the cases is under review.*

As you can see, this was normal business, conducted by me as a recognised and legally-protected union representative – and I was, incidentally, proved right on every single count.

But, following this meeting, Steven Boyle had gathered statements from some of the managers present, and my contribution to the session as union convener was later cited as another example of my unacceptable behaviour in the 'disciplinary'.

I had the opportunity to read the statements by these managers at my ultimately successful, even joyous, tribunal, but the lies and false representation from management were sickening.

Just before the Christmas break, and immediately prior to our being evicted from our office at a few days' notice, I was told two things.

One was that I was subject to an investigation, on the grounds that I had not stopped our regional secretary from truthfully responding to the *Daily Record*, and that I had faithfully and properly represented my members in a meeting to which the company had invited me. This really did make for a relaxing and enjoyable break! It was, of course, the intention to put me and my family under pressure and ruin our holiday.

The other thing I was told was that I was to go back on to shift work at the rail loading station. Working at the station, run by our excellent members, is an honourable profession, of course, but let me remind you that I had come on to trade union daywork at the request of management some years before all this.

The Hydrocracker, where I had worked before I became a full-time convenor, was the most complex area of the refinery, with the highest graded jobs. I was now going to the station which was the lowest graded area. I agreed to go without complaint, however, because I did not want to give them the satisfaction of forcing me down there.

At the end of the day I had done nothing wrong, and the temptation was to walk away from my job at the site. I don't think anyone would have blamed me if I had done so, but I still had responsibilities to look after my family and I needed to work.

I asked our troops down at the rail loading station if I would be welcome and they joked that they would welcome me on the first morning under their raised and crossed shunting poles as a guard of honour. They said they had renamed the shunting train the 'Che Guevara', and that we would launch the revolution together from the loading gantry.

You see. This is what these people don't understand. This is why they can never oppress us and box us off for long. The spirit of our members will always rise up again. The humour, resilience and warmth from my brothers and sisters made me feel re-energised and restored.

But it was not to last.

I think the managers were hoping that they had harassed and victimised me to such an extent that I would resign in order to avoid coming back to the treatment they had indicated was on the way.

Not in this lifetime friends.

I came back to work after the Christmas holidays and went to the station. It was actually great to be out with the troops again, and I had missed that more than I had realised. The guys on the station are brilliant and I was made to feel extremely welcome and looked after very well.

The supervisor down there had told me to do my safety induction, sort my lockers, etc, get a look round the area and then head off mid-afternoon. This is exactly what I did.

That evening I got a text from Boyle accusing me of being 'away sharp' and telling me that a letter was being hand-delivered to my house.

Sure enough, two security guards in full high visibility clothing came right up to my door and delivered the letter. It was an obvious act of intimidation and harassment. I have no doubt that they were specifically instructed to do this.

The letter was, of course, a notification of a disciplinary hearing, at which I know it had already been decided that I was to be sacked, on the trumped-up charges as set out above. My belief is that they wanted to spoil my break over Christmas and wait to see if I would show up for work. When I did return, much to their disappointment, they resorted to the fall-back plan and moved to sack me.

My confirmed and certain belief is that Ratcliffe had instructed that, hell or high water, there was no way I was to be allowed to continue at the site in Grangemouth.

Maclean has been foolish enough to confirm this openly in talks with some of our senior officers.

Medication, support and spies

I guess everyone thinks they are bulletproof, and in our game it can become a more or less accepted occupational hazard that you will be badly treated by rogue employers, but this was just a bit too much.

I am not going to cover this period in too much detail because it is personal, but I was made very ill by this treatment.

I was not able to attend the disciplinary hearing as I had been diagnosed as being unwell by my doctor and advised not to go at this stage.

I was tried in my absence and sacked in February 2014.

The chairman of the hearing was … Declan Sealy. I had an appeal heard in my absence in due course as I was still unwell, and the chairman was … Tony 'Behavioural Safety' Traynor. What manner of justice is that?

My appeal against dismissal was denied.

An uplifting element came when Labour MPs and MSPs moved emergency motions condemning the treatment I had received at the hands of Jim Ratcliffe's Ineos. The Early Day Motions were widely signed by Westminster and Holyrood representatives. It was satisfying to see these people exposed, shamed and humiliated in such a public way.

Early Day Motion 1046 in Westminster read:

> That this House expresses serious concern at the anti-trade union behaviour of INEOS at its petrochemical plant in Grangemouth where it has dismissed Mark Lyon, the UK Vice-President of Unite The Union, for carrying out his responsibilities as the elected convener of Unite The Union at the Grangemouth complex; notes that INEOS refuses to accept the Unite shops stewards elected by the workforce to represent them and is acting against the International Labour Organization (ILO) Declaration on Fundamental Principles and Rights at Work 1998, particularly ILO Convention 87 on Freedom of Association and Protection of the Right to Organise 1948, and ILO Convention 98 on The Right to Organise and Collective Bargaining, 1949; further notes that INEOS is acting in contravention of the rights set out by the UK Government on the gov.uk website sections on Trade union membership: your employment rights and the role of your trade union rep; is concerned that INEOS is in line to receive £9 million in grants from the Scottish Government and has applied for loan guarantee fund support from the UK Government of £150 million; calls on the Government to make it clear to INEOS that actions in breach of ILO conventions and in contradiction of UK law on the rights of employees to be represented by a trade union and to take part in trade union activities is not acceptable in the UK in the 21st century; and further calls for the reinstatement of Mark Lyon and a negotiated settlement

of points of difference between INEOS and trades unionists in its employment.

The EDM was signed by over 100 MPs.
Motion S4M – 08956 in Holyrood read:

INEOS and Trade Unions

That the Parliament expresses its serious concern at what it considers the anti-union behaviour of INEOS at its petrochemical plant in Grangemouth; understands that it has dismissed Mark Lyon, the UK vice-chair of UNITE, for carrying out his responsibilities as the plant's elected trade union convener; believes that INEOS is refusing to accept the role of UNITE's shop stewards, despite them being elected by the workforce; considers that the company is acting against the ILO Declaration on Fundamental Principles and Rights at Work 1998; is concerned that what it sees as this aggressive anti-union action comes at a time when INEOS is in line to receive £9 million in grants from the Scottish Government and has also applied for £150 million in loan guarantee fund support from the UK Government; believes that the UK and Scottish governments must make it clear to INEOS that actions in breach of ILO conventions and that contradict the right of an employee to be both represented by a union and to take part in union activities are not acceptable, and calls for the immediate reinstatement of Mark Lyon and a negotiated settlement between INEOS and the unions that represent its employees.

The motion was signed by every Labour MSP in the house.

I am a Roman Catholic but not a very good one. I have gone through sporadic spells of attending mass as an adult, but cannot claim to be a pillar of the church.

I guess you take theological knocks sometimes, and books like the *Ragged Trousered Philanthropists* and *Strumpet City* make you wobble on organised religion, but recently I have found myself applauding the stance of various clergy, including Archbishop Vincent Nichols of the Catholic Church and, from the Church of England, people like Kennington parish priest Giles Fraser, who has opened his London church as a homeless shelter and has been critical of the lack of action from the government. Many others from the religious communities have stood up for working people, commented on the rampant inequality in our society and given practical assistance to food banks and other aid projects.

In fact there can sometimes be a big overlap between the trade union movement and the church, especially in community involvement. Our branch was also involved in raising funds and collecting donations for foodbanks, specifically for the Trussell Trust, and on one occasion in early 2013 we gave them a significant financial contribution. The local chair subsequently reported to us that his multi-faith group had prayed for intervention since they had a problematic rent bill to cover, and the amount the branch had donated was just about identical to what they needed.

I make these somewhat out of context references so that I can tell you about a touching and nourishing incident at my own church, when my wife was attending evening mass one Saturday. It was just after I had been sacked quite publicly, and around the time of press interest and commentary in both the Scottish and Westminster parliaments denouncing Jim Ratcliffe and his company for their actions.

Part of the proceedings at mass is to offer 'bidding prayers', and normally the congregation will hear petitions from the parish priest. For example, he may say that we pray for the sick, we pray for the recently departed, we pray for peace in the world, we pray for the poor and hungry, etc. Each petition is punctuated by the priest saying 'Lord hear us', to which the congregation responds 'Lord graciously hear us'.

Anyway, this must have been the weekend immediately after my unfair dismissal, and our parish priest, Canon Leo, the most compassionate, brilliant, inspiring, gentle and humble man you could meet, looked out to the congregation and declared in a slow, determined and deliberate voice:

Let us pray for anyone who has lost their job through no fault of their own …
Lord hear us …

Sometimes an act of kindness played out in an instant can remain with you for a lifetime.

I will also tell you a couple of personal low moments from around this time, since it's just you.

The first came when I was given some medication to take the edge off. I had been warned it could make me a bit nauseous, and, though I will spare you the details, it made me quite physically ill. At that time it hit home that I had actually been made so ill by the actions of a few people who I had worked for. I had devoted my life to the site, and my only crime had been to try and improve the lot of the members who had chosen me to represent them. The actions of these people were ultimately carried out because I was an obstacle to their agenda – which, when distilled right down, was the greedy pursuit of even more money.

My considered position is that these individuals may have money and wear the cloak of respectability, but ultimately they are beneath contempt.

In only one respect I am glad my parents have passed away. The treatment I have received at the hands of these people would have crushed them.

The other low moment came after I had attended an appointment with a psychiatrist that had been arranged for me in Edinburgh. The appointment was at 7pm on a weekday evening as this was the first appointment available. I had been referred for an assessment of my mental health because good friends and comrades were worried about me, given the way I had been treated.

My wife came with me to offer support, and we went right through to Edinburgh after she had finished work. We had not had anything to eat because of the timings, so on the way back from the appointment we dropped into a restaurant near the station to grab a bite. We were in that restaurant for about 45 minutes and back home before 10pm.

The company wrote to my lawyers shortly afterwards saying that I had been seen in a restaurant in Edinburgh, and that I was 'acting normally'. This shameful episode upset my wife more than any other, and the thought that they might be watching my home and my family, and tracking our movements, was very troubling.

I believe that private investigators were hired under the instructions of Ratcliffe to follow me during this time, in the hope that they would uncover something – anything – that they could use to justify their despicable actions. There is no way for me to be certain of that, but it is my belief.

In common with every other aspect of support from the union, the legal assistance I got was astonishing, and if anyone wonders why it is a good idea to be in a union, the access to legal help is one of a million other good reasons to join.

Howard Becket is our Director of Legal Services and he has guided me through the legal process with great expertise and devotion. Our team from Thompsons Solicitors have been brilliant as well. Lindsay Bruce, Kenny Gibson and Patrick McGuire have worked tirelessly to help me and I will be forever grateful.

The blues

Another thing that helped me through this period when I was trying to come to terms with being out of work after thirty-three years of continuous gainful employment, was music, specifically, blues music.

Very often, it is evident from the conversations of trade unionists when they get together that we suffer from a condition which means that our interests, hobbies and pastimes are all related to the union and political aims. But when, because of all that had happened, I found myself ill and confined to home for months, one positive was that it allowed me to reflect, and to enjoy things that usually had to be rushed, and squeezed in amid the madness of trade union life. I was now able to listen more to the blues music that I have loved as long as I can remember. The music and words have an authenticity and truth for me. I need a daily fix of those simple repetitive chord sequences, coupled with exquisite lead instrument lines and grinding vocals.

So I thought I would take time out of my story here to tell you more about the music that helped sustain me in this very low period.

I began playing the guitar very late in life for most people, in my twenties, around the time I rejoined BP in the early 1980s. I was playing in a band formed with mates who shared a passion for the music. The Smokehouse Blues Band had a variety of members over the years but the core was made up of Ian Moffat on guitar, Bruce Tait on bass and vocals, Sandy Black on harmonica, vocals and latterly saxophone, and myself on guitar.

We enjoyed some degree of success, and played hundreds of gigs across Scotland and England, and even toured for a spell in Germany.

We also produced a number of recordings, including a CD album called *Live to Work* which was recorded at the famous CaVa studio in Glasgow where such artists as Deacon Blue, Paolo Nutini and even Billy Connolly have worked.

I think I have long realised that my passion for the music far exceeded my talent as a guitarist and I have not played for many years. I did enjoy most aspects of life on the road though, and there were many memorable events over the years.

We did a number of gigs for a guy called Lenny Boyle in a pub in a town called Bo'ness. Lenny was known as a good natured bloke but a rough diamond. There was once a notable incident when, apparently, some kids were driving Lenny crazy with ball games in the street, and, after some unproductive sharp exchanges with the juveniles – and the continuing bounce of the ball off his walls – our Lenny stepped out onto the street of the council estate and discharged a firearm into the air in order to emphasise his displeasure!

Naturally, Lenny was captured and removed to a secure location for the safety of the public, and I believe the ball games were, at least temporarily, suspended.

Anyway, prior to this we met Lenny at his pub to have a few beers and discuss the gig. He was very enthusiastic about having our band play, and we must have performed there half a dozen times. When it came to the arrangements, Lenny had an unconventional approach. He declared that he would prefer to pay our modest expenses as 'half and half'. We all looked at each other then asked the question. 'Half in cash and half in hash' was our erstwhile barkeep's response ... But I never inhaled.

While I was awaiting my tribunal date, I had the opportunity to visit Clarksdale Mississippi. I had always wanted to go there as it is recognised by many blues fans as the birthplace of the musical style. Within a short distance of each other are the birthplaces of people like Muddy Waters, Howling Wolf and the outstanding and iconic BB King.

Clarksdale is also the location of the legendary folklore surrounding Robert Johnson. The story goes that Johnson was a very average guitar player until he did a deal with the devil to sell his soul, after which he became an extraordinary player overnight. Johnson died in mysterious circumstances in 1938 aged 27, and I suppose this has added to the legend.

'The Thrill is Gone' BB King 16 September 1925 – 14 May 2015

On the morning of May 15, 2015 my phone lit up with messages about the death of BB King and I feel like I want to mention him.

I first went to see BB King play live around 1986 at the Playhouse Theatre in Edinburgh and I have seen him on many more occasions over the years. His command of the stage, the audience and, above all, his beloved guitar 'Lucille' was always an event to remember. I met him a few times but only at the usual after-concert autograph 'meet and greet' but I think everyone who loved his music felt like they knew him.

James Brown used to be known as the 'hardest working performer in the industry' but BB King gets my vote. Around 100 gigs a year right up to his death and this was his idea of slowing down! In 1956 he played no less than 342 shows.

No prizes for guessing the pick of my playlist on May 15, 2015. BB King was a champion of workers' rights, having been the son of a poor sharecropper in Ole Miss. That day I listened to and reflected on the lyrics of his song 'Big Boss Man'.

The idea of the 27 club and the occurrence of premature deaths among musicians has grown with Amy Winehouse, Jimi Hendrix, Janis Joplin, Jim Morrison and Kurt Cobain. On my reckoning Johnson was a founder member of this club.

The crossroads where he is reputed to have met the devil is at the meeting of highways 61 and 49. I don't know what I expected when I got there. I guess atmospheric rolling mist and flurries of sand coupled with the odd passage of tumbleweed. In reality the crossroads is a very busy place with heavy trucks and greyhound buses continually screaming by.

Wendy and I ate and imbibed of Jack Daniel's at the Ground Zero blues club, now owned by Morgan Freeman, and took in some delightful tunes.

You probably think Mississippi is pretty far removed from our story. But there are parallels. I was shocked by the continuing poverty and ramshackle housing in Clarksdale. This state of the USA was born and raised on enormous wealth created for individuals on the sweat and blood of workers who shared in none of the spoils, and now that much of the industry is gone, along with the proceeds, the area and its residents have been left to suffer the consequences.

I realise I have strayed from our story a bit here, but this episode of discrimination and unfair dismissal from employment, and period of inactivity, made me realise how important it is to have interests outside the labour movement.

The mighty Engelman

Pat Rafferty had suggested that my case was worthy of an application to the employment tribunal for what is called 'Interim Relief', and Howard Becket agreed.

Interim Relief is granted on very rare occasions, and the legal hurdle for securing it is generally considered to be quite high. The benefits of winning an unlawful dismissal case at that stage, i.e. before the tribunal itself, would be that I would be placed back on full wages and conditions pending a full hearing of the tribunal.

The interim Tribunal hearing took place on 9 March, and it was a joy. Barrister Philip Engelman was magnificent. Over about three hours he ground out our case and dismantled the company's arguments line by line. He spoke of the protections afforded to union representatives and the case law on acceptable conduct by recognised representatives like me. No aspect was neglected. At the end of his submission I just felt enormously relieved, and delighted that, regardless of the decision, my name had been cleared and the flimsy, contrived, case of the company had been utterly destroyed.

We had a big team on the day from Unite and Thompsons, and I was so happy to be supported and share the day with so many fine people.

The only poor soul from Ineos who had been instructed to come along to suffer this drubbing was Ian Fyfe (who used to be a Grade One Referee). If his head had gone any lower during the ferocious assault of the mighty Engelman, I believe he would have toppled from his chair.

Ineos's solicitor tried to progress the argument that they were right to sack me because I should have done more to stop Pat from talking to the press. They argued that it was me who routinely told Pat what to do, so I should have stopped him talking to the Daily Record.

Remember the previous contrived 'disciplinary', where the company had said that I had been instructed by my union to retract the note to members about the smear campaign, because the union routinely told me what to do.

Now they were saying that, no, it was actually me who was in charge!

Even the judge at the interim hearing pointed to this ridiculous conflicting argument in open session and shook his head.

During this exchange one of our team wrote in a notebook and showed me the words 'this is painful!'.

Our barrister was asked if he wanted to respond to this conflicting submission, and I imagined that he would talk for some time about the incredible and, frankly, embarrassing, line being set out by their lawyer.

His immortal words live with me still. His withering putdown made redundant thousands of years of putdowns in the course of human oratorical exchanges.

No putdown will ever be valid again.

Friends, just like expletives ... there are no putdowns left.

Philip Engelman, in response to the offer to reply, simply said this: 'Only to say that my friend's entire case is ... chaotic and contradictory'.

The presiding Judge, Stewart Watt, took a very short adjournment to consider the case and came back to report that, in his view, 'there was no material evidence that Mr Lyon had been guilty of any wrongdoing', before awarding me the interim relief. I was to be on full wages and all conditions up to the full tribunal hearing. Judge Watt also observed that 'it was likely that Mr Lyon would win his case'.

The only mild disappointment was that Sealy, Maclean, Boyle, Grant and Ratcliffe were not there to see it. I would have given anything to be on a party line when they told Ratcliffe that they had been smashed, wasted and destroyed and now lay prostrate and face-down in the street before the might and majesty of Unite the Union.

Alright ... I know, but give me a bit of licence – it had been a mildly difficult year for me you know!

Unite ran the story below in the days following the hearing, as a press release and on our Unite and Grangemouth branch websites.

Chaotic and contradictory!

What a result!! In support of Mark Lyon, your ex-convenor who fought so bravely for your rights, the Union has offered all legal resources. Following the incredible decision of Ineos [I will use Ineos to generally describe the associated companies as well as Mark's specific employer – Petroineos Manufacturing Scotland Ltd] to dismiss Mark, while he was absent from work on stress related illness, we issued a claim in the Employment Tribunal.

The application to the Employment Tribunal accused Ineos of victimising Mark for reasons of his trade union representation and of unfairly dismissing Mark for reasons of his trade union representation and membership. A decision was also taken to make an application for an Interim Relief Order. Interim relief exists to allow those unfairly dismissed for trade union reasons to make an application for an early (interim) judgement of the tribunal. That judgement would either say an individual is likely to win a full hearing, or not. The applications are very rare, in Mark's case the Tribunal Chair commented on how few cases had been before the Glasgow Tribunal in all of his years of sitting as a Chair.

One of the reasons the applications are rare is because they must be made within 7 days of dismissal. In other words, within 7 days of the date of dismissal Mark had to present his full pleadings to the Tribunal outlining exactly why he was unfairly dismissed. More importantly, to be successful with the application Mark would have to show a Tribunal that he is 'likely' to win a final hearing, not that his case is better than the defence of his employer but that his case is 'likely' to succeed. A high threshold by any standards. We had two advantages to the case. Firstly the truth and secondly Ineos's defence! Amazingly Ineos's defence amounted to admitting Mark was dismissed for trade union representation. The defence admitted Mark was acting in his capacity as a Trade Union Representative but claimed that the representation was to further a personal agenda, on making such a claim the burden became to show that Mark had acted 'dishonestly or with malice or wholly unreasonably'. In detail the allegations against Mark were that he could have prevented the Unite Regional Secretary from making comments to the press (an article that Ineos did not claim contained any inaccuracies) and failed to do so; that in voicing concerns about the number of safety reps appointed he had failed to commit to the 'survival plan' and in voicing concerns that some proposed shift changes would be unwelcome amongst the workforce he was again failing to show commitment to the 'survival plan'. During the hearing itself the case against Mark became that he was deserving of dismissal as clearly he had failed to 'toe the line'!

Perhaps the best way to describe the Ineos defence was as described by Mark's Counsel in final submissions. The defence, said Counsel, was 'chaotic and contradictory'. Mark's case for interim relief was successful on all grounds. The tribunal found that there was no evidence at all to suggest Mark had stepped outside the duties of a convenor (or outside the boundaries of what could be expected in the normal cut and thrust of industrial relations), that his conduct (including a letter of support for Stevie Deans for which Mark received a final written warning) was done in the course of acting in his role as a trade union representative and, crucially, that there was not a single piece of evidence to suggest dishonesty or malice on the part of Mark.

The tribunal commented that a convenor who failed to challenge an employer's decisions, when concerned about the impact of those decisions, would not be carrying out his or her duty as a trade union representative. Where a trade union representative acts in the course of their duties they have protection from dismissal – the tribunal found that Mark is likely to be said to have such protection at a final hearing. From now until the final hearing Ineos must pay Mark his loss of earnings (including pension). The final hearing will be many months away.

This is a victory not just for Mark but for all trade union representatives. It is a victory for all trade union members. The victory says clearly that Unite will support our representatives in the workplace and fight for our members to be entitled to elect their representatives without fear of reprisals from an employer. Where now on legal actions against Ineos? Mark's case followed the successful defence of a defamation action brought by Ineos against the union, Len McCluskey and Pat Rafferty for an article, released during the dispute, saying that Stevie Deans had been victimised. Following a defence that the comment was truthful Ineos chose to discontinue the proceedings meaning they are responsible for Unite's substantial legal costs. Unite stood by the article and continues to do so.

Mark's case will now be prepared to final hearing where we will openly challenge the real decision maker – Jim Ratcliffe – to attend tribunal to justify his decisions. Mark will have the full resources of the Union. We won't stop there – the Data Protection Act complaints to The Information Commissioners Office (against Ineos and their media companies) will continue and we will apply to the High Court for access to all information Ineos hold on Mark Lyon, Stevie Deans and others. The DPA actions arise because one question remains unanswered – who leaked private emails to national newspapers? We won't rest until we find the answer to this question.   .

Where does all this leave us in Grangemouth? Well we are sending a clear message of support for you and for your chosen representatives. Most of all our actions should be a clear message to Ineos – accept the findings of the Tribunal and treat our members and trade union representatives with the respect they deserve and the respect required by law. This is a landmark decision and let's hope Ineos take note.

Howard Beckett, Executive Director for Legal, Membership
and Affiliated Services Unite the Union

Discrimination is discrimination

There are no acceptable forms of discrimination in my opinion. It might be possible to create a hierarchy of discrimination in your mind and categorise offences committed by people according to the scale, but I don't consider that to be in any way credible.

Ask yourself for a moment: what would be at the top of the league of injustice? Race discrimination? Disability? Sex? Hate crimes against LGBT?

I can instinctively feel some issues are further up the tree than others, but I know this is the wrong approach. My reason for throwing this around, of course, is to ask you how you feel about trade union discrimination. In some ways it feels a bit further down the pecking order to me, because of the despicable actions associated with the other forms of discrimination, but, again, I think that's the wrong approach.

My assertion is not that people who discriminate in any respect are lost and worthless. People can always be reformed, and this should always be our aim. But the people who discriminated against our members by disproportionally and savagely slashing their terms, who singled out our representatives and told them they were not fit to be stewards, as well as those who contrived and lied or had any part in my unfair dismissal, and who acted so disgracefully towards Stevie Deans – all these reside in the dreadful malignant tent of those who discriminate.

Let's not offer the mitigation that one form of discrimination is somehow preferable to another. No. These shamed individuals are forever and indelibly marked with the horrible stain of prejudice.

I often wonder if I will meet any of these lost souls when I am out and about locally. I always hope I will, so that they can be confronted with their actions. I imagine it must be very difficult for the worst offenders among them to even leave the house, for fear of meeting the good people from our site and suffering the corresponding embarrassment.

The site in 2016

At the time of writing this last section of the book, early in 2016, the site is not in a good place. A very significant proportion of experienced and knowledgeable employees have left the company. The loss of experienced and trained employees has led to lower productivity, and to occasions when the plant and equipment is being run without the previously prescribed safe number of employees in control. I have been briefed from employees at the site who talk about a raft of reports from an Ineos system called Traction, showing such instances of 'running light', as it is called in the industry, and recording a raft of safety incidents and accidents.

There are many job opportunities in our chemical and oil sector, and every employee who leaves has the potential to take more people with them, because bounties are offered by some firms to workers who successfully encourage others to join them. Despite the drop in oil price in recent times there are still job opportunities in our sector and people continue to haemorrhage from the site.

The safety performance at Grangemouth is something that everyone who works at the site who I meet in the street, the pub or the supermarket seems to be very troubled by. I think this is as a result of the lack of experience, lack of safe staffing levels, the destruction of all the previous safety structures and the derecognition of our safety representatives.

In early 2014, all the stewards who had been involved in any aspect of our talks before the plot was completed were taken in one by one and told they were not fit to be representatives because they did not agree with the company.

The reputation of the site as having poor conditions and the most aggressive employer has made the site extremely unattractive to anyone even considering applying for work if they already have a position with a credible multinational.

Predictably, weasels and sycophants come into their own in this type of climate, and the company has now set up a cost saving-suggestion scheme. Everyone I meet tells me about it with incredulity and mirth. Such ideas as recycling old jackets, printing in a thinner font because it will up use less ink and asking plant operators to undertake gardening have emerged so far. These are the operators that we don't have, by the way, because they are leaving in droves as a reaction to their treatment.

Gardening services are certainly needed. I am told the site looks like a wasteland, with weeds and vegetation sprouting everywhere. This will cause dangerous damage to pipes in the long run, as I explained earlier. It's funny how lessons are never learned and how history repeats itself over and over (see Gertrude).

The self-same managers who so robustly advocated the slashing of everyone's terms save their own are now frantically going round the site grovelling and trying to persuade our people to stay and not abandon the site. This snivelling display is in sharp contrast to the smug and loud-mouthed approach at the end of 2013. Our members are saying that the damage they have caused to relationships can never be repaired.

At the end of 2013 we were being told bullishly by this crowd that 'there is no plan B'. By 2015 they had to back down and were offering retention payments and a return of some of the holidays they had withdrawn from our troops. These were acts of blind panic because our members were continuing to leave. You may think this backing down is positive, but they have spectacularly messed this up as well. There are big differences between what different operators have been offered. People with less than five years' experience have been offered nothing, while some areas within the site have also been offered nothing regardless of job description; the plan is not consistent across the different areas of the site. It is a shambles. They have managed to upset just about everyone all over again.

In a few short years Ineos have managed to convert one of the most valued workplaces in Scotland, to which people would devote their entire working lives, into a third-rate and discredited factory where the workforce detest the management and the future is uncertain.

The incessant and nonsensical ranting of Ratcliffe in the press is also doing nothing to raise the reputation of the site, and it is difficult to see the way forward. Ratcliffe's well-rehearsed mantra amounts to this: tax us less but give us more of the taxpayers' money; don't trouble us with regulation of our business or restrictions concerning the environment; and introduce legislation to remove the voice of anyone who even dares to challenge anything I say, especially the unions.

I understand that the trade organisations are looking through their fingers and cringing as they wait for the next episode. The Carr review proposals were bad enough, but Ratcliffe's representation to the outgoing President of the European Commission in March 2014 was even more breathtaking. In an open letter to José Barroso, he told him, among other things, that, when it came to the chemicals industry in Europe, 'we have got our trousers down'. I do hope this translates well or we may all end up on some kind of register. Ratcliffe has also lectured us on energy costs, fracking and a host of other enlightening topics.

There are definitely people without whom the world would be a better place.

As 60s comedian Terry-Thomas would say … They are an absolute shower.

The sands of time

Even without reference to Old Moore's Almanac, you can tell that the future is littered with certainties and some highly predictable occurrences. Let's examine the things we know. Well, we know that the company has borrowed lots of money to build this tank, and that the tank is being built and is visible from all around the local area. We know that once that money is handed over the plant does not really belong to the company any more, it belongs to the banks – so the threat to close the site becomes less credible.

We know that the company is getting £9 million as a grant from people like us who pay tax. We don't think any conditions are attached to this gift, but you would like to think there are some very robust ones.

We know that the company is building ships especially to bring fracked gas from the USA to Grangemouth at a considerable cost.

We know that long-term contracts to take the gas from the USA have been signed.

We know that the company will make an absolute fortune once the tank is built, and the cost of any stoppage, given they have a heavy debt to pay off, will be difficult to bear.

We know that the workforce will be significantly different by the time the project is completed – that is, if the factory survives this period of disastrous management. But we also know that folks are folks, and that it is an absolute certainty that the union will be organised, have a massive membership and be in a strong position in the future. This is not a possibility. It is a certainty, as night follows day. It is an absolute certainty.

The other assurance we should offer each other right now is that the first line of our collective agenda should not be to restore our terms and conditions – that should be the second line.

The first line of our agenda should be to insist that the managers at the site who have continued to treat our members so poorly must be punished for their actions. These barrel-chested go-getters who have so bravely committed acts like cutting the pay of the seriously ill will, no doubt, be abandoned by the company the instant it becomes financially beneficial for them to do so during talks with us.

We know that, don't we? We have seen it all before. And, more to the point, the industrial heroes involved know in their heart of hearts that this is true, and that our letter is in the post.

Maybe you have a couple of years, take advantage while you can …
but keep your eyes open.

At the end of this account I return to the question I asked at the
beginning. Who is to blame for the situation at Grangemouth? The
drivers, or those who have handed over the keys? Employers or governments? Policy-makers? Financiers who fund the hopeless and the
unqualified?

One thing for sure is that it ain't the fault of the men and women
who have to put up with the peaks and deep troughs created by the
decision-makers. The fine people who work in pursuit of a decent life
for themselves and their loved ones, and in the hope of a retirement at
some level of dignity and comfort, carry no blame.

In the case of Grangemouth, the drift from public ownership to
private ownership, from protective government oversight to the aban-
donment of nationally important assets to anyone who can raise the
cash in the short term, has proved disastrous.

The model whereby organisations running utilities or providing
vital services are operated with the principal motive of making a profit,
rather than provision of said services, is very dangerous. They become
vulnerable to short-term thinking or just plain poor decision-making.

It is bad enough when companies are run by boards of directors,
who are permitted to pick and mix from expansion, contraction or
offshoring product lines with no other reference than the balance
sheet. But at least there are some checks and balances in place in such
companies.

In a company like Ineos, however, one man has the power to do
almost anything without constraint, and this can be disastrous.

People need to recognise the difference between their ambitions
and their capabilities.

Unless life or death services like health or the essential production
of oil, electricity and gas are secured within public ownership, there is
no way to ensure supply. The power industry is a classic case: we have
all paid through the nose to build electricity generation stations and
have subsidised them to death, but we have handed the assets over to
shareholders at knock-down prices and we are still talking about
struggling to keep the lights on.

The environmental debate is also lost unless an honest broker can
be found. One who can see the big picture and make interventions
accordingly. Right now it is like the Wild West out there.

Let's hope some lessons can be learned from all this, so that working people need not pay the price again for the inadequacy of our political system and the incompetence that resulted from it.

But what do I know?

Be sure to let me know what you think.

Epilogue

THE MAIN TEXT of this book was completed in mid-2015 and I think it is worth reviewing some of the issues. I am writing this section in early 2016.

I guess the main setpiece political drama of 2014 was the Scottish referendum – the 55 per cent vote against independence with an extraordinarily high turnout, and the continuing party political fallout from all that.

I would describe myself as a weak Yes in the referendum. I voted with the losing 45 per cent.

This was not as a result of a misplaced shortbread tin or 90-minute soccer patriotism on my part. I just felt that the task of repositioning the UK Labour Party with even a mildly socialist agenda was a very long-term project and that the agenda the people of Scotland want might never be delivered within the UK. The subsequent election of Jim Murphy as Labour Party leader in Scotland did nothing to alleviate my anxiety. I feel there is a growing discomfort with Labour among trade union members and working-class folks in general.

The key political event of 2015 was the general election, in which the worrying and predicted collapse of the Labour vote in Scotland did in fact materialise, and this contributed significantly to the overall majority gained by the Conservatives nationwide.

The standing joke in Scotland among Labour supporters used to be that there were more Pandas in Scotland than Tory MPs. Two Pandas were brought to Edinburgh Zoo in 2011 and at that time the Conservatives held one Westminster seat: that of Dumfriesshire, held by David Mundell. Alas, the reality now is that the SNP has now won every seat save three in Scotland, and that Labour, the Conservatives and the Liberal Democrats all hold only one seat each.

A remark made by regional secretary Pat Rafferty at a Unite presentation ceremony in 2015 underlined the parlous state of the Labour Party in Scotland. Pat was presenting a special award to three retired members, John Keenan, Robert Somerville and Bob Fulton, who had worked at the Rolls Royce plant based near Glasgow airport in the early 1970s. They had refused to service engines from aircraft which had been used by the fascist junta in Chile to bomb their own citizens. Their brave stand grounded the airforce and saved many lives. In his speech Pat remarked that, given the virtual wipe-out suffered by Scottish Labour MPs in the general election, the members in question were loath to leave their seats to accept the award in case the SNP got them. (As well as Chile's highest award available to foreign nationals, the three were presented with Unite's gold medal.)

For the record, I am still a member of the Labour Party and hope things can be turned around for the party. The track record of our excellent local MP, Michael Connarty, prompted me once more to mark my cross next to the rose, but sadly Michael lost his seat.

I don't think Labour's attitude during the Ineos debacle can be seen as a key reason for the avalanche of activists and voters who have left the party for the SNP and other parties. I don't think it is so high in the consciousness of people in that way. But I think the positioning of Labour was a clear demonstration of the degree to which the party has lost its way, and of the need for radical change. The outcome of the Labour leadership election in Scotland after the general election was a graphic illustration of the fact that the party had remained determined to pursue a 'business as usual' approach.

Jim Murphy initially tried to continue as Scottish party leader after the general election rout in our country. I felt this illustrated two things: firstly that his judgement was seriously flawed in thinking he was the person to lead us to better times since his brand of 'newish' Labour had brought us to defeat in the first place; and, secondly, that he was willing to put his own interests before the party and selfishly hang on like a limpet for another round of Scottish elections in 2016 with the same old policies and with a predictable outcome.

I don't know why things have gone so wrong for Labour in the birthplace of James Keir Hardie, and where we have enjoyed such support from the people over the years. I have listened carefully to more analysis than you could shake a stick at, and there is probably no single reason for the collapse, but there are a few factors worth remembering.

Shortly after 2011, when Johann Lamont became Scottish Labour leader, there was a party conference and one of the issues in everyone's mind was the forthcoming independence referendum in 2014. Our union had put forward a motion calling for a second question on the ballot paper to give the electorate the choice of more powers for the parliament in preference to outright separation – the so called devolution-max or 'devo-max' option. This would have allowed us to campaign on a positive alternative and I believe the Scottish people would have voted comfortably for this option.

It would also have meant that Labour would not have entered into the 'better together' campaign with the Tories and Liberals and would not have been seen as being in bed with David Cameron and his chums. This was a fatal move in my opinion.

Our union was persuaded to withdraw the two-question proposal at the request of the party hierarchy, who were supremely confident that the people would vote overwhelmingly against independence; that the SNP would be put to the sword and be never heard of again; and that, in some strange kind of Enid Blyton fantasy, we would all be home in time for hearty congratulations and back-patting at our cleverness and to take tea and scones washed down with lashings of ginger beer.

In the event the second question was effectively later introduced as a possibility by Gordon Brown, in the panic-stricken days just before the referendum vote, when it became apparent that the northern Barbarian hordes were about to vote Yes. At this point Brown started to promise all kinds of things, though without a hint of any mandate or authority to do so. The vision of the three party leaders, Miliband, Cameron and Clegg, flying north as one, is something that people are still talking about as a key reason that swathes of support were lost for Labour.

Another element, I think, is the way decisions are taken in the Labour Party, and the lack of internal democracy. I don't think the voters go around thinking about this in those terms, but it feels like there is an intangible malaise; that everything is controlled and sanitised and, frankly, stitched up. I have heard quite a few people saying that it is pointless to go to branch and constituency meetings as no real decisions are made there. The annual conference is more like a US-style convention these days and any decisions can be ignored by the leadership. This needs to change. The furious reaction to our entirely democratic and proper actions as a union over the Falkirk candidate selection just seems to illustrate all this perfectly.

Jeremy Corbyn

The other notable event for Labour in September 2015 was, of course, the landslide victory of Jeremy Corbyn in the leadership election. This decisive win was the clearest possible indication that the party needs to change course and adopt a more progressive stance.

The country is crying out for an alternative to the failed austerity agenda and constant pandering to big business and the financial institutions.

It is worth reflecting that the result of the leadership election would have almost certainly been the same under the old party rules. However the changes made as a result of the Collins review of party procedures, included a scheme to give 'registered supporters' a vote in the leadership election in return for £3. That made Corbyn's victory even more decisive.

Disloyal but influential members of the party, who continue to try to undermine Corbyn and his leadership were, in many cases, the same crew who wrongly called foul in Falkirk. This was a shameful episode for the right wing of the party in many ways, but, ironically, it was also a chapter of history that may have contributed to real change and enhanced party democracy.

Industrial developments

In terms of industrial economics the big news has been the drop in oil prices, from more than $100 a barrel to below $50 in 2015, and to around $33 in January 2016.

BP and others with heavy commercial footprints in oil exploration are currently continuing with their recent moves to cut jobs, and to press government for tax breaks and financial incentives to shore up their businesses.

It is important to reflect again on the strategic philosophy adopted by BP and other oil majors as I described earlier in the book. The decision to exit from most of their manufacturing operations and concentrate on nothing but harvesting crude oil may have been extremely successful while the oil price was so high, but the lack of a mixed portfolio of exploration, refining and chemical divisions is now demonstrating the vulnerability that comes from placing all a company's eggs in one basket.

The potential for dramatic economic shifts as a result of the financial levers at the easy disposal of organisations like OPEC is one of the reasons why key industries that are integral to the security of supply of vital products such as fuel should remain within public control.

In December 2015, Ineos announced it had bought all the North Sea gas fields belonging to Deutsche Erdoel AG, and was forming a new company called Ineos Breagh. Leaving aside for one moment the problem of even more of this country's energy assets now being under the control of JAR, there seems to be a contradiction here with previous Ineos statements: in 2013, when JAR was threatening to close the plant unless they got investment for their tank for US imported gas. At that time North Sea gas production was portrayed by Ratcliffe as a rapidly declining source of supply.

The situation at the Ineos Grangemouth site unfortunately continues to worsen. Morale is at rock bottom and the number of people who have left or continue to leave is high.

Safety concerns

As we have seen (see p196–7), safety continues to be a cause for concern at Grangemouth. There have been a number of very serious safety incidents at the site in the last couple of years, including a gas leak that caused the closure of the main arterial road in the town, and the confinement of local children inside their nursery for their own protection.

On 9 September 2015 a massive explosion and fireball rocked the town during the demolition of still more manufacturing capacity on the site. I was working away from home that evening, but my wife called me to say that the blast had shaken our house, which is located a number of miles away. I have viewed the 'controlled' explosion on YouTube and it was frightening to see that members of the public were so close to the blast zone, and that debris can be seen landing behind them. One of our members had strongly advised his wife not to go down to see the demolition, because he knew the site would be covered in polymer dust, and that an explosion was likely.

Then in January 2016 there was a very serious incident when one of the plants in the Refinery, the DHT (Distillate Hydrotreater), ended up in an unsafe condition; and in the same month a fire broke out around extruders in the Polymers area of the Chemical site.

In response to a request under freedom of information law, the Health and Safety Executive released a report on Ineos at Grangemouth in Scotland which stated that, after problems uncovered by a major hazard inspection in December 2014, HSE had issued Ineos with an 'action legal' requiring them to properly identify 'safety critical tasks' associated with 'major accident hazards' at its ethylene plant at the site. One of the hazards identified was 'a leak or rupture from the top of the propylene tower with the potential for a fireball or vapour cloud explosion which could give rise to multiple on-site fatalities'. The company was given until the end of April 2016 to comply.

A subsequent HSE inspection in May 2015 concluded that 'there were no designated competency standards for the safety critical tasks', and 'a lack of clarity around exactly what was required and who could perform it'. There was also 'some ambiguity around the importance of safety measures such as cordoning' and 'some room for improvement' on one task.

According to the HSE enforcement database, Ineos was also served an improvement notice on 4 September 2015, originally due to be complied with by 16 October 2015, then postponed until 27 November 2015 and then again until 11 March 2016. The notice was because of 'a failure to make a suitable and sufficient assessment of the risks to the safety of persons which arise from dangerous substances (namely stabilised gasoline) for the task of draining water from the floor drain of storage tank ST-410'. This was the twelfth improvement notice served by HSE on INEOS at Grangemouth since September 2011.

In addition, the Scottish Environment Protection Agency (SEPA) rated the environmental performance of the Ineos refinery at Grangemouth as 'poor' in 2014 under two control regimes. One rating has been challenged by INEOS and is being reviewed by SEPA. The other is 'due to loss of vapour recovery unit following pump failure' leading to 'unabated emissions'. The INEOS refinery has been rated as poor by SEPA under one regime or the other in four of the last five years.

The actions of the HSE and SEPA suggest that health, safety and environmental performance at INEOS Grangemouth are not what they should be

I am also concerned that potentially dangerous equipment is consistently being run without the previously prescribed number of people in control – a recipe for disaster. I have personally been involved in meetings with the Health and Safety Executive to highlight unsafe practices such as these and encouraged it to act. It is disappointing to report that such practices are still being allowed despite the potential consequences.

One of the priorities for our union is to restore some sanity and rigour to the safety procedures at the site.

An edifice

The clearance of manufacturing equipment that caused the blast and fireball was carried out to allow a massive shiny Ineos office block to be built on Inchyra Road. I can only assume that the cash for this development came partly from the cuts to our members' shift allowance and overtime rates, and from the withdrawal of benefits to our sick and disabled members.

I recently read that the decline in the performance of a major retailer could be directly traced to the loss of key experienced individuals, which had resulted in a drop in the consistency of 'customer-faced delivery'.

The difference between this retailer and Ineos Grangemouth is that there may have been a steep drop in the sales of beans at the former, but at the latter a lack of experience could lead to deaths among employees and members of the public.

Oh how the foolhardy Ineos decision-makers must rue the day they embarked on this crazy crusade to slash and burn.

Quite apart from the potentially deadly consequences, the business has been hit hard financially. Cuts to production due to lack of competent people in key positions have reduced substantially any perceived financial benefit the company may have hoped for by cutting employee wages and benefits.

Most concerning, I think, is that the company appears to have learned nothing from this self-inflicted disaster, and is still refusing to recognise key Unite representatives. It is continuing to pretend that all is well at the site, and is hell-bent on pursuing its disastrous bogus consultation with employees.

If there is a positive from all this it comes from seeing the approach of other employers in our oil and chemical sector. You would have been forgiven for thinking that the brutal attack on the Grangemouth workforce would be taken as a blueprint for other installations.

Nothing could be further from the truth. Our senior representatives, with the possible exception of one UK site, report that Ineos has become a byword for poor practice and undesirable industrial relations. Management teams recognise the costly consequences of such actions and have spoken to our representatives with the objective of avoiding such a calamity at their own sites. Ratcliffe has indeed provided an example for our industry ... a very poor example.

The other announcement we have all been treated to by Jim Arthur was his intention to get into oil exploration. Remember that advert? I think it was for VW, I recall it went something like this: 'This is the man who put a million on black and it came up red, this is the man who moved into gold, just as the smart money was moving out.'

Frack me!

In 2015 Ratcliffe made a fascinating address to the nation concerning his intention to frack for gas all across the central region of Scotland. Some of the licenses had been previously held jointly between Ineos and Dart Energy, which is associated with Lynton Crosby – Cameron's special advisor on fracking!

Crosby was given a knighthood in the 2016 New Year list, on the recommendation of the Conservatives ... what a surprise! Do you think any of our other notable friends will be so honoured in the future or do you have to have your interests within taxable reach of Blighty? We shall see.

There is fierce opposition to this destructive fracking process from the community, and I am involved in a number of organisations campaigning to ensure this environmentally disastrous project is halted.

The risks of fracking that we have learned about from the USA include water table contamination, carcinogenic chemical leakage, methane gas releases and minor earthquakes. New York State, Texas, Ohio and California have all banned such destructive exploration. Planning permission to frack has also been denied in France, Germany and Switzerland (where, you will remember, Ineos moved to avoid tax).

Quite apart from the environmental destruction which would be visited on Scotland by fracking, I think we should also remember the track record of Ineos, and its willingness to threaten to close national assets and walk away at the drop of a hat. This should never be forgotten. The idea that it could now be allowed to further meddle with the fabric and economy of Scotland is almost unbelievable.

The Smith Commission on Scottish devolution moved licensing control nearer to the Scottish Parliament, and, thankfully, a moratorium on unconventional gas extraction is in place as I write. You have to hope – and expect – that a total ban will result from the clearly expressed opposition to fracking among the people of our nation.

In 2015, Ineos declared that it was going to have a series of public meetings to try to convince people that it was a good thing to drill holes under their homes and liberate toxic and flammable gas, using similarly toxic chemicals.

Tom Crotty from Ineos remarked that 'we will be drinking gallons of tea in village halls' as they embarked on the charm offensive.

When I went to one of the meetings in the town of Denny, it was abundantly clear that not one person in the hall wanted fracking to take place. This is a community which had already suffered for years because of a privately run incinerator that released dangerous dioxins into the atmosphere. At the time the public were told the process was quite safe. It took years for the truth to come out, but not before babies had been born with birth defects, and livestock had to be destroyed for the same reason. This resulted from the same kind of complacency that now surrounds fracking.

I made a contribution at the meeting and was applauded when I said we did not want this process to go ahead in Scotland.

Ineos answered questions live on a blog to try to convince people. The front man for Ineos was a poor soul called Tom Pickering. Below are a selection of the questions asked.

Will fracking be taking place near Mr Pickering's land, or is it just beneficial around everyone else's land?

What compensation will I get if my house price falls because I live near a fracking site?

Ineos, your proposals would create a major public health hazard and do great damage to our tourist industry. It is pretty clear by now that almost nobody wants their community to be fracked. Do you actually care, or is it all about making quick profits that you can squirrel away offshore to avoid paying any corporation tax?

Ineos in Grangemouth already have a poor track record for safety – 34 health and safety breaches in the last four years, officially rated as 'poor' by the SEPA (Scottish Environment Protection Agency) for three years in a row. How do you possibly expect communities in the central belt to trust Ineos?

What do you intend to do with the millions of gallons of radioactive polluted water that you pump back out of the fracked wells?

As Ineos is a company with a dubious industrial relations record that just threatens to sack an entire workforce if they don't immediately comply with a management decision, can we expect you to use the same hard-nosed techniques to try and convince people that fracking is safe?

How does it feel to be running a business that is guaranteed, by past records, to be detrimental to human health, the environment, water supplies and air?

How many million gallons of drinking water mixed with carcinogenic chemicals used for fracking will never be drinkable again?

And so on. I don't think there was a single question welcoming this process in our country but the grind goes on. Maybe they consider the public too stupid to decide and that they know better – just like they thought our union representatives were too stupid to understand the issues in negotiations?

Maybe you will need more tea than you thought Tom!

Media?

I find it astonishing that Ineos has enjoyed so much positive media coverage about the Grangemouth site – about the massive gas storage tank being built and about the ships under construction to bring the gas from the USA.

We were all told on national television and in the press when the company got planning permission to build the tank. When the tank was partially built, we had a two-page spread picture of it in the *Daily Record*, and we heard from Ineos one year on, about how well things were going despite the obvious difficulties. I guess we can expect to

For immediate release: 22 October 2013

Child labour PR specialists help Ineos swindle Scottish workers

Ineos, the company that has forced Scotland's biggest industrial site into extreme shutdown and announced plans to cut the wages, jobs and pensions of all its workers, is using a public relations firm specialising in protecting companies hit by child labour accusations.

Media Zoo is a London-based PR firm which advertises itself as having 'extensive experience of dealing with crisis situations including industrial disputes, fatal accidents, profit warnings, child labour, product failures, customer service issues, redundancies and restructuring.'

The firm has been running what the Unite union described as a 'campaign of fear' designed to terrify the 1,400 strong workforce into believing that the site is on the verge of collapse, despite a buoyant energy market, in order to force through swingeing cuts to their pay, jobs and pensions.

Unite is warning the PR firm that, by enthusiastically engaging with a management team that has taken such a ruthless approach to its workforce and Scottish energy supplies, it risks serious reputational damage.

The PR firm's claims to be 'renowned as a leading crisis comms agency' with a specialism in 'industrial relations' confirms Unite's suspicions that Ineos has sought to target a convenor at the plant, Stephen Deans, in a deliberate effort to undermine the workforce's faith in their union and so force them into accepting inferior working conditions.

Ineos' group communications manager has said 'We look to Media Zoo to thoroughly prepare our spokespeople.'

hear when the tank is finished, when the gas arrives, when the gas is being used and so on.

The disappointing thing about all this, of course, is that none of the news about the site seems to make any reference to its recent history. I believe that every time the name Ineos is used we should be reminded about the appalling treatment of its workforce in 2013, and the fact that it continues to avoid paying tax despite receiving massive hand-

Pat Rafferty, Unite Scottish secretary, said: 'Employing Media Zoo, a PR agency that helps businesses shrug off allegations of child labour and celebrates its skills in redundancies and restructuring, which is little more than PR shorthand for grinding down decent working men and women, shows that Ineos has a determined strategy to spin its way through its efforts, waging a campaign of fear to make this workforce pay for its profits.

'But Media Zoo should not be celebrating this contract. By working with such a ruthless company, they could face reputational damage themselves as a result, particularly in light of the company's strange accounts, and claims to financial distress that are in direct contradiction to the 56 per cent jump in operating profits last year. Scottish finance minister, John Swinney, this morning even said that the company's claims of being financially 'distressed' were inappropriate given Ineos' business strength.

'Opinion formers ought to think very carefully about the propaganda they receive on behalf of Ineos as neither the intention nor the content comes with any integrity.

'Media Zoo ought to be thoroughly ashamed. It is colluding in the ruination of a vital national asset, the skilled jobs that support it, and the community that depends on it. The PR industry is seriously damaged by the existence of companies that tout for business on such an immoral basis.

Unite pointed to recent claims made by the company as evidence of its strategy to misrepresent events, including claims that the business was in 'financial distress' when an independent review of the accounts revealed that sales in the last year increased by 50 per cent, gross profits grew by a margin of 20 per cent and the operating profit grew by 56 per cent.

outs from the tax payer and underwritten loans from the public. Ineos should continually be linked to the stigma it has deserved.

In June 2015 I was contacted by a member of the press asking if I knew about the invitations that Ineos had extended to certain people in the media asking them to attend the launch of one of the ships that had recently been built to transport gas from the USA to Grangemouth and Rafnes in Norway. The journalist told me that they had been invited to travel to the site and stay in a nice hotel so that they could dutifully report on the launch.

You may be wondering which hotel the company chose. Presumably one near the Clyde shipyards in Glasgow, where you might assume the vessels are being built? And perhaps the tour would include a visit to the UK steel mill where the fabric of the ships was being made? Not so my friends. The journalists were going to China to cover the event. At the risk of sounding repetitive, can I just ask why it was not a condition of the handouts taxpayers gave Ineos that manufacturing would take place in, and benefit, the UK. Other stipulations might well have been that workers' rights and conditions would be restored in Grangemouth; that the company would pay the maximum rather than the minimum in tax; that every penny of the handouts would be repaid to us once the project was complete; and that a portion of the spoils would also be paid to the government and used to support other manufacturing industries.

It is worth pointing out that Ineos pay substantial money for media spin, and this may go some way to explaining the press coverage they appear to be able to attract.

The involvement of PR firm Media Zoo, who acted for Ratcliffe both during the 2008 dispute and in 2013, was exposed by our union in the Unite press release reproduced on pp212–3.

Media Zoo's latest engagement with Ineos has been to help them spin the case for fracking, and I was pleased to hear in June 2015 that their posh offices in Imperial Wharf, Chelsea Harbour, were occupied by environmental protesters, with banners proclaiming 'Fracking is shit. You can't polish a turd'. Kind of sums it up.

Me

On a personal note, you will remember that I was placed on full wages up to the full employment tribunal hearing, and that this was as a result of our fantastic victory at the interim proceedings. I am constrained from revealing the outcome of the process for legal reasons, but think I can tell you that when it came to the steps of the court house, Ineos showed great desperation to avoid a full exploration of the issues, and that I settled only after securing industrial objectives as part of the outcome.

We made an application to have Jim Ratcliffe ordered to take the stand at the tribunal. This would have given us an opportunity to interrogate him about his actions, and also given him an opportunity to have his say. Unfortunately he launched a strenuous, and ultimately successful, legal objection and did not have to appear.

I am now employed and working hard as an industrial organiser for a global union federation, the International Transport Workers' Federation. One of my key responsibilities is organising in Grangemouth around a new concept called hub organising. The idea is to bring together activists from across trade unions and international organisations to support each other in good times and bad. In the case of Grangemouth, workers from oil, chemical road transport construction, docks public services and community, youth, retired and equality are among the participants in this excellent and progressive work.

Stevie Deans

It may please you to know that Stevie has secured full time employment with Unite the Union as an officer, and that his family are, once again, enjoying some security – as they assumed they were doing during the decades of faithful and diligent service that Stevie gave to our site.

Blacklisting

It is disappointing to report that some Unite members who were told they were not fit to be representatives by Ineos (see p197) continue to be blacklisted in this way.

Trouble in paradise

In April 2015 we were all witness to an undignified public scrap between Ratcliffe and former Ineos CEO Calum Maclean, who had left the organisation to become chief executive of Synthomer, a supplier of speciality polymers and manufacturer of rubber gloves. Apparently, and according to newspaper reports, the erstwhile twosome were all hot and bothered about wee Calum poaching highly paid help from Ineos. It was reported that big Jim was threatening to sue and banging on about 'trust and confidence', and that the actions reflected badly on the reputation of Maclean's company.

The former big mates were now behaving like rats in a sack.

One of the questions all this brings to mind is what attitude will be adopted by rampant sycophants like Stuart Duncan, who is a junior manager in the refinery, and who used to mist over every time the names Ratcliffe and Maclean were mentioned. Who, out of the two, will he have as his screen saver now?

The most serious and sickening part of this story was that, according to press reports, Maclean left Ineos with a pay-off of tens of millions. If these reports are true, it is outrageous that this organisation was masquerading as a 'distressed business', scrounging money from us as tax-payers against the threat to close Grangemouth, while all the time having enough cash in hand to later line the pockets of the very character who had fronted up the disgraceful events of 2013 at our site.

An insider in the senior management team has conveyed to our members a credible account of why Maclean actually left the company to pursue his rubber related new career. His assertion is that after Ratcliffe had decided to stage the closure of the Grangemouth Chemicals business in 2013, Maclean approached him to ask if he could buy it, and progress the lucrative fracked gas project. The story goes that Jim saw this as a big act of disloyalty, and from that moment on wee Calum's jacket was on a shoogly nail! If this is true it tells you all sorts, including – as we suspected anyway – that there had never been the smallest intention to close the chemicals business: it had always been a desirable business, despite the strenuous efforts to show it in a different light.

Gordon Grant left a few months after he was side-lined by Sealy; Sealy is now a stores-related guy in Europe for Ineos, but has been removed from the Grangemouth site. Unite, of course, is still a strong presence on the site.

Big Mensa

Big mouth strikes again … I said earlier that I would not let the insults from Declan Sealy stand without reply, and I am happy to close this book by telling you about an encounter I had with him around April 2015. Here is what happened.

I was on a flight from London when who should get on but the Nugget. He tried to stare me out as he shuffled up the aisle, but then decided to wink at me as he approached my seat. I responded verbally as you would expect, and he muttered that he would see me in Edinburgh. Oh Joy.

I was off first so I waited downstairs for him. His face was a picture as he rounded the corner and saw me. I had no intention of threatening or assaulting this buffoon and I didn't, but he was clearly terrified. In fact I merely pointed out to him that there was no table to hide behind now, and asked him where his big mouth was today.

I will spare you the histrionics, but needless to say Sealy was revealed as a very small man that day, and I would be surprised if he is stupid enough to wink at me again if I ever I have the misfortune to see him on my travels.

I hesitated to tell you this story as it may make me appear aggressive and I am not naturally like that. But this is a very extreme set of circumstances, and I am resolved that people of low character like Sealy must be confronted and must answer for their actions. It is a classic case of the bully brought to heel when someone stands up to them.

Now that I have gained personal satisfaction and put this man in his place I feel a bit better. I will, however, work relentlessly to right the wrongs of the disgraceful events at Grangemouth, and will do so through every available industrial, political and social avenue open to me.

A happy ending?

Not every story has a happy ending – and the end of this one has not been decided yet.

In 2013 the company's directors elected to use the nuclear option. The missile has been launched and detonated, and casualties taken on all sides, though mostly involving devastating harm to their own side.

Ineos no longer holds that type of weaponry.

The threat to close our factory is no longer viable. If there is so much as a whisper of such a threat by this mob again, after such substantial public investment and all the sacrifices made by the workforce, then Ratcliffe, in my view, should be driven from our country, and the highly profitable factory should be nationalised without compensation.

In February 2015 CEO Gary Haywood claimed the site could be in jeopardy if fracking did not go ahead. But the company was forced to retract and 'clarify' the assertion in double quick time, through a statement by John McNally, another of the plethora of Ineos CEOs, who stated that the site was safe for at least fifteen years regardless.

Closure is not an option.

The key to restoring justice at the Grangemouth site lies with the workforce and our many supportive organisations. The good news is that with every passing day the decks become stacked more and more towards the Unite union membership and away from Ineos. The situation, as I understand it, is that the majority of the workforce detest the company. Ineos is in serious hock to the banks, and its substantial loans are underwritten by the government. The tank they keep boasting about is nearing completion, as are the ships being built to fill it.

The three year no-strike deal that was forced on the union in 2013 evaporates at the end of 2016 and wage negotiations will then start.

Ineos can ill afford industrial action and it has no place to go with its well-rehearsed threats routine.

Our Unite organisation, in contrast to Ineos, grows stronger every day. We elected workplace stewards at a meeting I convened in June 2015, and preparations for delivering our agenda will proceed and accelerate in the coming months.

The end of the three year no-strike deal must have appeared a long time away to Ratcliffe in 2013, but every second, minute, hour and day moves us closer to its conclusion.

This is not about revenge. Far from it. This is about justice. And justice is also a dish that can be served cold.

Our strategy should be neither secretive nor devious. We must build our membership and prepare for the struggle ahead, when Ineos is no longer in a position to threaten our nation and does not have any restrictive labour agreements to hide behind. Confidence among our members will be key and this may take some time to build, given how they have been treated. But we should be in no rush as we prepare and move forward.

We can still live in hope that the company will come to its senses – and apologise to the workforce, the people of Grangemouth and the taxpayers of the UK, try to make amends for their behaviour in 2013, and begin to work constructively with our members.

Given their track record, I fear this may be a vain hope.

I fully expect them to try and launch some sort of charm offensive now that they are in a tight spot, and to hand back a fraction of what they took from our members in an attempt to avoid disputes they can't now win. This would be pleasing, but any gains must be judged against the baseline of where we were at the end of 2013.

As well as the industrial agenda, we need to work diligently for however long it takes to demand an inquiry into the conduct of all those involved in the plot, including those from the world of politics.

We must all vigorously campaign for justice in Grangemouth.

January 2016

The greedy thieves who came around
And ate the flesh of everything they found
Whose crimes have gone unpunished now
Who walk the streets as free men now

They brought death to our hometown, boys
Death to our hometown

Death to my Hometown, Bruce Springsteen

The cast

The union side

Howard Beckett	Legal director of Unite
Stephen Deans	Secretary of Unite branch SC 126, chair of the Unite Scottish region, chair of Labour Party in the Falkirk constituency
Philip Engelman	Barrister
Scott Foley	Regional officer of Unite
Mark Lyon	Convener for Unite branch SC126, vice chair of Unite's executive council, chair of Unite's international committee
Len McCluskey	General Secretary of Unite
Jim Mowatt	Unite national officer for Ineos sites
Karie Murphy	Prospective candidate for the Falkirk parliamentary seat in 2013
Ian Proudlove	Chair of Unite branch SC 126
Pat Rafferty	Regional secretary of Unite

Ineos side

Steven Boyle	O&P UK HR manager, Ineos, from the beginning of 2013 (previously in other Ineos management roles)
Tom Crotty	Director of Ineos for corporate affairs and communications
Ian Fyfe	HR director at Ineos Grangemouth and a 'Grade One Referee'
Gordon Grant	Ineos Grangemouth general manager
Gary Haywood	Ineos CEO for refinery, then chemicals business, then CEO Ineos Upstream (i.e. shale exploration)

Calum Maclean	CEO Ineos (now CEO Synthomer)
Gordon Milne	Chemicals operation director
James Arthur Ratcliffe	Chairman and CEO of Ineos
Declan Sealy	Procurement and supply chain director, Grangemouth (now Operations Director, Ineos O&P Europe)
Helen Stewart	HR manager up to 2013

Timeline

Pre-Ineos

1924

A simple refinery was built in Grangemouth and opened in 1924. The location was chosen because it was close to the docks where crude oil from the Middle East could be imported. Many of the workers from early shale oil works in the surrounding towns came to work at the new facility.

The site ceased operation from 1939 to 1946 because the war meant no crude could be delivered by ship.

1940s

The refinery reopened in 1946 and a year later the first of many chemical plants were commissioned next to the BP refinery under the ownership of the newly formed British Hydrocarbons company.

1952

The refinery was connected by pipeline to the deep water ocean terminal at Finnart in the West of Scotland. This allowed large sea tankers to bring crude oil from around the globe to feed the Grangemouth site.

1975

Crude oil was discovered in the North Sea and began flowing by pipeline to Grangemouth. A third business called BP Forties Pipeline System opened to pipe the oil to the refinery so that it could be 'stabilised'. This involved removing gas and some contaminants from the oil prior to it being sold or processed at the refinery. Three businesses operated in co-operation at Grangemouth during this period, but on paper they were entirely separate companies: BP Oil Refinery; BP Forties Pipeline System; and British Hydrocarbon Chemicals

1977

The process of privatisation of the site began under a Labour government led by Jim Callaghan. The government retained a 'golden share' to ensure the site was run in the public interest and that poor decisions didn't place the site in jeopardy.

1979

The golden share principle was abandoned and the drive to sell off the entire BP group of companies was progressed.

1990s

By now BP had reformed the businesses and changed the names but the site still consisted of three businesses: BP Refinery, BP Chemicals and BP Forties Pipeline System. But now it moved to bring the three component sites under one management structure. During this period the terms and conditions and working practices across the three businesses at the site began to be aligned. Early on in the decade the company had withdrawn recognition from our unions across these plants for the purposes of collective bargaining, but during this process collective bargaining was restored.

2001/2002

A significant management review led to some 800 full-time in-house job losses. Our branch successfully resisted compulsory redundancies. We secured a one year stay of execution for all employees regardless of union membership, and the placement within BP Grangemouth of many people who were at risk of redundancy.

2004

BP announced it was going to sell the chemicals division by separating it out again and making an Initial Public Offering (IPO) of shares. The refinery was later also included in the IPO, but eventually attempts to float the company were abandoned.

Ineos period

2005

The chemicals division and the refinery, which were both part of the IPO, were sold to Ineos for $9bn. Most, if not all, of this money was borrowed from banks, so the site was suddenly laden with debt again. The only part of the site retained by BP was the exploration-linked Forties Pipeline System.

2006-2008

Ineos arrived at the site in the shape of Tom Crotty who was one of their CEOs. Crotty announced at our very first meeting that Ineos did not believe in final salary pension schemes and that it would be closing ours. Our scheme was fully funded at the time and the company was very profitable.

2007

As a consequence of the financial crash, Ineos found itself in potentially significant trouble over finance covenants. The company was required to renegotiate arrangements with the banks in order to avoid breaching agreed covenant parameters.

2008

Ineos embarked on an ill-advised battle with our union in an attempt to close our final salary pension scheme. Some 97 per cent of Unite's members voted for a strike, which lasted 48 hours, from 27 to 29 April. We won a decisive victory, but the episode was no cause for celebration.

2010

Ineos moved its headquarters and 'tax residence' to Switzerland, with projected tax savings of around €450m between 2010 and 2014.

2011

Ineos sold half the refinery to the state-owned Chinese oil company PetroChina for $1bn. The site was thus once again split asunder, and our pension schemes and union agreements were substantially altered.

2012/2013

The company was deep in thought around the circumstances it would later use to threaten to close the site unless the union agreed unprecedented concessions. The company was also preparing to extract financial assistance from the Scottish and UK governments.

False allegations were made by Labour that Unite had unlawfully 'packed' the Falkirk Labour Party with its own members ahead of a ballot to replace the disgraced MP Eric Joyce. Ineos used the row to put pressure on Stevie Deans, who was chair of the constituency party, and they also used the situation to cause industrial relations agitation. Unite members voted for industrial action in defence of Stevie Deans unless the company dropped its accusations.

Meanwhile the company offered a 'survival' plan requiring employees to accept greatly reduced terms and conditions, and particularly, reduced pensions. Employees were asked to sign up to the plan prior to any consultation and the vast majority of our members refused to do so.

Ineos then threatened to close the plant and, to avoid what would amount to a devastating blow to the Scottish economy, Unite was forced to accept the company's plan. On 25 October 2013 Ineos announced that the plant would stay open. Unite had agreed to take no strike action for three years, to move to a new pension scheme, and to accept a three-year pay freeze.

On 28 October, after months of harassment and intimidation by the company, Stevie Deans resigned from Ineos.

2014

On January 6 I was notified that I was to be subject to disciplinary action for allegedly failing to stop someone else from giving his opinion to the *Daily Record*. The other allegation was that I had raised safety concerns at a union-management meeting! I was never to return to the site as an employee. I was dismissed from employment in February 2015.

Following the imposition of the 'survival plan' during 2014, people left their jobs in droves, as we had predicted. The company was forced to close plants ahead of schedule. Job losses among Ineos employees and its contractors accelerated. Serious safety problems emerged including gas releases. Hazardous equipment was operated without enough trained people.

2015

Gordon Milne, the chemicals business director, wrote to employees in February saying that safety performance since the start of the year had been really poor. 400 safety-related incidents had occurred since January and 20 people had been injured.

The environmental performance had also been unacceptable over the three years from 2010 to 2012. The Scottish Environmental Protection Agency had rated the pollution performance of the refinery as 'poor'.

The company now expressed its determination to carry out fracking.

The chemicals business is a shadow of its former self with previously operational plants reduced to rusting and redundant hulks. There is comparatively little viable production left since massive factory areas have closed, including the installations known as G4, BE3 and a Benzene plant. A massive tank, underwritten and paid for by taxpayers, is being built, but this will only hold the imported gas supply for one plant, the KG. Many full-time employee posts have been lost due to this deterioration as well as many more contractor and agency jobs.

The refinery continues in production with discussions continuing about investments. This is positive, but we will see who is asked to underwrite the finance and provide handouts to pay for it.

In November 2015, my employment and outstanding legal business with Ineos was concluded without the need for a full tribunal hearing.

Index

Agency staff *see* contractors
Allison, Mairi 9

Baird, Ross 138
Balls, Ed 44
Beckett, Howard 103, 188, 191, 195, 203
Black, Sandy 188
Bowen, Cliff 162
Boyle, Steven 66, 118, 147, 159, 171, 172, 174, 175, 176, 180, 181-2, 183, 192
British Petroleum (BP) 3, 11, 12, 13, 14, 15-17, 18, 19, 21, 26, 27, 28, 29, 30-1, 32, 38-40, 42, 43, 44-5, 46, 48-9, 51, 52, 54, 81, 102, 113, 114, 135, 169, 205
  BP steam pipeline 134-6, 153
  Deepwater Horizon 42-3
  Innovene (BP subsidiary) 40-1
  and pensions 26, 33, 53-4
  share scheme 51-2
  Texas City 42
Brown, Gordon 68, 204
Browne, John 45, 46
Bruce, Lindsay 188
Buchanan, Ian 79
Burke, Tony 78, 114, 162
Butler, Nicola 117, 119

Cameron, David 140, 171, 204, 209
Carr, Bruce 132
Carr Review 131-2, 150, 152, 198
Christie, Campbell 27
Clarksdale, Mississippi 189, 190-1
Collins, Ray 100
Collins Review 100, 205
Connarty, Michael 41, 73, 75, 94, 162
Conroy, Tam 162
Contractors 12-13, 23, 24, 26, 40, 61, 62, 76, 81-2, 96, 97, 122, 167
Cook, Marianne 138
Corbyn, Jeremy 92, 95, 101, 205
Coryton 43, 44, 46
Conservative Party, Conservatives 77, 111, 202, 209
Crosby, Lynton 209
Crotty, Tom 45, 47, 56, 139, 147, 210
Cullinane, Jackson 108
Cunningham, Mhairi 9

Daily Record 160-1, 178, 179-80, 182, 191, 212-3
Deans, Harry 175-6
Deans, Stephen 4, 36, 50, 57, 59, 66, 68-9, 73, 74, 75, 78-9, 82,

86, 89, 91, 96, 124, 134, 140,
145, 147, 215
and Falkirk Labour Party 90-5,
99-100, 101, 102-3
suspension by Ineos (including
union response) 102-19, 136,
141, 148, 150, 151, 152-8,
161, 162, 170, 171-5, 194,
195, 196, 212
De-recognition 26-7, 29, 33, 34,
75, 196
Dhokia, Umesh 181
Dubbins, Simon 78
Duncan, Ian 97, 106-7
Duncan, Stuart 216
Durie, Mark 66

East, David 139
Engelman, Philip 174, 191-2
Ewing, Fergus 139

Fair Pley 109
Falkirk 6, 7-8, 9, 52
Falkirk Herald 14
Falkirk Labour Party dispute
90-119 *passim*, 120, 137, 153,
161, 170, 176, 204, 205
Foley, Scott 97, 108, 154, 162, 173
Forties Pipeline System 48
Fracking 43, 198, 199, 209-11,
214, 216, 218
Fraser, Giles 185
Fyfe, Ian 53-4, 55, 60, 62, 89,
104, 105, 106, 110, 112, 114,
115, 116, 118, 145, 148, 152,
153, 175, 176, 177, 180, 191

Gardner, Andrew 74, 111, 138,
139

George, Trevor 19, 24, 33, 34-5
Gibson, Kenny 188
Grangemouth complex 4, 11-12,
13-15, 18-19, 20, 25-6, 38-9,
41-2, 44, 45, 48-9, 50, 51,
126-7, 164, 168-9, 196-8,
199-200, 206, 208, 209, 214,
216, 218-9
Battle for Grangemouth, The
(management film) 155
Chemicals site 3, 9, 11, 15, 19,
32-3, 35, 38, 40-1, 44, 45, 47,
128, 136, 164, 165, 180, 207,
216
Benzene Plant 180
BE3 plant 180
G4 cracker 164, 180
KG ethylene cracker 48, 125,
62, 135-6, 164
See also Innovene, Olefins and
Polymers
Ethane tank 70-2, 122, 133,
134, 136, 199, 206, 212-4,
218
Integration and de-integration
30, 32-6, 40-1, 48, 49, 86,
88, 137
maintenance 12-13, 19, 21, 23,
30-1, 40, 46, 48, 49, 81
management 13, 20, 34, 39, 45,
46, 49, 51, 59, 60, 62, 65, 75,
82, 83-4, 145, 148, 163, 199
Refinery 11, 15, 18, 19, 21, 27,
30, 32-3, 35, 40-1, 44, 45, 48,
65, 85, 165, 181, 207
Hydrocracker 25, 26, 31, 181,
182
See also BP, Ineos, safety, Unite
Grangemouth branch

Grant, Gordon 28, 38, 55, 56, 57, 60, 62, 65, 70, 71, 72, 73, 81, 82, 83, 84, 85, 86-7, 89, 91, 95, 104, 105, 106, 107, 108, 110, 111, 112, 113, 114, 115, 116, 122, 123, 124, 130, 138, 139, 141, 142, 145, 146-7, 152, 153, 155, 167, 192, 216
Greatrex, Tom 78
Guthrie, Jonathan 138

Hart, Steve 78
Harvey, George Vincent 7-8
Haywood, Gary 73, 111, 132-4, 156
Health and Safety Executive (HSE) 39, 58, 130, 144, 154, 155, 164, 207, 208
Holland, Diana 82
Hooper, Sharon 65, 181
Hope, Bob 12, 13-14
Hughes, Andy 63-4
Hunt, Chris 76
Hutton, John 134

ICI 43-4, 64, 68, 69
Ineos Group 3, 4, 28, 38, 41, 44, 45, 46, 47, 48, 49, 50-2, 60, 61, 62, 63, 65, 73, 79, 88, 122, 126-8, 138-9, 175, 184-5, 196-8, 199, 200, 208, 209, 210, 212-3
    European Works Council 41, 59-60, 62, 66-7
    and grants 3, 64, 68, 70-1, 102, 166, 168, 184, 185, 199, 214
    and HR 66, 80-1, 82, 142, 143; see also Grangemouth/
        management; Boyle, Steven; Fyfe, Ian; Stewart, Helen
Ineos Breagh 206
Ineos Capital 61, 62, 72, 84, 104, 105, 106, 108, 112, 113, 114, 116, 122
Ineos Chlor, Runcorn 62, 63, 64
Ineos Grangemouth Ltd 132-4
    and litigation 54, 57, 64, 73, 141, 194-5
    Mark Lyon dismissal and tribunal, 54, 66, 77, 81, 106, 123, 145, 148, 171-5, 177-8, 179-84, 185, 186, 187, 191-5, 214-5
    November 2013 dispute, 120-70 passim
    and pensions 3, 46, 50, 52, 60, 61, 85, 86, 88, 89, 102, 113, 115, 120-5, 126, 127, 141, 142, 159, 160, 161, 178
    management pension pot 89
    pension scheme dispute 2007-8 53-60, 134, 137
    strike-breaking plan 2013 128-30
    and Switzerland 67-9, 71, 72, 210
    see also BP steam pipeline; Deans, Stephen; Falkirk Labour Party; fracking; Grangemouth site; PetroChina; safety
Ireland, John 138, 139

Johnson, Robert 188, 189
Joyce, Eric 77, 90, 91, 92

Kane, Lorraine 176
Kane, Tommy 138

Kemp, Alexander 16
King, BB 189, 190

Labour Party 9, 16, 29, 74, 77,
    78, 134, 171, 174, 175, 202-4,
    205; see also Falkirk Labour
    Party dispute
Lamont, Alan 162
Lamont, Gary 162
Lamont, Johann 203
Loftus, Tony 20, 29, 59
Lyon, Cecily 9, 15
Lyon, Hugh (author father) 9, 11,
    13, 15, 19
Lyon, Hugh (author grandfather)
    8
Lyon, Hugh (author great-great-
    uncle) 9
Lyon, Wendy 25, 187, 190, 206

McCluskey, Len 76, 100, 107,
    108, 112, 141, 148, 167, 174,
    177, 194
McCulloch, Linda 78, 108, 114,
    154
McGuire, Patrick 188
McKay, Colin 162
Maclean, Calum 57, 71, 72, 78,
    84, 86-7, 88, 95, 111, 123,
    124, 127, 138, 146, 147, 148,
    149, 151, 152, 156, 157, 159,
    160, 163, 164, 165, 167, 183,
    192, 216
McLean, Colin 39
McMonagle, Mary 7, 8
McNally, John 139, 218
Mann, Russell 65, 111
Media Zoo 176, 212-3, 214

Milne, Gordon 155, 164
Mitchell, Ian 138
Moffat, Ian 188
Morris, Bill 175
Mossmoran 73
Mowatt, Jim 26
Murphy, Karie 90-5, 96, 99, 110
Murphy, Jim 202, 203
Murphy, Richard 126-7

National Oil Refining Co-
    ordinating Committee
    (NORCC) 74-5, 76, 78, 111
Nichols, Archbishop Vincent 185
North Sea Oil 15, 16, 18, 70,
    113, 134, 136, 153, 206

Olefins and Polymers (O&P) 40-
    4, 45, 48, 49, 128, 132-3, 207

Pensions see BP/pensions and
    Ineos/pensions
PetroChina 84-8, 111, 126
Petroplus 43, 44, 46
Pickering, Tom 138, 139, 210-1
Proctor, Martin 66
Proudlove, Ian 29-30, 33, 35, 36,
    82, 86, 96, 97, 107, 110, 114,
    124, 134, 156

Rafferty, Pat 59, 86, 103, 108,
    127, 141, 144, 147, 148, 156,
    157, 160, 162, 178, 179-80,
    191, 194, 202, 213
Ratcliffe, Jim (JAR) 3, 4, 19, 20,
    29, 37, 46, 47, 55, 56, 57, 60,
    61, 63, 65, 68, 69, 71, 72, 80,
    83-4, 85, 88, 104, 105, 106,
    107, 108, 112, 113, 115, 116,

117, 118, 119, 122, 130, 131, 132, 134, 135, 137, 138, 139, 142, 148, 150, 152, 153, 157, 162, 165, 167, 168, 169, 175, 176, 177, 178-9, 183, 184, 186, 187, 192, 195, 198, 206, 209, 214, 215, 216, 218

Redundancies (proposals for and resistance to) 25, 26, 37-8, 39, 40, 143, 159, 213

Religion 21, 185-6

Robertson, Arthur 21

Safety 25, 28, 29, 31, 32, 42, 144, 164-5, 196, 197, 206-8, 211
  behavioural safety 66-7
  during industrial action 57-8, 114, 129, 135, 151, 154, 155, 167
  and union representation 27-8, 36, 39, 49, 82-3, 143-4, 164-5, 178, 181, 194

Salmond, Alex 58, 138, 160

Scottish Environment Protection Agency (SEPA) 207, 211

Scottish independence 101, 202, 204

Scottish National Party 101, 111, 155, 160, 202, 203, 204

Scottish TUC 54, 144, 162, 169

Sealy, Declan 28, 123, 133, 145-7, 149-50, 151, 152, 154, 155, 156, 157, 165, 167, 168, 171, 173, 174, 175, 176, 177, 178, 180, 184, 192, 216, 217

Simpson, Derek 61, 174

Smith, Amy 81

Smith, Grahame 162, 168-9

Smokehouse Blues Band, the 188-9

Stein, Gertrude 64, 197

Stewart, Helen 62, 65, 93, 97, 103, 110, 118, 147

Sturgeon, Nicola 139

Swinney, John 101, 139, 147

Tait, Bruce 188

Tanker drivers 26, 76, 162

Thatcher, Margaret 16, 17

Thompsons Solicitors 144, 188, 191

Transport & General Workers Union 9, 18, 19, 23, 33, 23, 100; *see also* Unite

Traynor, Tony 67, 172, 184

Tressell, Robert 9, 16

Unite the union (national) 3, 54, 66, 68, 75, 76, 77, 125-6, 147, 148, 152, 160, 166, 171, 177, 191, 192, 194, 195, 208, 212-3
  Refining our future 78

Unite Grangemouth (before 2007 Transport & General Workers Union) 30, 32-3, 34-6, 39, 40, 48-9, 51, 66, 68, 80, 81-2, 83, 87-8, 120-5, 143-4, 150, 153-4, 160-1, 166, 168-9, 177-8, 181-2, 184, 185, 186, 199, 204, 215, 216, 218
  November 2013 dispute, 120-70 *passim*
  political activity in collaboration with Ineos management 68-79

See also Ineos/pensions/pensions
    scheme dispute; Falkirk
    Labour Party dispute; safety
United Kingdom Petroleum
    Industry Association
    (UKPIA) 74, 76, 77

Watterson, Andrew 82
Welsh, Peter 156
Wishart, Brian 35
Woodhouse, Tony 108, 162
Woodley, Tony 61, 174
Wright, Stephen 109

Jim Ratcliffe, the boss of the Ineos concern which victimised Mark, has a better-stocked bank account to be sure. But reading this book, he is surely not richer in the things that matter – family, friendships, community, principle, service to his fellows, courage and integrity. There, Mr Ratcliffe may be overdrawn in fact, while Mark Lyon's credit rating is triple A. I am certainly proud that, through Unite, I have been able to do what I can to support Mark and our other members at Grangemouth. And it is certain that there will be another turn.

I hope that more grass-roots leaders in our movement follow the example of Mark Lyon and write down their experiences of life and work. Such accounts are worth more than most textbooks explaining socialism and its values. Through his part in the struggle, and then through this memoir, Mark has laid two stones on the highway to the future.

Barrie Clement, former Labour editor of *The Independent*

Countless fawning accounts are published about the captains of industry in the business sections of newspapers – and online.

You can imagine the inquisition to which such businessmen are subjected: How clever do you think you are on a scale of nought to ten? What has been the highlight of your career so far? What are your ambitions, if you can possibly have any left?

This book redresses the balance. Mark Lyon has exposed the ruthlessness of James Ratcliffe, chief executive, chairman, founder and 60 per cent shareholder of Ineos, a Swiss-based private company which took over the Grangemouth petrochemical complex in 2005.

Mark tells how Ratcliffe plotted the emasculation of Unite at the site and the unfair removal of its leaders, including himself.

He shows how the billionaire tax exile relieved British taxpayers of every possible handout – some of it in questionable ways – to support his drive for ever increasing appetite for profit.

And he exposes the foolishness of allowing such a man and such an organisation to control an installation of such key importance to the British economy.

Mark suffered personally for his refusal to be cowed by Ratcliffe. He deserves our deepest respect and this book deserves a wide audience.

Jackson Cullinane, head of Unite Scotland politics, research and campaigns unit

Mark Lyon's 'inside story' of the events at Ineos in 2013 (and their roots) is an excellent and revealing account of the disgraceful circumstances faced by trade union reps at Grangemouth, the workforce they represent and their families.

Contrasting sharply with the portrayal of such events by the 'mainstream media', Mark's book should be compulsory reading for all who wish to understand the true nature of the events at Grangemouth, the background to them and their consequences.

His account, however, raises questions far beyond the issue of the relationship between Ineos and its Grangemouth workforce. It is, above all, an illustration of the need to address the abuse of power exercised by powerful companies and those who own them.

Perhaps the most disturbing feature of the Grangemouth events was the manner in which one man, while himself ensconced in a luxury yacht, made such demands of the workforce, community and elected governments, at both Scottish and UK levels.

Everyone should admire and appreciate the principled roles played by people such as Mark Lyon and Stevie Deans who, like hundreds of thousands of other trade union activists, are driven by their decency, care and commitment to apply their time, energy and skills to promoting the needs of their community and their fellow workers.

And they should also support and be active in their own unions, politically as well as industrially. It is precisely because strong trade union organisation is feared by those who benefit from the current concentration of wealth and power in too few hands that trade unionists such as Mark Lyon are attacked by the worst employers, who are backed by anti-union laws and their proponents in politics and the media.

They understand, as we all should, that strong and active trade unions are key, not only in defending people at work but also in leading the case for an alternative to victimisation, austerity, benefit cuts, privatisation, environmental damage, inequality and the decimation of communities.

In his detailing of the events at Ineos, Mark Lyon makes a tremendous contribution to an understanding of the need for an alternative way forward, founded on the principles of solidarity, the redistribution of wealth and power and the extension of democracy – in politics, at the workplace and in economic ownership.

Stevie Deans, former Grangemouth vice convenor

I am honoured to have been asked to contribute to this insightful account of the shared history of our community in Grangemouth, a town built on the blood, sweat and tears of generations of working-class trade unionists – in its docks, shipyards and factories: driving the trains and lorries, refining fuel and making chemicals, working in the timber industry, making soap, bottling whisky, or working any one of the many other industries that have given Grangemouth its existence and character.

The book gives an informative account of the origins of the town's industry, the changing approach taken towards its workers by their employers, and the gains for members secured by their trade unions for their families and the wider community.

The role played by the trade union movement – and Unite and its predecessors in particular – in protecting, advancing and defending their members and community is clear to see. The role of the Labour Party as the political voice of the working class and the trade union movement is also evident – until the Blair years when it started to desert its people. In fact, as Mark shows in this book, it was events in the Labour Party that offered the immediate excuse – if one was required – for Jim Ratcliffe to embark on his attempt to undermine Unite at Grangemouth. The Labour Party debacle over the selection of its Falkirk parliamentary candidate came about because of its weak and supercilious UK leadership and ineffective and invisible Scottish leadership, and the moral bankruptcy of some among Falkirk's local Labour councillors.

I congratulate Mark on what is not just a great read but also a vital contribution to Scottish and UK social, political and industrial history.

Karie Murphy, provisional Labour parliamentary candidate for Falkirk in 2013

In 2012 Eric Joyce, the MP for Falkirk, was expelled by the Labour Party for violent and drunken conduct. In 2000 Joyce had been parachuted in as candidate by the party machine, to replace Dennis Canavan, a working-class hero despised by New Labour and expelled by them from the party. The once proud local party was moribund. Cronyism and rifts were the order of the day. It was against this backdrop that the move to rejuvenate Labour in Falkirk began.

Unite, alongside other unions, had a political strategy to engage local party members in policy decisions and the selection of representatives. Its aim was to counteract the disengagement of voters and activists. The union was permitted to present its strategy in workplaces, including at Ineos Grangemouth. Change and hope were on offer and hundreds were inspired to join the party.

The first suggested replacement candidate, Stevie Deans, decided to opt out as the local situation became more pernicious, and I was then nominated and became the parliamentary candidate.

The Labour Party had been completely abreast of everything Unite was doing at Falkirk. But when the party machine woke up to what was happening, outrage was expressed. It should be Scottish ministers and their mates in party HQ that ran the machine, not trades unions. There was seen to be a clear threat to the hierarchy, and an instruction now came directly from the Leader's office to the general secretary's office at Unite to stop the selection.

A witch hunt and media onslaught ensued. Unite stood firm in defending its activists, but still the machine ploughed on. There were secret meetings, off-the-record press briefings and scandalous manipulation of facts. The allegation was that Stevie Deans and I had broken the rules in order to secure my selection as candidate. Evidence was duly manufactured and labelled as a Labour Party 'report', but, shamefully, there was no attempt made by the report's authors to communicate with the people it was accusing. Against its own legal advice, Labour then reported individuals to Police Scotland. This farce was on show for all to see, and it did not go unnoticed at Ineos, where Stevie Deans was vice convenor, and where industrial relations had been strained since the company arrived in 2006.

Stevie Deans and I were duly exonerated by both party and police. We had done nothing wrong in Falkirk except challenge the Labour Party machine. Throughout this period we were given brilliant support by our movement, particularly from the members of Mark Lyon's Ineos branch.

So Unite was vindicated over Falkirk, but Grangemouth workers were subsequently bullied and a country held to ransom. However, after all the setbacks, Unite Grangemouth continues to defend its members' interests, and Unite remains an integral part of civic Scotland.

Grahame Smith, general secretary Scottish TUC

There are many perspectives from which to view what happened at Ineos in the autumn of 2013. There is the geo-politics of global energy policy. There is the staggering but largely surreptitious influence of private equity capital and high net-worth individuals on the global economy and our democratic wellbeing. There is Scotland's constitutional politics and the Independence Referendum. And then there are the internal machinations of the Scottish Labour Party, its waning popularity and subsequent annihilation at the 2015 General Election. Each, in its own way, is part of the Grangemouth story and its aftermath.

The perspective I prefer is that of the workforce, its Unite representatives and the local community. People like Mark Lyon, Stevie Deans, Ian Proudlove and Pat Rafferty – the people who had worked at the plant for decades, raised families locally and supported local businesses and community activities, people whose stake in the plant's continued operation far outweighed that of its absentee owner.

These people demonstrated remarkable solidarity and dignity in the face of extreme intimidation, from an employer who favoured imposition over negotiation, and who placed them in the invidious position of having to accept cuts to their pay, pensions and other conditions, or else see their jobs and community sacrificed, and the Scottish economy destabilised.

The weekend after the dispute ended I was interviewed by John Humphries on Radio Four's *Today* programme. The line was that the Ineos dispute was an echo of industrial relations from the 'bad old days', from an era of rogue shop stewards propagating a hard left political ideology and misleading their members, and of union General Secretaries being parachuted in to resolve disputes.

This was, of course, a deeply prejudiced characterisation of 1970s industrial relations. But it was also a perverse, lazy and ignorant caricature of the Ineos dispute, and betrayed a mind-set that pervades into the deepest reaches of the British state and its elite. It is the same mind-set that spawned the Carr Review, established in the aftermath of the dispute. Despite being abandoned by its Chair, Bruce Carr QC, due to the lack of evidence submitted by employers and unions and meddling by Tory ministers, the Review was intended to lay the ground for an attack on unions, on the right to strike and on the fundamental freedoms of speech, association and assembly; and these have now been incorporated in the Tory government's Trade Union Bill.

Fearing the assault on unions signalled by the setting up of the Carr Review, in November 2013 the STUC persuaded the Scottish government to take a different approach and to establish its own Independent Review into the positive role of unions. The Working Together Review, published in the same week that the Carr Review was abandoned, produced Scotland's recently created Fair Work Convention, and a public recognition of the positive role of unions and collective bargaining in advancing the interests of workers and achieving a wide range of economic and social objectives.

Some might consider it ironic that the approach to unions and industrial relations being pursued in Scotland in the period since Grangemouth was in the headlines stands in such stark contrast to that of the UK government. However, securing in Scotland the constructive approach to industrial relations espoused by the Working Together Review would be a fitting legacy of the events at Grangemouth. After all, the desire of the Ineos workforce and their union Unite was simply to have the opportunity to negotiate and reach agreement with the employer in good faith. Unfortunately, it was a desire the employer did not share.

Howard Beckett, Unite Director of Legal Services

History will have the last word. This was a dispute like no other – an industry so vital to the economy yet under the control of one man; and a Labour leader hungry for a chance to show his personal independence from the trade union movement. History will find that this dispute, against all the odds, awakened forces for good; that it gave light to what is best about our movement. Three good people – Stevie Deans, Mark Lyon, Karie Murphy – had to fight to stop the destruction of their lives. Lambasted by the media, the prime minister, their employer and the Labour Party, they fought for their dignity. They survived, and flourished, and each will go on to achieve much for our movement because of this battle. Unite survived and our members, whose jobs and communities had been threatened, stayed strong and to this day remain a collective ready to demand their rights in the workplace. The Labour Party became a democratic party of the many, the largest socialist movement in Europe. There were dark days, darkest for Stevie, Mark and Karie; and the forces of the media, the establishment and the business oligarchy did their worst. But history will record a moment when the forces of good stood firm and ensured that our movement kept to the right path. Those dark days are behind us, and what remains is a victory for our members at Grangemouth; a victory for Stevie, Mark and Karie; a victory for the true Labour Party; and a victory for our movement.